The
ENCYCLOPEDIA
of
U-BOATS

The
ENCYCLOPEDIA
of
U-BOATS
From 1904 to the Present Day

EBERHARD MÖLLER and WERNER BRACK

Translated by Andrea Battson and Roger Chesneau

Greenhill Books, London
Stackpole Books, Pennsylvania

2529917

Greenhill Books

The Encyclopedia of U-Boats: From 1904 to the Present
First published 2004 by Greenhill Books
Lionel Leventhal Limited, Park House, 1 Russell Gardens,
London NW11 9NN
info@greenhillbooks.com   www.greenhillbooks.com
and
Stackpole Books, 5067 Ritter Road, Mechanicsburg, PA 17055, USA

Translation by Andrea Battson and Roger Chesneau from
Enzyklopädie deutscher U-Boote: Von 1904 bis zur Gegenwart

Copyright © Motorbuch Verlag, Stuttgart, 2002
English language edition copyright © Lionel Leventhal Ltd 2004

British Library Cataloguing in Publication Data:
Möller, Eberhard, 1924–
The encyclopedia of U-boats: from 1904 to the present
1. Submarines (Ships) – Germany – History
2. Submarine Warfare – Germany – History
I. Title   II. Brack, Werner
623.8′257′0943

ISBN 1-85367-623-3

Library of Congress Cataloging-in-Publication data available

Edited, designed and typeset by Roger Chesneau
Printed in Thailand by Imago

Title-page illustration:
One of the most famous U-boats of all time—Günther Prien's U 47,
a Type VIIB, seen here returning to Wilhelmshaven having sunk the British
battleship *Royal Oak* at Scapa Flow, 14 October 1939.

Contents

Preface

I was born on 5 April 1924 in Detmold (Lippe) as the son of a municipal officer; nowadays his position would be probably be called 'city treasurer'. Five years later my sister was born. My father died of a heart attack at the age of only forty.

I spent my childhood and youth in my parental home in Altenberndstrasse in the beautiful city of Lippe-Detmold. From 1930 I attended primary school and from 1934 the classical grammar school (Leopoldinum), starting to study Latin, and later adding French, Greek and English.

Normally it would have taken eight years until Arbitur (school-leaving examinations), but in the meantime war had broken out and it was possible to shorten this period by six months. If one decided to pursue the career of an active officer in one of the three services of the armed forces and one were accepted, the school issued a so-called Reifevermerk (leaving note) instead of the Abitur certificate. This note was supposed to entitle one to access to university after the war.

I applied for the Kriegsmarine (Navy), was invited for the enlistment examination and went to Kiel on 22 July 1941. The whole exam took three days—a test of knowledge on the first day, a test of sports on the second and 'psychological exam' on the third, the last being a test option that the Navy had only just discovered. This involved presenting oneself in reports to and conversations with psychologists and Kriegsmarine officers.

Anyway, I assume that I must have done reasonably well: I was accepted as an Ingenieuroffizier candidate and soon went to Danholm (a small island between Stralsund and Rügen), where the basic training for all officers of the German navies had taken place since the times of the Kaiser. At the end of 1941 we then went to the Marineschule in Flensburg-Mürwik for our first technical instruction course.

On 1 March 1942 we went from there by train and ship to our first front-line posting—aboard the battleship *Tirpitz*, which at that time was berthed in Fättenfjord near Trondheim. We arrived in the night of 5/6 March, and a few hours later the *Tirpitz* put to sea for her first sortie against a convoy in the area between Bear Island and Jan Mayen.

I stayed on *Tirpitz* for almost six months—with sorties in the North Sea or, between these excursions, at moorings in fjords and elsewhere in Norway.

On 19 September 1942 I went from Narvik to an officer course at the Marineschule in Flensburg-Mürwik; a second, technical course followed.

On 1 May 1943 I joined 36. Minensuchflottille (36th Minesweeper Flotilla) in Ostend and in the middle of May 42. Minensuchflottille at Les-Sables-d'Olonne. This was not a happy time, because my ship in the 36th Flotilla was sunk in combat and that of the 42nd Flotilla ran on to a mine and also sank. I was therefore quite pleased when, on 5 July 1943, I was given orders for to attend U-boat training at Pillau. This type of training, which took place also at Gotenhafen and Hela, was of the usual variety, aiming for the position of Leitend Ingenieur (Chief Engineer) on U-boats. In between I had front-line duty on U-boats as a midshipman (cadet) and Wachoffizier (Officer of the Watch).

At the end of the year and at the beginning of 1945 I was attached to one of the very latest U-boats—a Type XXI—as Leitend Ingenieur, although at that time the boat was still in the building yard at Blohm & Voss in Hamburg. It was common practice to send the technical branches of the crew for 'construction instructions' as early as possible, in order to make them familiar with all the details. My U-boat was damaged by bombs for the first time on 11 March and finally put out of action on 8 April.

Amongst others, the U-boats to which Ali Cremer and Gerhard Thäter had been assigned suffered the same fate at more or less the same time. As there was no chance of transferring to another U-boat, we formed, through our own initiative (and, of course, voluntarily), an anti-tank command to face the British, who were advancing between Bremen and Hamburg. At the end of April, when Grossadmiral Karl Dönitz was nominated Hitler's successor, the latter wanted some U-boat staff with him, so we drove, in a private car, to Plön and then to Flensburg-Mürwik, where the Provisional Reich Government resided until 23 May 1945—in the Marineschule, in fact, where everything had started for me.

When, on that day, all notable representatives of the Reich Government— Dönitz, Generalfeldmarschall Jodl, Lüdde-Neurath etc.—were picked up by the British, the latter did not really know what to do with us Navy soldiers. We were not even taken prisoner, and soon afterwards we drove home—everyone by himself.

I was fortunate enough to find my parents' home in Detmold undamaged, and so, after making up for the Abitur in Göttingen—the Reifevermerk of 1941 was, of course, no longer valid!—I was able to start studying electrical engineering on 1 December 1945 in Hanover. I finished my studies there in April 1949.

Soon after this I started a job with Siemens as a junior engineer. I worked there in various positions and at many different places until 1982, the last sixteen years as a Technical Director.

During my time at Siemens my hobby was 'extreme' mountain climbing in the Alps, including the climbing of almost all the Viertausender (mountains 4,000 metres high or more) and skiing, including, amongst other things, making the longitudinal crossing of the Alps by the legendary Haute-Route on three occasions.

When, following a serious illness, I retired from Siemens in 1983, I naturally started looking for a new and meaningful occupation. The historian Professor Dr Wilhelm Treue, a friend of mine, suggested to me that I should not totally abandon my engineering career: I had obtained my certificate in 1949 at the Technische Hochschule (Technical College) in Hanover and should study for a degree in a technical/historical subject. After many conversations we chose as the subject of a possible thesis 'The Historical Development of Submarine Propulsion Systems, from the Seventeenth Century to the Present Day'. This extensive work, written over several years (and requiring a good deal of research both at home and abroad) was accepted by the Technische Universität (Technical University) in Berlin, where I graduated in April 1989 as a Doktor-Ingenieur (Doctor of Engineering).

Since then I have been writing books and articles and giving lectures about technical naval history, my most important publications being *Deutsche Marineruestung 1919–1942*, in collaboration with Prof. Wilhelm Treue and Kapitän zur See Werner Rahn (Herford, 1992); *Kurs Atlantik: Die deutsche U-Boot-Entwicklung bis 1945* (Stuttgart, 1995); *100 Jahre Dieselmotoren für fünf deutsche Marinen*, in collaboration with Dr Werner Brack (Hamburg, 1997); and *Marine-Geheimprojekte: Hellmuth Walter und seine Entwicklungen* (Stuttgart, 2000).

I would like to offer my special thanks to the people who have helped me on my way through life, beginning with my mother, Frieda Möller. When my father died unexpectedly in 1932, my mother was alone with two children; I was eight years old, my sister only three. A few years before, my father had built a house containing three flats that was mortgaged almost 100 per cent. My mother nevertheless managed to keep the house and make it possible for us children to go on to higher education—and at that time one still had to pay fees for the privilege. She always showed understanding for my wishes and ideas, also for my desire to volunteer for the Kriegsmarine at the age of only seventeen. She also supported my decision to start studying at university after the war. She always showed great interest in my professional career. I still remember how proud she was when I once showed her my job as a Technical Director of Siemens A. G. in Düsseldorf at the beginning of the 1970s. My mother reached the age of 91. During the last years she was living with my sister in Leer. When I visited her there a few days before her unexpected death, she told me as a farewell, '*Mein Junge*, you have always ever given me only joy.'

I would like also to thank my class-teacher at grammar school, the classical scholar Dr Walther Hoffmann, who not only taught us, but taught us the joy of antiquity and the Latin and Greek language.

In the Marine, I would like to thank Oberleutnant (Ing.) Paul Zajusch, my first Gruppenoffizier (section leader) at the Marineschule in Flensburg-Mürwik, and Oberleutnant (Ing.) Walter Junge, who taught me the capabilities necessary for the technical command of a submarine.

I acknowledge my debt also to Georg Wilbig, the Personnel Director at Siemens, who not only shared my enthusiasm for the work at the company but also my pleasure in mountain climbing. I should also like to remember Hans Imboden and Hans Hary, my guides during my mountain-climbing expeditions.

Finally, I would like to mention Prof. Dr. h.c. Wilhelm Treue, who guided me through my graduation to my work in technical naval history.

For the present work, I must acknowledge the help of Katharina Rohde, who spent almost two years keying the text on computer, putting it in the required format and incorporating the changes arising from new information; and of Franz Seliger, who kindly made illustrations from his extensive archive available to the authors. The following also gave invaluable assistance by providing illustrations and information: Rainer Busch, René Greger, Hans H. Hildebrand, Siegmund Mainusch, Dr Rolf Nahrendorf, Prof. Theodor F. Siersdorfer and Heiner Theuerkauf.

Eberhard Möller

Editor's Note
Acknowledgement is due to Dr Ron Bicknell, Jack Clamp and Eddie Jones for their kind assistance concerning a number of technical matters.—R.D.C.

Introduction

The following is a basic list of all U-boats to have served with the German Navy (in its various forms), with details of their fates, their successes and the loss of life sustained by their crews.[1]

IMPERIAL NAVY

IN SERVICE

Pre-First World War U-boats	41
UA series	1
Mobilisation U-boats	68
UE Type I minelayers	10
UE Type II minelayers	9
Large U-boats (forerunners of U-cruisers)	2
U-cruisers	4
Converted commercial submarines	7
Sub-total, Fleet U-boats	**142**
UB series U-boats	136
UC series U-boats	95
Grand total	**373**

FATES

FATES	Fleet boats	UB series	UC series	Total
To museum	1	—	—	1
Scrapped, decommissioned or scuttled	7	9	7	23
Delivered	70	56	30	156
Lost	60	63	47	170
Accidentally lost	3	1	7	11
Interned	1	2	4	7
Transferred to allied navies	—	5	—	5
Totals	**142**	**136**	**95**	**373**

LOSSES

5,249 dead, corresponding to about 50 per cent of submarine crewmen.

SUCCESSES

In the First World War, 6,394 merchant ships were sunk, totalling 11,848,702grt. In addition, the following warships were sunk:

Battleships	10
Armoured cruisers	10
Protected cruisers	2
Light cruisers	4
Minelaying cruisers	1
Aircraft depot ships	1
Monitors	1
Destroyers	21
Torpedo boats	8
Gunboats	4
Sloops	14
Patrol boats	2
Minelayers	4
Minesweepers	8
Submarines	10
Total	**100**

KRIEGSMARINE

U-BOATS IN SERVICE (863 commissioned)

UA	1
Type IA	2
Type IIA	6
Type IIB	20
Type IIC	8
Type IID	16
Type VIIA	10
Type VIIB	24
Type VIIC	659
Type VIID	6
Type VIIF	4
Type IXA	8
Type IXB	14
Type IXC	54

Type IXC/40	87
Type IXD1	2
Type IXD2	28
Type IXD/42	1
Type XB	8
Type XIV	10
V-80	1
Type Wa 201	2
Type Wk 202	2
Type XVIIB	3
Type XXI	118
Type XXIII	62
Foreign-built	4
Captured submarines	9
Total	**1,169**

STATUS

In-service losses:

To enemy surface ships	243
To enemy aircraft	258
To enemy surface ships/aircraft combined	45
To enemy submarines	22
To mines	11
To unknown cause (missing without trace)	40
To collisions at sea (operational)	7
To foundering as a result of combat damage	16
To capture	7
To scuttling/demolition overseas	11
Subtotal	**660**

Losses etc due to other causes:

To enemy action at overseas bases	16
To enemy action at home	39
To diving accidents	6
To collisions at home while building	16
To mines in home waters	7
Decommissioned before end of war	56
Sunk in error by German torpedo boat	1
Surrendered to Japan	8
Scuttled in German coastal waters by end of war	198
At sea at end of war, scuttled after capitulation	4
At homeports at end of war	108
At sea at end of war, taken to Allied ports	30
At sea at end of war, returned to homeports	16
Subtotal	**509**
Grand total	**1,169**

LOSSES

30,003 dead, out of a total of some 40,000 crewmen—the figure given by Dönitz as being crewmen who took part in at least one wartime sortie. The percentage loss was thus approximately 75.

SUCCESSES

During the Second World War, 2,840 merchant ships were sunk, totalling 14,333,082grt, along with the following warships:

Aircraft carriers	6
Battleships	2
Light cruisers	5
Cruiser-minelayers	1
Destroyers	34
Destroyer-escorts	18
Frigates	2
Corvettes	26
Sloops	13
Fleet minesweepers	10
Submarines	9
Submarine-chasers	3
Gunboats	1
Fast minesweepers	3
Landing ships	13
Depot ships, aircraft tenders	3
Total	**149**

BUNDESMARINE

SERVICE

240 class (*Hai* and *Hecht*)	2
241 class (*Wilhelm Bauer*)	1
201 class	3
202 class	2
205 class	11
206 class	18
Total	**37**

FATES

To museums	3
Decommissioned, scrapped	12
Target boat	1
Sonar trials boat	1
Currently in service	12
Total	**37**

Early Submersibles

The *Brandtaucher*

Wilhelm Bauer was born on 23 March 1822 in Dillingen and died on 18 June 1876 in Munich. From 1848 he was involved in the construction of submersibles, about which there was much discussion during the German–Danish War and for which there were high hopes at the time. He sketched his first submersible in 1850, a single-case type with transverse frames and riveted 6mm iron plating. Bauer's original sketch shows two floodable compartments and one control compartment, but this design was not implemented: instead 20 tons of iron in the keel served as ballast, trim being controlled by an adjustable 0.5 ton weight. Propulsion was achieved by means of two pedal-wheels with a two-stage transmission on a drive shaft connected to a propeller. This first draft, including as it does floodable and control compartments, has all the basic essentials required for a functional submarine. Indeed, in

the opinion of the British author Burgoyne, Bauer made a greater contribution to the development of the submarine than any other inventor.[1] However, the completed boat did not reflect all of Bauer's early ideas.

The submersible displaced between 28.2 and 30.95 tons and had a length of 8.07m (26ft 6in), a beam of 2.01m (6ft 7in) and a draught of 2.63m (8ft 8in). Construction was begun at the Hollersch Glassworks, Rendsburg, in 1850, additional work being undertaken by Schweffel & Howaldt in Kiel.

The boat sank in a diving accident during acceptance trials in Kiel harbour on 1 February 1851, although fortunately there were no casualties. The wreck was discovered in 1887 during dredging operations at Ellerbeck and was raised on 5 July 1887. It was first placed on display at the Naval Academy in Kiel, then from 1906 in the Museum für Meereskunde (Museum of Oceanography) in Berlin. In 1963–65 the boat was restored at Rostock and in 1965 was placed in the German Army Museum at Potsdam. It was transferred in 1972 to the Army Museum at Dresden.

Friedrich Otto Vogel's Boats

Vogel was born on 10 February 1844, in Dresden. Soon after completing his training as a teacher, he left the profession in order to devote his time to the study of submersibles and submarines and, in particular, the possibilities of using steam propulsion underwater.

His first boat was built in the winter of 1867/68 in the workshop of Friedrich Raschke, a locksmith, in Friedrichstadt, Dresden. Vogel's son has written that, however, 'the hull proved not to be watertight, as a result of shortcomings in

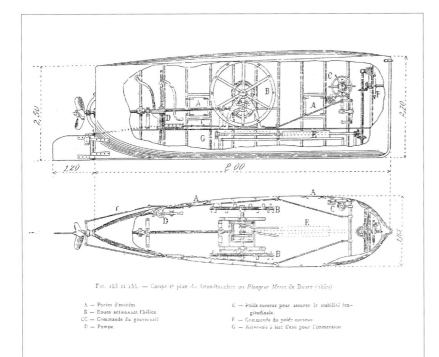

Fig. 153 et 154. — Coupe et plan du Brandtaucher ou Plongeur Marin de Bauer (1850).

A — Portes d'entrées
B — Roues actionnant l'hélice
CC — Commande du gouvernail
D — Pompe.

E — Poids curseur pour assurer la stabilité longitudinale.
F — Commande du poids curseur.
G — Réservoir à lest d'eau pour l'immersion

Left: A sketch showing Bauer's *Brandtaucher* (literally, 'Fire Diver') of 1850.

Left: Wilhelm Bauer's *Brandtaucher*—the first German submersible, and the foreunner of the U-boat.

Right: A sketch of one of Vogel's boats.

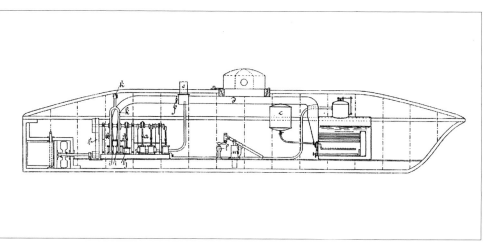

the riveted iron construction and, moreover, was insufficiently robust.'[2] The craft was broken up.

Vogel placed an order with Otto Schlick's Schiffs- und Maschinenbauanstalt (Institute of Ship and Mechanical Engineering) at Dresden for a second submersible. This, according to his own records, had a length of 10m (32ft 10in). However, because his personal finances were exhausted, Vogel approached the Königlich Sächsische Ministerium (Royal Ministry of Saxony) and the Königlich Preußische Marineministerium (Royal Naval Ministry of Prussia) for assistance. Both refused him.Vogel's design was favourably received, but it was never tested. His son again: 'The inventor's funds came to an end, and the shipbuilder did not have the capital to support the project, so the craft lay uncompleted and was later scrapped, as a result of which the inventor was financially ruined.'[3]

In 1868–69 Vogel tried once more to obtain some financial backing for another project, his final efforts being set down in a report dated 17 April 1869, about which the *Dresdner Journal* carries some detailed information. Vogel indicated that an underwater endurance of three hours

would be possible, although he never explained how steam would be produced from the machinery during this time. On one occasion he referred to heating the boiler underwater in the same way as it would be on the surface, on another of a superheater for the boiler, and later still of 'reboiling' to relieve the steam pressure. Following his failure to attract any funding, Vogel destroyed all his plans and in 1876 resumed his teaching career in Saxony. He later lived in Leipzig.

Vogel survived just long enough to learn of the successes achieved by Otto Weddigen with U 9 on 22 September 1914 against three Royal Navy armoured cruisers. These sinkings may have brought him some satisfaction that his ideas of 50 years earlier had justification. He died on 22 October 1914.

Howaldt Boat, 1891
This craft is mentioned for the first time in 1902 by Delpeuch.[4] He refers to a length of 30.25m (99ft 3in), a displacement of 180 tons and a range of 24nm surfaced and 1.5nm submerged.

The 24 November 1902 issue of the French newspaper *Le Matin* reported on the boat, amending Delpeuch's dimensions—length 15m (49ft 4in), diameter 2m (6ft 7in)—and even providing an illustration, which shows a spindle-shaped hull with clearly defined, continuous, longitudinal external ribbing. In 1903, Burgoyne maintained that this picture was taken in 1891 at Howaldt in Kiel—information that was repeated over the ensuing decades by many authors who refer to the 'Howaldt boat'.[5]

The truth was revealed to the author in 1989, prompted by a message in *Reports from the Branch of Maritime Affairs* of 1902 following investigations in the Federal and Military archives in Freiburg: the illustration has nothing to do with Howaldt, nor, indeed, Germany.[6] The Inspectorate of Torpedoes, following a brief visit (not to Kiel, but to Petersen's Dock in Hamburg) wrote to the Secretary of State in the Imperial Navy Office, as follows:

> The submarine arrived in Hamburg aboard the steamer *Pennsylvania*, and, according to a memorandum in the Hamburg-Amerika Line's records, belongs to a Mr Hermann Reiche, whose address in Hamburg is Große Bleichen 3 III.
>
> The boat is high and dry at Petersen's Dock and will remain there until spring 1903, at which time it is to be taken into the water and trials will be commenced. On questioning the above-mentioned Mr Reiche concerning a tour of the boat, only during next summer might such be offered: the boat is guarded day and night, so that an inspection of the boat's interior is unfortunately not permissible at the moment.
>
> Occasionally, on journeys through Hamburg, Geheimrath Veith has noticed the boat at the Petersen dock: it was hanging in the floating crane, in order to have its weight checked. It was originally stated that the weight was 15 tons, but it must in fact have been more than 30 tons since the 30-ton capacity of the crane was insufficient for the cradle.

The boat is constructed of wood, with copper or sheet-brass plating. It is about 15 metres long and 3 metres at its largest diameter, the cross-section being almost circular. It has a wooden superstructure deck, with an iron cylinder-like structure, about 0.8 metres in diameter, rising from it. Its deck can be closed by means of a cover, providing access to the interior of the boat. There is no vertical rudder at the stern, but horizontal rudders [*sic*] could be seen on either side. Propellers were not visible, [but] a tube about 400 millimetres in diameter jutted out at the stern—possibly some sort of propulsion device. Similarly, no torpedo launching system could be seen.

The owner of the boat was present at the weighing and was anxious to keep inquisitive eyes away from it. To any direct questions put to him concerning the internal arrangements and intended use of the boat, he answered only generally, and, from the information given, no sense of the internal arrangements could be deduced.

The boat, in its current configuration, is unsuitable for naval purposes: the attitude of the owner and the incorrect weight declaration in the shipping manifest do not exactly inspire confidence in the thing. However, inspection will continue, and reports will be made in due course.[7]

The identity of the boat's American builders, and its fate after it arrived in Germany, will probably remain a mystery.

Howaldt Boat No 333[8]

This boat was built in 1897 at Howaldtswerke in Kiel and was first mentioned in print in 1898:

> An underwater torpedo boat was manufactured at Howaldtswerke shipbuilders at the mouth of the Schwentine, on behalf of a firm in Berlin and based on plans prepared by a German torpedo officer. The craft, shaped like a torpedo, is fifteen metres long and two metres at its maximum diameter.[9]

Left: The 1891 Howaldt boat.

Forelle

Designer	d'Équevilley
Builder	Germaniawerft, Kiel
Completion date	20 June 1903
Length	13.0m
Diameter of pressure hull	1.66m
Beam (over torpedo tubes)	2.82m
Displacement	15.5 tonnes surfaced, 16.5 tonnes submerged
Propulsion system	Electric motor, 65hp
Batteries	108 (later 94) cells
Maximum speed	
without torpedo system	7.55 knots surfaced, 7.73 knots submerged
with torpedo system	6.55 knots surfaced, 6.50 knots submerged
Range	
without torpedo system	6.0nm at 4.5 knots
with torpedo system	3.5nm at 4.5 knots

The lower part of the hull comprises a box-shaped keel designed to accommodate either compressed air or water, depending upon whether the vessel is required to surface or submerge. In the second week of October, the boat commenced trials in the coastal waters off Kiel. During the first of these, which lasted three hours, the craft managed to submerge to a depth of two metres, although it could have gone deeper, and just as readily in the horizontal as in the vertical plane, thanks to the two horizontal [stabilisers] and single vertical rudder for steering. The propulsion system is electrical; the torpedo armament is situated in the bows of the craft. The boats will be taken in hand for further small modifications, after which trials will be resumed.

Lawrenz has furnished the following data, published in 1938 in his book *100 Jahre Howaldt*:[10]

Propulsion, both surfaced and submerged, was by means of a steerable electric motor of 120hp, speed 6–7 knots, underwater performance not quoted.

On 18 March 1902 the Inspectorate of Torpedo Systems at the Reichsmarineamt wrote as follows:

> Trials with the Howaldtswerke submarine have been aborted owing to a lack of adequate batteries.
> Following the death of Herr Howaldt, further tests have aroused particular interest—a consequence of the great enthusiasm for the project shown by the company management.[11]

The electric motor was a constant-speed device, connected in parallel, and had an output of 65hp. Speed was varied by rotating wingbolts

The batteries, designed by Dr Kisertzki, were supplied by Watt-Akkumulatoren-Fabrik in Zehdenick. They comprised 108 cells each weighing 65kg and having a capacity of 715 amp-hours and a discharge of ten hours. Turfs of

Above left: The so-called 'Leps'sches Tauchboot' tests the water, 1903.
Left: *Forelle* en route by rail to St Petersburg in 1904. The name of the boat, in Cyrillic script, can be discerned at the bow.

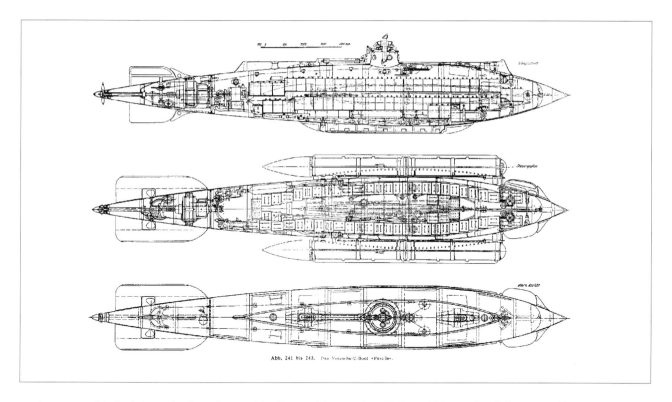

peat were used to isolate each plate. Later, 14 cells would be used, in order to increase stability.

The boat first took to the water on 20 June 1903, Kritzler reporting in detail on the tests conducted off Kiel and in Eckenförde. As a result of various modifications, displacement rose to 17.5 and then to 19.0 tonnes.

In 1904 Germaniawerft received orders for the Russian boats *Karb*, *Karas* and *Kambala*. *Forelle*—as the Howaldt boat had been named— was included in the selling price,

and on 20 June 1904 was loaded on to a railway transporter at Kiel, bound for St Petersburg, where Kritzler trained a Russian crew.

The boat was then taken to Vladivostok by rail to participate in the Russo–Japanese War, but saw no action in that conflict because suitable targets were never encountered in the waters in which she operated. However, her mere presence was, according to the Russians, the reason the Japanese refrained from attacking Vladivostok.

Above: Inboard general-arrangement drawings for *Forelle*.
Right: *Forelle* under hoist at Germaniawerft, Kiel.

U-Boats in Service

KAISERLICHE MARINE

U 1

Type	Prewar boat
Design and development	Coastal, double-hull type. Design by Friedrich Krupp, Germaniawerft, 1904–05. Based on *Karp*, *Karas* and *Kambala* (sold to Russia).
Builder	Germaniawerft, Kiel
In service	1906
Type displacement	238 tonnes surfaced, 283 tonnes submerged
Dimensions	42.39 × 3.75 × 3.17m
Speed	10.8 knots surfaced, 8.7 knots submerged
Range	1,500nm at 10 knots surfaced, 50nm at 5 knots submerged
Propulsion	
surfaced	Two 6-cylinder, two-stroke Körting petrol engines = 400hp
submerged	Two Deutschen Elektromotorenwerke Garbe-Lahmeyer combined motor/generators = 300kW
Armament	One 45cm torpedo tube
Crew	Two officers and 10 men (later three officers and 19 men)
Fate	To Deutsche Museum, Munich, in 1921

Below: The Russian submarine *Karp* was built at Kiel and was based on *Forelle.* It served as a blueprint for U 1.

U 2

Type	Prewar boat
Design and development	Coastal, double-hull type. Official design (1905).
Builder	Kaiserliche Werft, Danzig
In service	1908
Type displacement	341 tonnes surfaced, 430 tonnes submerged
Dimensions	45.42 × 5.5 × 3.05m
Speed	13.2 knots surfaced, 9.0 knots submerged
Range	1,600nm at 13 knots surfaced, 50nm at 5 knots submerged
Propulsion	
surfaced	Two 6-cylinder, four-stroke Daimler petrol engines = 600hp
submerged	Two SSW electric motors = 460kW
Armament	Two 45cm bow and two 45cm stern torpedo tubes
Crew	Three officers and 19 men
Fate	Scrapped 1920

Above: Two photographs depicting U 1 under way in the Baltic.

U 3, U 4

Type	Prewar boats
Design and development	Official design. Ocean-going, double-hull type.
Builder	Kaiserliche Werft, Danzig
In service	1909
Type displacement	421 tonnes surfaced, 510 tonnes submerged
Dimensions	51.28 × 5.6 × 3.05m
Speed	11.8 knots surfaced, 9.4 knots submerged
Range	3,000nm at 9 knots surfaced, 55nm at 4.5 knots submerged
Propulsion	
surfaced	Two 6-cylinder, two-stroke Körting petrol engines = 600hp
submerged	Two SSW electric motors = 760kW
Armament	Two 45cm bow and two 45cm stern torpedo tubes, plus (until late 1914) one rotary cannon or (from 1915) one 5cm gun
Crew	Three officers and 19 men
Fates	
U 3	Sunk by accident 17 November 1911 at Kiel (3 fatalities); raised by *Vulcan*, surrendered; sank 1 December 1918 under tow off Preston
U 4	Scrapped 1919

U 5–8

Type	Prewar boats
Design and development	Ocean-going, double-hull type. Design by Germaniawerft (Dr Techel).
Builder	Germaniawerft, Kiel
In service	1910–11
Type displacement	505 tonnes surfaced, 636 tonnes submerged
Dimensions	57.3 × 5.6 × 3.55m
Speed	13.4 knots surfaced, 10.2 knots submerged
Range	3,300nm at 9 knots surfaced, 80nm at 5 knots submerged
Propulsion	
surfaced	Two 6-cylinder, two-stroke and two 8-cylinder, two-stroke Körting petrol engines = 600hp
submerged	Two SSW electric motors = 760kW
Armament	Two 45cm bow and two 45cm stern torpedo tubes, plus one rotary cannon and (U 6 and U 8 additionally from 1915) one 5cm gun
Crew	Four officers and 24 men (U 8: 25 men)
Fates	
U 5	Sunk with all hands 18 December 1914 in English Channel (by mine?)
U 6	Sunk 15 September 1915 off coast of Norway (24 fatalities)
U 7	Sunk 21 January 1915 off coast of Netherlands by torpedo from U 22 (26 fatalities)
U 8	Sunk 4 March 1915 in English Channel (no of fatalities unknown)

Far left, upper: U 1 and U 2 with the submarine tender *Vulcan*, at Swinemünde.
Far left, lower: A photograph of U 3.
Below: U 7 under way at full speed.

U 9–12

Type	Prewar boats
Design and development	Ocean-going, double-hull type. Official design.
Builder	Kaiserliche Werft, Danzig
In service	1910–11
Type displacement	493 tonnes surfaced, 611 tonnes submerged
Dimensions	57.4 × 6.0 × 3.13m
Speed	14.2 knots surfaced, 8.1 knots submerged
Range	3,250nm at 9 knots surfaced, 80nm at 5 knots submerged
Propulsion	
surfaced	Two 6-cylinder, two-stroke and two 8-cylinder, two-stroke Körting petrol engines = 1,000hp
submerged	Two SSW electric motors = 860kW
Armament	Two 45cm bow and two 45cm stern torpedo tubes, plus one rotary cannon (U 9, U 10, U 12 until late 1914: one rotary cannon; U 9, U 10 from 1915: one rotary cannon and one 5cm gun; U 9 March–December 1916: mines only, for experimental purposes; U 10: one 8.8cm)
Crew	Four officers and 25 men
Fates	
U 9	Surrendered 16 November 1918; scrapped at Morecambe 1919
U 10	Final sortie 27 May 1916; lost with all hands in the Gulf of Finland
U 11	Sunk by mine 9 December 1914 in English Channel (29 fatalities)
U 12	Sunk 10 March 1915 in North Sea (20 fatalities)

Below: U 11 making way. Bottom: U 14. The two-stroke petrol engines produced highly visible smoke trails.

U 13–15

Type	Prewar boats
Design and development	Ocean-going, double-hull type. Official design.
Builder	Kaiserliche Werft, Danzig
In service	1912
Type displacement	516 tonnes surfaced, 644 tonnes submerged
Dimensions	57.88 × 6.0 × 3.44m
Speed	14.8 knots surfaced, 10.7 knots submerged
Range	4,000nm at 9 knots surfaced, 90nm at 5 knots submerged
Propulsion	
surfaced	Two 6-cylinder, two-stroke and two 8-cylinder, two-stroke Körting petrol engines = 1,200hp
submerged	Two SSW combined motor/generators (after modification) = 860kW
Armament	Two 45cm bow and two 45cm stern torpedo tubes, plus one rotary cannon (U 14: one 5cm gun)
Crew	Four officers and 25 men
Fates	
U 13	Sunk with all hands 12 August 1914 in the North Sea
U 14	Sunk 5 June 1915 in the North Sea (1 fatality)
U 15	Sunk with all hands 9 August 1914 in North Sea

U 16

Type	Prewar boat
Design and development	Ocean-going, double-hull type. Design by Germaniawerft (Dr Techel).
Builder	Germaniawerft, Kiel
In service	1911
Type displacement	489 tonnes surfaced, 627 tonnes submerged
Dimensions	57.8 × 6.0 × 3.36m
Speed	15.6 knots surfaced, 10.7 knots submerged
Range	4,500nm at 9 knots surfaced, 90nm at 5 knots submerged
Propulsion	
surfaced	Two 6-cylinder, two-stroke and two 8-cylinder, two-stroke Körting petrol engines = 1,200hp
submerged	Two SSW combined motor/generators = 860kW
Armament	Two 45cm bow and two 45cm stern torpedo tubes, plus (until late 1914) one rotary cannon or (from 1915) one 5cm gun
Crew	Four officers and 25 men
Fate	Sunk en route to internment 8 February 1919

Below: U 16 entered service in 1911. The boat was equipped with two bow and two stern torpedo tubes.

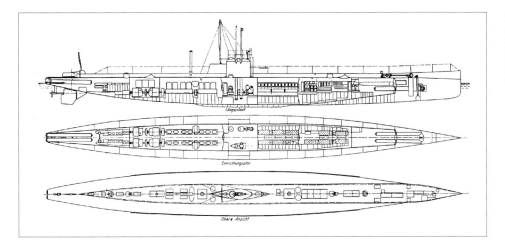

Left: General-arrangement drawings of U 16.
Below left: U 18 was built at the Kaiserliche Werft in Danzig (now the Polish port of Gdansk).

U 17, U 18

Type	Prewar boats
Design and development	Ocean-going, double-hull type. Official design.
Builder	Kaiserliche Werft, Danzig
In service	1912
Type displacement	564 tonnes surfaced, 691 tonnes submerged
Dimensions	62.35 × 6.0 × 3.4m
Speed	14.9 knots surfaced, 9.5 knots submerged
Range	6,700nm at 8 knots surfaced, 75nm at 5 knots submerged
Propulsion	
surfaced	Four 8-cylinder, two-stroke Körting petrol engines = 1,400hp
submerged	Two AEG combined motor/generators = 820kW
Armament	Two 45cm bow and two 45cm stern torpedo tubes, plus (U 17 only, until 1917) one rotary cannon or (U 17 thereafter) one 5cm gun
Crew	Four officers and 25 men
Fates	
U 17	Scrapped 1919–20
U 18	Sunk 23 November 1914 off the Orkney Islands (1 fatality)

Below: U 22, U 20, U 19 and U 21 in port.

U 19–U 22

Type	Prewar boats
Design and development	Ocean-going, double-hull type. Official design.
Builder	Kaiserliche Werft, Danzig
In service	1913
Type displacement	650 tonnes surfaced, 837 tonnes submerged
Dimensions	64.15 × 6.1 × 3.58m
Speed	15.4 knots surfaced, 9.5 knots submerged
Range	9,700nm (U 21: 7,600nm) at 8 knots surfaced, 80nm at 5 knots submerged
Propulsion	
surfaced	Two 6-cylinder, four-stroke MAN SM6×400 diesel engines = 1,800hp
submerged	Two AEG combined motor/generators = 880kW
Armament	Two 50cm bow and two 45cm stern torpedo tubes, plus one or (from 1916) two 8.8cm or (U 19 only, from 1917) one 10.5cm gun.
Crew	Four officers and 31 men
Fates	
U 19	Surrendered 24 November 1918; scrapped 1919–20 at Blyth
U 20	Stranded and sunk 5 November 1916 off Jutland; broken up 1925
U 21	Sunk 22 February 1919 en route to internment
U 22	Surrendered 1 December 1918; scrapped 1919–20 at Blyth

U 23–U 26

Type	Prewar boats
Design and development	Ocean-going, double-hull type. Germaniawerft design.
Builder	Germaniawerft, Kiel
In service	1913–14
Type displacement	669 tonnes surfaced, 864 tonnes submerged
Dimensions	64.7 × 6.32 × 3.45m
Speed	16.7 knots surfaced, 10.3 knots submerged
Range	9,910nm (U 25: 7,620nm) at 8 knots surfaced, 85nm at 5 knots submerged
Propulsion	
surfaced	Two 6-cylinder, two-stroke Germaniawerft diesel engines = 1,700hp
submerged	Two SSW combined motor/generators = 880kW
Armament	Two 50cm bow and two 50cm stern torpedo tubes, plus one or (U 25, on occasion) two 8.8cm guns
Crew	Four officers and 31 men
Fates	
U 23	Sunk 20 July 1915 in the North Sea (24 fatalities)
U 24	Surrendered 22 November 1918; scrapped 1921–22 at Swansea
U 25	Surrendered 23 February 1919; scrapped 1921–22 at Cherbourg
U 26	Sunk with all hands September 1915 in the Baltic Sea

Below: U 24 survived World War I and was surrendered with other German U-boats after hostilities had ceased.

U 27–U 30

Below right: General arrangement of U 31–U 37.

Type	Prewar boats
Design and development	Ocean-going, double-hull type. Official design.
Builder	Kaiserliche Werft, Danzig
In service	1914
Type displacement	675 tonnes surfaced, 867 tonnes submerged
Dimensions	64.7 × 6.32 × 3.48m
Speed	16.7 knots surfaced, 9.8 knots submerged
Range	8,420nm (U 30: 9,770nm) at 8 knots surfaced, 85nm at 5 knots submerged
Propulsion	
surfaced	Two 6-cylinder, four-stroke MAN S6V41/42 diesel engines = 2,000hp
submerged	Two AEG combined motor/generators = 880kW
Armament	Two 50cm bow and two 50cm stern torpedo tubes, plus (U 30 until 1916) one or (U 27 and U 28, and U 30 from 1916) two 8.8cm or (U 30 in 1918) one 10.5cm gun
Crew	Four officers and 31 men
Fates	
U 27	Sunk with all hands 19 August 1915 in the English Channel
U 28	Sunk with all hands 2 September 1917 in the Arctic Ocean
U 29	Sunk with all hands 18 March 1915 in the North Sea
U 30	Sunk with all hands 22 June 1915 in an accident in the Ems estuary; raised 22 November 1918, surrendered, scrapped 1919–20 at Blyth

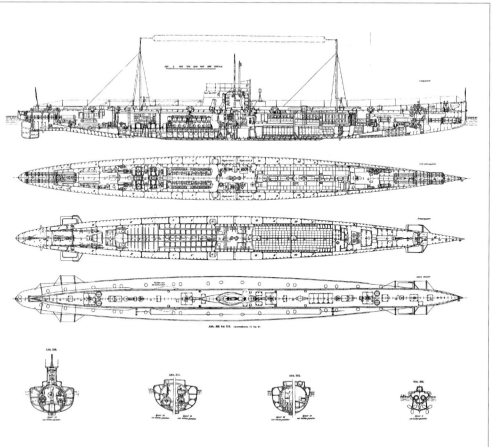

U 31–U 41

Type	Prewar boats
Design and development	Ocean-going, double-hull type. Germaniawerft design.
Builder	Germaniawerft, Kiel
In service	1914–15
Type displacement	685 tonnes surfaced, 878 tonnes submerged
Dimensions	64.4 × 6.32 × 3.56m
Speed	16.7 knots surfaced, 9.8 knots submerged
Range	8,790nm at 8 knots surfaced, 80nm at 5 knots submerged
Propulsion	
surfaced	Two 6-cylinder, two-stroke Germaniawerft diesel engines = 1,850hp
submerged	Two SSW combined motor/generators = 880kW
Armament	Two 50cm bow and two 50cm stern torpedo tubes, plus:
U 35	1914: one 7.5cm gun; 1915: one 8.8cm gun; 1916: one 10.5cm gun
U 32, U 36, U 37	Two 8.8cm guns
U 33, U 34, U 38–U 41	One 8.8cm gun
U 32–U 34, U 36–U 39	One 10.5cm gun from 1916–17
Crew	Four officers and 31 men
Fates	
U 31	Lost without trace January 1915 in the North Sea
U 32	Sunk with all hands 5 May 1918 north-west of Malta
U 33	Surrendered 16 January 1919; scrapped 1919–20 at Blyth
U 34	Sunk with all hands October 1918 in the Mediterranean Sea
U 35	Surrendered 26 November 1918; scrapped 1919–20 at Blyth
U 36	Sunk 24 July 1915 west of Rona, Hebrides (18 fatalities)
U 37	Sunk with all hands April 1915 by mine in the English Channel
U 38	Surrendered 22 February 1919; scrapped 1921 at Brest
U 39	Sunk 18 May 1918 off El Ferrol (2 fatalities); interned; surrendered 1919; scrapped 1923 at Toulon
U 40	Sunk 23 June 1915 in the North Sea (29 fatalities)
U 41	Sunk 24 September 1915 in the English Channel (35 fatalities)

Below: The most successful U-boat of all time, U 35, seen here under the Austro-Hungarian flag, at Pola, with an *Erherzog Karl* class battleship in the distance. Under four commanders, U 35 sank 223 merchantmen with an aggregate registered tonnage of 536,000. Right: U 35 off Cattaro (Kotor) in the southern Adriatic.

U 43–U 50

Type	War Mobilisation boats
Design and development	Ocean-going, double-hull type. Official design, War Contract A.
Builder	Kaiserliche Werft, Danzig
In service	1915–16
Type displacement	725 tonnes surfaced, 940 tonnes submerged
Dimensions	65.0 × 6.2 × 3.74m
Speed	15.2 knots surfaced, 9.7 knots submerged
Range	11,400nm at 8 knots surfaced, 51nm at 5 knots submerged
Propulsion	
surfaced	Two 6-cylinder, four-stroke MAN S6V41/42 diesel engines = 2,000hp
submerged	Two SSW combined motor/generators = 880kW
Armament	Two 50cm bow and two 50cm stern torpedo tubes, plus (U 43–U 46) one (later two) 8.8cm gun or (from 1916–17) one 10.5cm gun, plus (U 43, U 44, from 1916) mines
Crew	Four officers and 32 men
Fates	
U 43	Surrendered 20 November 1918; scrapped 1922 at Swansea
U 44	Sunk with all hands 12 August 1917 in the North Sea
U 45	Sunk 12 September 1917 west of the Shetlands (43 fatalities)
U 46	Surrendered 26 November 1918; became Japanese O 2; scrapped 1922 at Kure
U 47	Scuttled 28 October 1918 off Pola
U 8	Sunk 24 November 1917 in the Thames estuary and beached (19 fatalities)
U 49	Sunk with all hands 11 September 1917 in the Irish Sea
U 50	Missing with all hands September 1917 in the North Sea

U 51–U 56

Type	War Mobilisation boats
Design and development	Ocean-going, double-hull type. Official/Germaniawerft design, War Contract A.
Builder	Germaniawerft, Kiel
In service	1916
Type displacement	715 tonnes surfaced, 902 tonnes submerged
Dimensions	65.2 × 6.44 × 3.64m
Speed	17.1 knots surfaced, 9.1 knots submerged
Range	9,400nm at 8 knots surfaced, 59nm at 5 knots submerged
Propulsion	
surfaced	Two 6-cylinder, four-stroke MAN S6V45/42 diesel engines = 2,400hp
submerged	Two SSW combined motor/generators = 880kW
Armament	Two 50cm bow and two 50cm stern torpedo tubes, plus two 8.8cm or (U 52 from 1917) one 10.5cm or (U 53–U 55 from 1916–17) one 8.8cm and one 10.5cm gun
Crew	Four officers and 32 men
Fates	
U 51	Sunk 14 July 1916 in the Ems estuary (34 fatalities); raised 1968, scrapped
U 52	Sunk 29 October 1917 following a torpedo explosion at Kiel (5 fatalities); raised 31 October 1917, repaired; surrendered 21 November 1918; scrapped 1922 at Swansea
U 53	Surrendered 1 December 1918; scrapped 1922 at Swansea
U 54	Surrendered 24 November 1918; scrapped 1919 at Taranto
U 55	Surrendered 26 November 1918; became Japanese O 3; scrapped 1922 at Sasebo
U 56	Disappeared without trace some time after 2 November 1916 in the Arctic Ocean

U 57–U 59

Type	War Mobilisation boats
Design and development	Ocean-going, double-hull type. Official/Germaniawerft design, War Contract A.
Builder	A. G. Weser, Bremen
In service	1916
Type displacement	786 tonnes surfaced, 954 tonnes submerged
Dimensions	67.0 × 6.32 × 3.79m
Speed	14.7 knots surfaced, 8.4 knots submerged
Range	7,730nm at 8 knots surfaced, 55nm at 5 knots submerged
Propulsion	
surfaced	Two 6-cylinder, two-stroke MAN (Nürnberg) 8SS35 diesel engines = 1,700hp
submerged	Two SSW combined motor/generators = 880kW
Armament	Two 50cm bow and two 50cm stern torpedo tubes, plus two 8.8cm (U 57: one 10.5cm and from 1916–17 also one 8.8cm) or (U 58, U 59 from 1916–17) one 10.5cm and one 8.8cm gun
Crew	Four officers and 32 men
Fates	
U 57	Surrendered 24 November 1918; scrapped 1921 at Cherbourg
U 58	Sunk 17 November 1917 in the Bristol Channel (2 fatalities)
U 59	Sunk 14 May 1917 on a German mine in the North Sea (33 fatalities)

U 60–U 62

Type	War Mobilisation boats
Design and development	Ocean-going, double-hull type. Official/Germaniawerft design, War Contract A.
Builder	A. G. Weser, Bremen
In service	1916
Type displacement	768 tonnes surfaced, 956 tonnes submerged
Dimensions	67.0 × 6.32 × 3.74m
Speed	16.5 knots surfaced, 8.4 knots submerged
Range	11,400nm at 8 knots surfaced, 49nm at 5 knots submerged
Propulsion	
surfaced	Two 6-cylinder, two-stroke MAN S645/42 diesel engines = 2,400hp
submerged	Two SSW combined motor/generators = 880kW
Armament	Two 50cm bow and two 50cm stern torpedo tubes, plus one 10.5cm (U 60 additionally one 8.8cm) gun
Crew	Four officers and 32 men
Fates	
U 60	Surrendered 21 November 1918; ran aground while under tow; scrapped 1921
U 61	Sunk 16 March 1918 in the Irish Sea (36 fatalities)
U 62	Surrendered 21 November 1918; scrapped 1919–20 at Bo'ness

Left: A close-up view of U 61's conning tower.

U 63–U 65

Type	War Mobilisation boats
Design and development	Ocean-going, double-hull type. Official/Germaniawerft design, War Contract A.
Builder	Germaniawerft, Kiel
In service	1916
Type displacement	810 tonnes surfaced, 927 tonnes submerged
Dimensions	68.36 × 6.3 × 4.04m
Speed	16.5 knots surfaced, 9.0 knots submerged
Range	9,170nm at 8 knots surfaced, 60nm at 5 knots submerged
Propulsion	
surfaced	Two 6-cylinder, two-stroke Germaniawerft diesel engines = 2,200hp
submerged	Two SSW combined motor/generators = 880kW
Armament	Two 50cm bow and two 50cm stern torpedo tubes, plus one 8.8cm and (until mid-1918) one 10.5cm gun
Crew	Four officers and 32 men
Fates	
U 63	Surrendered 16 January 1919; scrapped 1919 at Blyth
U 64	Sunk 17 June 1918 south-east of Sardinia (38 fatalities)
U 65	Scuttled 28 October 1918 off Pola

U 66–U 70 (UD)

Type	UD
Design and development	Design by Germaniawerft (Dr Techel). Ocean-going, double-hull type. Built as U 7–U 11 for the Austro-Hungarian Navy, purchased, and completed under War Contract D.
Builder	Germaniawerft, Kiel
In service	1915
Type displacement	791 tonnes surfaced, 933 tonnes submerged
Dimensions	69.5 × 6.3 × 3.79m
Speed	16.8 knots surfaced, 10.3 knots submerged
Range	7,370nm at 8 knots surfaced, 115nm at 5 knots submerged
Propulsion	
surfaced	Two 6-cylinder, two-stroke Germaniawerft diesel engines = 2,300hp
submerged	Two SSW combined motor/generators = 880kW or (U 68– U 70) two Pickler combined motor/generators = 910kW
Armament	Four 45cm bow and one 45cm stern torpedo tube, plus one 8.8cm (U 69 one additional 8.8cm from 1916) or (all boats, from 1916–17) one 10.5cm gun
Crew	Four officers and 32 men
Fates	
U 66	Missing with all hands from 3 September 1917 in the North Sea
U 67	Surrendered 20 November 1918; scrapped 1921 at Fareham
U 68	Sunk with all hands 22 March 1916 west of Dunmore Head
U 69	Missing with all hands from 24 July 1917 in the Irish Sea
U 70	Surrendered 20 November 1918; scrapped 1919–20 at Bo'ness

Right, upper: U 64 in the Mediterranean.
Right, lower: U 69 in rough waters.

U 71–U 80

Type	UE Type I minelayers
Design and development	Ocean-going, single-hull type with saddle tanks. Official design, War Contract E or UE.
Builders	A. G. Vulcan, Hamburg and (U 73, U 74) Kaiserliche Werft, Danzig
In service	1915–16
Type displacement	745–755 tonnes surfaced, 829–832 tonnes submerged
Dimensions	56.8 × 5.9 × 4.86m
Speed	10.6 (U 73, U 74: 9.6; U 75–U 80: 9.9) knots surfaced, 7.9 knots submerged
Range	7,880nm (U 73, U 74: 5,480nm) at 7 knots surfaced, 83nm at 4 knots submerged
Propulsion	
surfaced	Two 6-cylinder, four-stroke Benz (U 73, U 74, U 77–U 80: two 6-cylinder, two-stroke Körting) diesel engines = 900hp
submerged	Two SSW combined motor/generators = 660kW
Armament	One 50cm bow and one 50cm stern torpedo tube, plus one 8.8cm gun (U 72 from 1917: one 10.5cm gun); two minelaying tubes for 38 mines
Crew	Four officers and 28 men
Fates	
U 71	Surrendered 23 February 1919; scrapped 1919–20 at Cherbourg
U 72	Scuttled 1 November 1918 at Cattaro (Kotor)
U 73	Scuttled 30 October 1918 off Pola
U 74	Sunk with all hands 27 May 1916 in the North Sea
U 75	Sunk by mine 13 December 1917 in the North Sea (23 fatalities)
U 76	Sunk 27 January 1917 in the Arctic Ocean (1 fatality)
U 77	Sunk with all hands some time after 5 July 1916 in the North Sea
U 78	Sunk with all hands 28 October 1918 in the North Sea
U 79	Surrendered 21 November 1918; became French *Victor Reveille*, scrapped in 1935
U 80	Surrendered 16 January 1919; scrapped 1922 at Swansea

U 81–U 86

Type	War Mobilisation boats
Design and development	Ocean-going, double-hull type. Official design.
Builders	Germaniawerft, Kiel
In service	1916
Type displacement	808 tonnes surfaced, 946 tonnes submerged
Dimensions	70.06 × 6.3 × 4.02m
Speed	16.8 knots surfaced, 9.1 knots submerged
Range	11,220nm at 8 knots surfaced, 56nm at 5 knots submerged
Propulsion	
surfaced	Two 6-cylinder, four-stroke MAN S6V45/42 diesel engines = 2,400hp
submerged	Two SSW combined motor/generators = 880kW
Armament	Four 50cm bow and two 50cm stern torpedo tubes, plus (U 81–U 83) one 10.5cm gun or (U 84–U 86 until 1917) two 8.8cm guns or (U 84–U 86 from 1917) one 8.8cm and one 10.5cm gun
Crew	Four officers and 31 men
Fates	
U 81	Sunk 1 May 1917 off the west coast of Ireland (24 fatalities)
U 82	Surrendered 16 January 1919; scrapped 1919–20 at Blyth
U 83	Sunk 17 February 1917 off south-west Ireland (36 fatalities)
U 84	Sunk with all hands 26 January 1918 in the Irish Sea
U 85	Sunk with all hands 12 Match 1917 in the English Channel
U 86	Surrendered 20 November 1918; sunk 1921 en route to shipbreakers

U 87–U 92

Type	War Mobilisation boats
Design and development	Ocean-going, double-hull type. Official design.
Builders	Kaiserliche Werft, Danzig
In service	1917
Type displacement	757 tonnes surfaced, 998 tonnes submerged
Dimensions	65.8 × 6.2 × 3.88m
Speed	15.6 knots surfaced, 8.6 knots submerged
Range	11,380nm at 8 knots surfaced, 56nm at 5 knots submerged
Propulsion	
surfaced	Two 6-cylinder, four-stroke MAN S6V45/42 diesel engines = 2,400hp
submerged	Two SSW combined motor/generators = 880kW
Armament	Two 50cm bow and two 50cm stern torpedo tubes, plus (U 87, U 89) one 8.8cm and one10.5cm gun or (U 90–U 92) one 10.5cm gun
Crew	Four officers and 32 men
Fates	
U 87	Sunk with all hands 25 December 1917 in the Irish Sea
U 88	Sunk with all hands by mine 5 September 1917 in the North Sea, off Terschelling
U 89	Sunk with all hands 13 February 1918 in the Atlantic Ocean
U 90	Surrendered 20 November 1918; scrapped 1919–20 at Bo'ness
U 91	Surrendered 26 November 1918; scrapped 1921 at Brest
U 92	Sunk with all hands 9 September 1918 in the North Sea

Left, upper: U 84, showing her 8.8cm deck gun.
Left, lower: U 72 at Pola, 1916. This Adriatic city was from 1797 until 1919 the most significant port of the Austro-Hungarian Empire.

U 93–U 98

Type	War Mobilisation boats
Design and development	Ocean-going, double-hull type. Official design.
Builders	Germaniawerft, Kiel
In service	1917
Type displacement	838 tonnes surfaced, 1,000 tonnes submerged
Dimensions	71.55 × 6.3 × 3.94m
Speed	16.9 knots surfaced, 8.6 knots submerged
Range	9,020nm (U 96–U 98: 8,290nm) at 8 knots surfaced, 52nm (U 96–U 98: 47nm) at 5 knots submerged
Propulsion	
surfaced	Two 6-cylinder, four-stroke MAN S6V45/42 (U 96–U 98: two 6-cylinder, two-stroke Germaniawerft) diesel engines = 2,400hp (U 96–U 98: 2,300hp)
submerged	Two SSW combined motor/generators = 880kW
Armament	Four 50cm bow and two 50cm stern torpedo tubes, plus one 8.8cm or (U 96–U 98) one10.5cm gun or (U 93–U 96 in 1918) one 8.8cm and one 10.5cm gun
Crew	Four officers and 32 men
Fates	
U 93	Lost with all hands January 1918 in the English Channel
U 94	Surrendered 20 November 1918; scrapped 1919–20 at Bo'ness
U 95	Sunk with all hands January 1818 in the English Channel
U 96	Surrendered 20 November 1918; scrapped 1919–20 at Bo'ness
U 97	Sunk by accident 22 November 1918 en route to hand-over
U 98	Surrendered 22 November 1918; scrapped 1919–20 at Blyth

Right: General-arrangement drawing of the U 93–U 98 class.

U 99–U 104

Type	War Mobilisation boats
Design and development	Ocean-going, double-hull type. Official design.
Builders	A. G. Weser, Bremen
In service	1917
Type displacement	750 tonnes surfaced, 952 tonnes submerged
Dimensions	67.7 × 6.32 × 3.65m
Speed	16.5 knots surfaced, 8.8 knots submerged
Range	10,100nm at 8 knots surfaced, 45.4nm at 5 knots submerged
Propulsion	
surfaced	Two 6-cylinder, four-stroke MAN S6V45/42 diesel engines = 2,400hp
submerged	Two SSW combined motor/generators = 880kW
Armament	Two 50cm bow and two 50cm stern torpedo tubes, plus (U 100 until 1918) one 10.5cm or ((U 101–U 104 until 1918) two 8.8cm or (U 100–U 104 from 1918) one 8.8cm and one 10.5cm gun
Crew	Four officers and 32 men
Fates	
U 99	Sunk with all hands 7 July 1917 in the North Sea
U 100	Surrendered 21 November 1918; scrapped 1919–20 at Swansea
U 101	Surrendered 21 November 1918; scrapped 1920 at Morecambe
U 102	Sunk with all hands September 1918 in the North Sea
U 103	Sunk 12 May 1918 in the English Channel (10 fatalities)
U 104	Sunk 5 April 1918 in St George's Channel (41 fatalities)

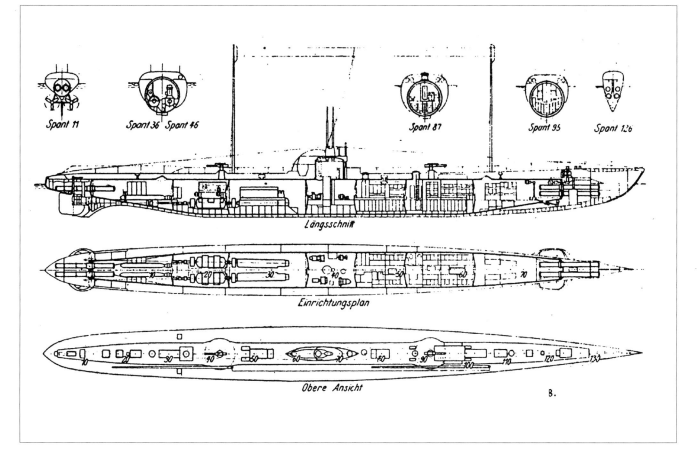

Spant 11   Spant 36   Spant 46   Spant 87   Spant 95   Spant 126

Längsschnitt

Einrichtungsplan

Obere Ansicht

8.

U 105–U 110

Type	War Mobilisation boats
Design and development	Ocean-going, double-hull type. Official design.
Builders	Germaniawerft, Kiel
In service	1917
Type displacement	798 tonnes surfaced, 1,000 tonnes submerged
Dimensions	71.55 × 6.3 × 3.9m
Speed	16.4 knots surfaced, 8.4 knots submerged
Range	9,280nm at 8 knots surfaced, 50nm at 5 knots submerged
Propulsion	
surfaced	Two 6-cylinder, four-stroke MAN S6V45/42 diesel engines = 2,400hp
submerged	Two SSW combined motor/generators = 880kW
Armament	Four 50cm bow and two 50cm stern torpedo tubes, plus one 10.5cm and one 8.8cm gun
Crew	Four officers and 32 men
Fates	
U 105	Surrendered 20 November 1918; became French *Jean Autric*; scrapped 1937
U 106	Sunk with all hands 8 October 1917 in the North Sea
U 107	Surrendered 20 November 1918; scrapped 1922 at Swansea
U 108	Surrendered; became French *Léon Mignot*
U 109	Lost with all hands January 1918 in the English Channel
U 110	Sunk 15 March 1918 north-west of Malin Head (39 fatalities)

U 111–U 114

Type	War Mobilisation boats
Design and development	Ocean-going, double-hull type. Official design.
Builders	Germaniawerft, Kiel (hulls built by Bremer Vulkan and Vegesack)
In service	1917–18
Type displacement	798 tonnes surfaced, 996 tonnes submerged
Dimensions	71.55 × 6.3 × 3.76m
Speed	16.4 knots surfaced, 8.4 knots submerged
Range	8,300nm at 8 knots surfaced, 50nm at 5 knots submerged
Propulsion	
surfaced	Two 6-cylinder, four-stroke MAN S6V45/42 (U 112–U 114: two 6-cylinder, two-stroke Germaniawerft) diesel engines = 2,400hp (U 112–U 114: 2,300hp)
submerged	Two SSW combined motor/generators = 880kW
Armament	Four 50cm bow and two 50cm stern torpedo tubes, plus one 8.8cm and (U 111, U 113 only) one 10.5cm gun
Crew	Four officers and 32 men
Fates	
U 111	Surrendered 20 November 1918; to USA
U 112	Surrendered 20 November 1918; scrapped 1922 at Rochester
U 113	Surrendered 20 November 1918; scrapped 1921 at Brest
U 114	Surrendered 26 November 1918; scrapped 1919 at La Spezia

U 117–U 126

Below: U 126, scrapped in 1923 at Upnor.

Type	U E Type II minelaying cruisers
Design and development	Ocean-going, double-hull type. Official design, War Contract L.
Builders	A. G. Vulcan, Hamburg (U 122–U 126: Blohm & Voss, Hamburg)
In service	1918
Type displacement	1,164 tonnes surfaced, 1,512 tonnes submerged (U 122– U 126: 1,163 tonnes surfaced, 1,468 tonnes submerged)
Dimensions	81.52 × 7.42 × 4.22m (U 122–U 126: 82.0 × 7.42 × 4.22m)
Speed	14.7 knots surfaced, 7 knots (U 122–U 126: 7.2 knots) submerged
Range	13,900nm (U 122–U 126: 11,470nm) at 8 knots surfaced, 35nm at 4.5 knots submerged
Propulsion	
surfaced	Two 6-cylinder, four-stroke MAN S6V45/42 diesel engines = 2,400hp
submerged	Two SSW (U 122–U 126: two BBC) combined motor/generators = 880kW (U 122–U 126: 910kW)
Armament	Four 50cm bow and two 50cm stern torpedo tubes, plus one 8.8cm or (U 117) one 8.8cm and one10.5cm or (U 123) two 10.5cm guns and (all) 42 mines
Crew	Four officers and 36 men
Fates	
U 117	Surrendered 20 November 1918; to USA
U 118	Surrendered 23 February 1919; scrapped 1922 at Brest
U 119	Surrendered 24 November 1918; became French *René Audry*; scrapped 1937
U 120	Surrendered 22 November 1918; scrapped 1919 at La Spezia
U 121	
U 122	Surrendered 26 February 1919; ran aground 1921 en route to shipbreakers
U 123	Surrendered 26 February 1919;ran aground 1921 en route to shipbreakers
U 124	Surrendered 1 December 1918; scrapped 1912 at Swansea
U 125	Surrendered 26 November 1918; became Japanese O 1; scrapped 1922 at Kure
U 126	Surrendered 22 November 1918; scrapped 1923 at Upnor

U 135, U 136

Type	Large U-boats (U-ships)
Design and development	U-cruiser prototypes. Double-hull type. Official design, War Contract M.
Builders	Kaiserliche Werft, Danzig
In service	1918
Type displacement	1,175 tonnes surfaced, 1,534 tonnes submerged
Dimensions	83.5 × 7.54 × 4.36m
Speed	17 knots surfaced, 8.1 knots submerged
Range	c.10,000nm at 8 knots surfaced, 50nm at 4.5 knots submerged
Propulsion	
surfaced	Two 6-cylinder, four-stroke MAN S6V53/53 diesel engines = 3,500hp
submerged	Two AEG combined motor/generators = 1,240kW
Armament	Four 50cm bow and two 50cm stern torpedo tubes, plus one 15cm gun
Crew	Four officers and 42 men
Fates	
U 135	Surrendered 20 November 1918; sunk 1921 off the east coast of Britain en route to shipbreakers
U 136	Surrendered 23 February 1919; scrapped 1921 at Cherbourg

U 139–U 142

Type	U-cruisers (largest U-boats in service)
Design and development	Prototypes. Double-hull type. Official design (Dr Techel, Germaniawerft).
Builders	Germaniawerft, Kiel
In service	1918
Type displacement submerged	1,930 (U 142: 2,158) tonnes surfaced, 2,483 (U 142: 2,785) tonnes
Dimensions	92.0 × 9.12 × 5.27m (U 142: 97.5 × 9.06 × 5.38m)
Speed	15.3–15.8 knots surfaced, 7.6 knots submerged
Range	12,630–17,750nm at 8 knots surfaced, 53nm at 4.5 knots submerged
Propulsion	
surfaced	Two 6-cylinder, four-stroke MAN S6V53/53 (U 142: two 10-cylinder, four-stroke MAN S10V53/53) diesel engines = 3,500hp (U 142: 6,060hp)
submerged	Two AEG combined motor/generators = 1,310kW
Armament	Four 50cm bow and two 50cm stern torpedo tubes, plus two 8.8cm and two 15cm guns (U 139: two 15cm only)
Crew	Six officers and 56 men, plus prize crew of one officer and 20 men
Fates	
U 139	Surrendered 24 November 1918; became French *Halbronn*; scrapped 1935
U 140	Surrendered 23 February 1919; to USA; sunk 22 July 1921
U 141	Surrendered 26 November 1918; scrapped 1923 at Upnor
U 142	Returned to shipyard, scrapped at Oslebshausen

Below: General-arrangement drawings of U 139–U 141.
Right: U 140, which was given the name *Kapitänleutnant Weddigen*.

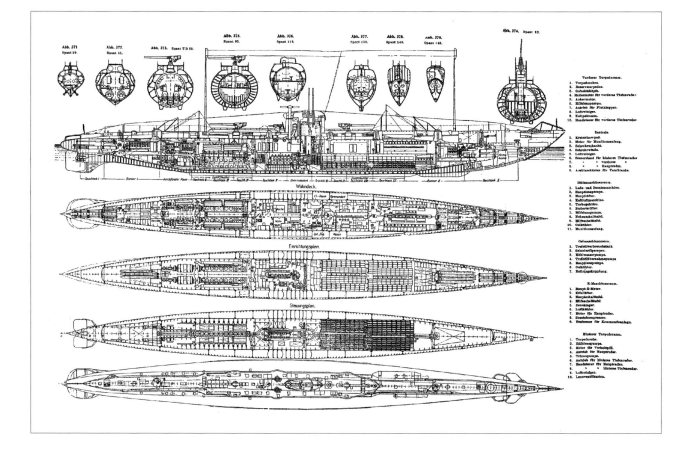

U 151–U 157

Type	Modified commercial (transport) submarines
Design and development	Double-hull type. Germaniawerft design (Dr Techel).
Builders	Flensburger Schiffsbaugesellschaft (U 152–154: Reihersteigwerft, Hamburg; U 165: Atlas Werke, Bremen; U 157: Stülken Sohn, Hamburg). Prefabricated at Germaniawerft, Kiel.
In service	1917
Type displacement	1,512 (U 155: 1,575) tonnes surfaced, 1,875 (U 155: 1,860) tonnes submerged
Dimensions	65.0 × 8.9 × 5.3m
Speed	12.4 (U 155: 10) knots surfaced, 5.2 (U 155: 6.7) knots submerged
Range	c.25,000nm at 5.5 knots surfaced, 65nm at 3 knots submerged
Propulsion	
surfaced	Two 6-cylinder, four-stroke Germaniawerft diesel engines = 800hp
submerged	Two SSW combined motor/generators = 590kW
Armament	Two 50cm bow torpedo tubes (U 155 only: six torpedo rails beneath the upper deck, plus two 15cm and two 8.8cm guns)
Crew	Six officers and 50 men, plus prize crew of one officer and 19 men
Fates	
U 151	Surrendered 24 November 1918; sunk 7 June 1921 by French as target
U 152	Surrendered 24 November 1918; sunk 1921 en route to shipbreakers
U 153	Surrendered 24 November 1918; sunk 1921 en route to shipbreakers
U 154	Sunk with all hands 11 May 1918 in the Atlantic Ocean
U 155	Surrendered 24 November 1918; scrapped 1922 at Morecambe
U 156	Sunk with all hands 5 September 1918 by mine in the North Sea
U 157	Surrendered 8 February 1919; scrapped 1921 at Brest

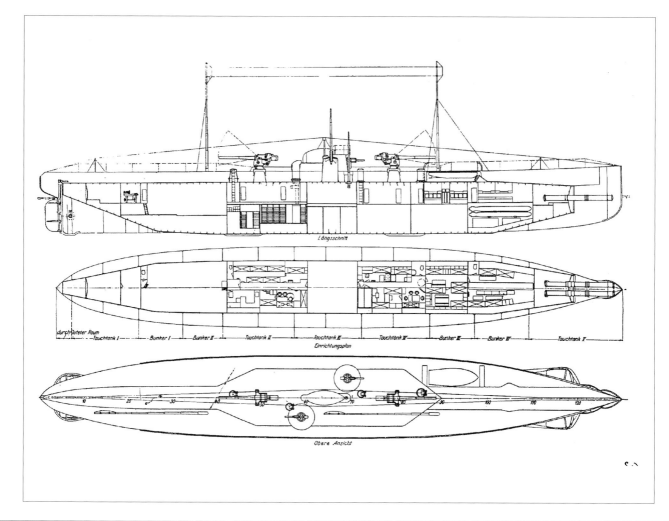

Längsschnitt

durch ljuteter Raum

Tauchtank I — Bunker I — Bunker II — Tauchtank II — Tauchtank III — Tauchtank IV — Bunker III — Bunker IV — Tauchtank V

Einrichtungsplan

Obere Ansicht

U 160–U 165

Left, upper: General arrangement of U 151–U 154. Left, lower: U 152 at Pola. Below: U 166 did not become operational in World War I but was transferred as booty to the French Navy, in which she served as *Jean Roulier*.

Type	War Mobilisation boats
Design and development	Ocean-going, double-hull type. Official design
Builders	Bremer Vulkan, Vegesack
In service	1918 (U 166, U 167 not completed)
Type displacement	821 tonnes surfaced, 1,002 tonnes submerged
Dimensions	71.55 × 6.3 × 3.88m
Speed	16.2 knots surfaced, 8.2 knots submerged
Range	8,500nm at 8 knots surfaced, 50nm at 5 knots submerged
Propulsion	
surfaced	Two 6-cylinder, four-stroke MAN S6V45/42 diesel engines = 2,400hp
submerged	Two SSW combined motor/generators = 880kW
Armament	Four 50cm bow and two 50cm stern torpedo tubes, plus one (U 160: two) 10.5cm gun(s)
Crew	Four officers and 35 men
Fates	
U 160	Surrendered 24 November 1918; scrapped
U 161	Surrendered 20 November 1918; ran aground 1921 en route to shipbreakers
U 162	Surrendered 20 November 1918; became French *Pierre Marrest*; scrapped 1935
U 163	Surrendered 22 November 1918; scrapped 1919 at La Spezia
U 164	Surrendered 22 November 1918; scrapped 1922 at Swansea
U 165	Sunk 18 November 1918 in an accident in the River Weser; scrapped 1919

UA

Type	Coastal (small) U-boat
Design and development	Double-hull type with limited ocean-going capability. Design by Dr Techel, Germaniawerft. Ex-Norwegian A 5, seized, commissioned into the Kaiserliche Marine 5 August 1914
Builders	Germaniawerft, Kiel
In service	1914
Type displacement	270 tonnes surfaced, 342 tonnes submerged
Dimensions	46.7 × 4.78 × 2.8m
Speed	14.2 knots surfaced, 7.3 knots submerged
Range	900nm at 10 knots surfaced, 76nm at 3.3 knots submerged
Propulsion	
surfaced	Two 6-cylinder, two-stroke Germaniawerft diesel engines = 700hp
submerged	Two SSW electric motors = 280kW
Armament	Two 45cm bow and one 45cm stern torpedo tubes, plus (from 1917) one 8.8cm gun
Crew	Three officers and 18 men
Fate	Surrendered 24 November 1918; scrapped 1920–21 at Toulon

Below: General-arrangement drawings of the UA type coastal U-boat.

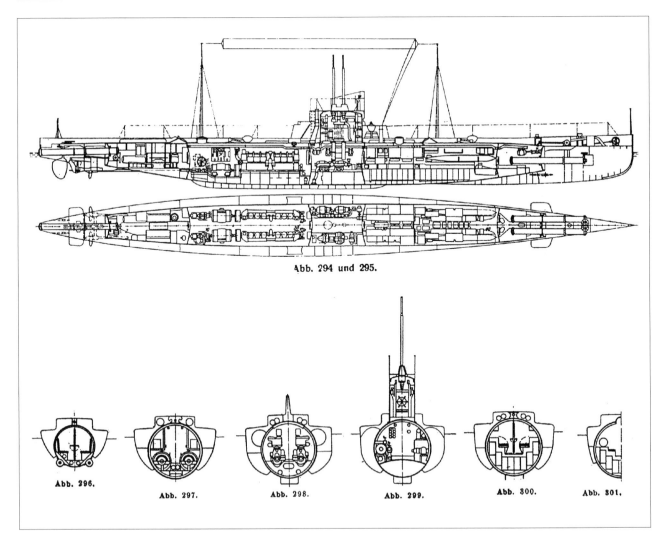

Abb. 294 und 295.

Abb. 296.

Abb. 297.

Abb. 298.

Abb. 299.

Abb. 300.

Abb. 301.

UB 1–UB 17

Type	UB I type (small) U-boats
Design and development	Coastal, single-hull type. Design by Dr Techel, Germaniawerft.
Builders	Germaniawerft, Kiel (UB 9–UB 17: A. G. Weser, Bremen)
In service	1915
Type displacement	127 tonnes surfaced, 142 tonnes submerged
Dimensions	28.1 × 3.15 × 3.03m (UB 9–UB 17: 27.88 × 3.15 × 3.03m)
Speed	6.47 (UB 9–UB 17: 7.45) knots surfaced, 5.51 (UB 9–UB 17: 6.24) knots submerged
Range	1,650nm (UB 9–UB 17: 1,500nm) at 5 knots surfaced, 45nm at 4 knots submerged
Propulsion	
surfaced	One 4-cylinder, four-stroke Daimler RS164 (UB 9–UB 17: Körting) diesel engine = 60hp
submerged	One SSW combined motor/generator = 90kW
Armament	Two 45cm bow torpedo tubes, plus one machine gun (UB 14 from 1917: one rotary cannon; UB 12 converted to minelayer 1918, with 8 mines embarked and torpedo armament deleted)
Crew	One officer and 13 men
Fates	
UB 1	Transferred to Austro-Hungarian Navy 12 July 1915 as U 10
UB 2	To Stinnes for scrapping 1920
UB 3	Sunk with all hands May 1915 in the Mediterranean Sea
UB 4	Sunk with all hands 15 August 1915 in the North Sea
UB 5	To Dräger for scrapping 1920
UB 6	Sunk 18 March 1917 after running aground off Hellevoetluis; interned; surrendered 1919; scrapped at Brest
UB 7	Sunk with all hands October 1916 in the Black Sea
UB 8	Transferred to Bulgarian Navy 25 May 1916 and redesignated U 18; scrapped 1921 at Bizerta
UB 9	To Dräger for scrapping 1920
UB 10	Scuttled 5 October 1918
UB 11	To Stinnes for scrapping 1920
UB 12	Missing, believed sunk with all hands 19 August 1918 after running aground
UB 13	Sunk with all hands 24 April 1916 off the Belgian coast
UB 14	Surrendered November 1918; scrapped 1920 in Malta
UB 15	Transferred to Austro-Hungarian Navy 18 June 1915 as U 11
UB 16	Sunk with all hands 10 May 1918 in the North Sea (15 fatalities)
UB 17	Sunk with all hands March 1918 off Flanders, cause and exact location unknown

Right: UB 13, typifying the UB 1 class of coastal U-boat. This particular vessel was lost off Belgium in 1916.

UB 18–UB 29

Type	UB II type coastal (small) U-boats
Design and development	Coastal, single-hull type with saddle tanks. Official design.
Builders	Blohm & Voss, Hamburg (UB 24–UB 29: A. G. Weser, Bremen)
In service	1915–16
Type displacement	263 (UB 24–UB 29: 265) tonnes surfaced, 292 (UB 24–UB 29: 291) tonnes submerged
Dimensions	36.13 × 4.36 × 3.7m (UB 24–UB 29: 36.13 × 4.36 × 3.66m)
Speed	9.15 (UB 24–UB 29: 8.9) knots surfaced, 5.81 (UB 24–UB 29: 5.72) knots submerged
Range	6,450–6,650nm (UB 24–UB 29: 7,200nm) at 5 knots surfaced, 45nm at 5 knots (UB 24–UB 29: 45nm at 4 knots) submerged
Propulsion	
surfaced	Two 6-cylinder, four-stroke Daimler RS20 (UB 20, UB 23: Körting) diesel engines = 284hp (UB 24, UB 25, UB 27, UB 28: two 6-cylinder, four-stroke Benz DS25u diesel engines = 270hp)
submerged	Two SSW combined motor/generators = 200kW
Armament	Two 50cm bow torpedo tubes (UB 34, UB 35, UB 41 also two above-water torpedo launchers), plus one 8.8cm and one 5cm or (UB 18, from 1917) one 5cm gun only or (UB 20, UB 26, UB 28, UB 29) one 8.8cm gun only, plus (UB 21, UB 22, UB 23, UB 24 only in 1916–17, UB 26 from 1916–17, UB 27) 14 mines
Crew	Two officers and 21 men
Fates	
UB 18	Sunk with all hands 9 December 1917 in the English Channel
UB 19	Sunk 30 November 1916 in the English Channel (8 fatalities)
UB 20	Missing, believed sunk with all hands 29 July 1918 after running aground off Flanders
UB 21	Surrendered 24 November 1918; foundered 1920 en route to shipbreakers
UB 22	Sunk with all hands 19 January 1918 by mine in the North Sea
UB 23	Surrendered 22 February 1919; scrapped 1921 at Brest
UB 24	Surrendered 24 November 1918; scrapped 1921 at Brest
UB 25	Sunk 19 March 1917 at Kiel following a collision with V 26; raised 26 November 1918, surrendered; scrapped 1922 at Canning Town
UB 26	Sunk 5 April 1916 at Le Havre; raised, became French *Roland Morillot*; scrapped 1931
UB 27	Sunk with all hands 29 July 1917 in the North Sea
UB 28	Surrendered 4 November 1918; scrapped 1919–20 at Bo'ness
UB 29	Sunk with all hands 13 December 1916 in the English Channel

UB 30–UB 41

Type	UB II type coastal (small) U-boats
Design and development	Coastal, single-hull type. Official design (1915).
Builders	Blohm & Voss, Hamburg
In service	1916
Type displacement	274 tonnes surfaced, 303 tonnes submerged
Dimensions	36.9 × 4.37 × 3.75m
Speed	9.06 knots surfaced, 5.71 knots submerged
Range	7,030nm at 5 knots surfaced, 45nm at 4 knots submerged
Propulsion	
surfaced	Two 6-cylinder, four-stroke Benz DS25u (UB 36, UB 38–UB 41: Körting) diesel engines = 270hp (UB 36, UB 38–UB 41: 284hp)
submerged	Two SSW combined motor/generators = 200kW
Armament	Two 50cm bow torpedo tubes (UB 34, UB 35, UB 41 also two above-water torpedo launchers), plus one 8.8cm gun, plus (UB 34, UB 35, UB 41 only) 14 mines
Crew	Two officers and 21 men
Fates	
UB 30	Sunk with all hands 13 August 1918 in the North Sea
UB 31	Sunk with all hands 2 May 1918 in the English Channel
UB 32	Sunk with all hands 22 September 1917 in the English Channel
UB 33	Sunk with all hands 11 April 1918 in the English Channel
UB 34	Surrendered 26 November 1918; scrapped 1922 at Canning Town
UB 35	Sunk 26 January 1918 in the English Channel (21 fatalities)
UB 36	Sunk with all hands 21 May 1917 in the English Channel
UB 37	Sunk with all hands 14 January 1917 in the English Channel
UB 38	Sunk with all hands 8 February 1918 by mine in the English Channel
UB 39	Sunk with all hands 15 May 1918 by mine in the English Channel
UB 40	Scuttled 5 October 1918 off Zeebrugge
UB 41	Sunk with all hands 15 October 1917 by mine in the North Sea

UB 42–UB 47

Type	UB II type coastal (small) U-boats
Design and development	Coastal, single-hull type. Official design (1916).
Builders	A. G. Weser, Bremen
In service	1916
Type displacement	279 (UB 43–UB 47: 272) tonnes surfaced, 303 (UB 43–UB 47: 305) tonnes submerged
Dimensions	36.9 × 4.37 × 3.75m (UB 43–UB 47: 36.9 × 4.37 × 3.68m)
Speed	8.82 knots surfaced, 6.22 knots submerged
Range	6,940nm at 5 knots surfaced, 45nm at 4 knots submerged
Propulsion	
surfaced	Two 6-cylinder, four-stroke Daimler RS206 diesel engines = 284hp
submerged	Two SSW combined motor/generators = 200kW
Armament	Two 50cm bow torpedo tubes, plus one 8.8cm gun
Crew	Two officers and 21 men
Fates	
UB 42	Surrendered 26 November 1918; scrapped 1920 in Malta
UB 43	Transferred 30 July 1917 to Austro-Hungarian Navy (retained designation)
UB 44	Sunk with all hands 4 August 1916 in the Ionian Sea
UB 45	Sunk 6 November 1916 by mine in the Black Sea (14 fatalities)
UB 46	Sunk with all hands 7 December 1916 by mine in the Black Sea
UB 47	Transferred 30 July 1917 to Austro-Hungarian Navy (retained designation)

Above: UB 40 in dry dock. Left: The Type UB II boat UB 18. Not one crew member survived when the boat went down in the English Channel on 9 December 1917.

UB 48–UB 53

Type	UB III type coastal (medium) U-boats
Design and development	Ocean-going, double-hull type. Official design (1915–16).
Builders	Blohm & Voss, Hamburg
In service	1917
Type displacement	516 tonnes surfaced, 651 tonnes submerged
Dimensions	55.3 × 5.8 × 3.68m
Speed	13.6 knots surfaced, 8.0 knots submerged
Range	9,040nm at 6 knots surfaced, 55nm at 4 knots submerged
Propulsion	
surfaced	Two 6-cylinder, four-stroke MAN S6V35/35 diesel engines = 1,100hp
submerged	Two SSW combined motor/generators = 580kW
Armament	Four 50cm bow and one 50cm stern torpedo tube, plus one machine gun (UB 14 from 1917: one rotary cannon; UB 12: rebuilt 1918 as a minelayer, with 8 mines embarked and torpedo tubes deleted)
Crew	Three officers and 31 men
Fates	
UB 48	Scuttled 28 October 1918 at Pola
UB 49	Surrendered 16 January 1919; scrapped 1922 at Swansea
UB 50	Surrendered 16 January 1919; scrapped 1922 at Swansea
UB 51	Surrendered 16 January 1919; scrapped 1922 at Swansea
UB 52	Sunk 23 May 1918 in the southern Adriatic Sea (32 fatalities)
UB 53	Sunk 3 August 1918 in the Strait of Otranto (10 fatalities)

Left: UB 45 under inspection by naval officers, some of whom are looking at mine damage at the bow.
Right: UB 49, one of the UB III Type 'medium' U-boats.
Below: UB 48 at Bocca di Cattaro (Kotor). The warship in the left background is the Austro-Hungarian cruiser *St Georg*.

UB 54–UB 59

Type	UB III type coastal (medium) U-boats
Design and development	Ocean-going, double-hull type. Official design (1915–16).
Builders	A. G. Weser, Bremen
In service	1917
Type displacement	516 tonnes surfaced, 646 tonnes submerged
Dimensions	55.85 × 5.8 × 3.72m
Speed	13.4 knots surfaced, 7.8 knots submerged
Range	9,020nm at 6 knots surfaced, 55nm at 4 knots submerged
Propulsion	
surfaced	Two 6-cylinder, four-stroke Körting diesel engines = 1,060hp
submerged	Two SSW combined motor/generators = 580kW
Armament	Four 50cm bow and one 50cm stern torpedo tube, plus one 8.8cm (UB 59 from 1918: one 10.5cm) gun
Crew	Three officers and 31 men
Fates	
UB 54	Missing, believed sunk some time after 1 March 1918 in the English Channel
UB 55	Sunk 22 April 1918 by mine in the English Channel (23 fatalities)
UB 56	Sunk with all hands 19 December 1917 by mine in the English Channel
UB 57	Sunk with all hands 14 August 1918 by mine off Flanders
UB 58	Sunk with all hands 10 March 1918 by mine in the English Channel
UB 59	Scuttled 5 October 1918 off Zeebrugge

UB 60-UB 65

Type	UB III type coastal (medium) U-boats
Design and development	Ocean-going, double-hull type. Official design (1915–16).
Builders	A. G. Vulcan, Hamburg
In service	1917
Type displacement	508 tonnes surfaced, 639 tonnes submerged
Dimensions	55.52 × 5.76 × 3.7m
Speed	13.3 knots surfaced, 8.0 knots submerged
Range	8,420nm at 6 knots surfaced, 55nm at 4 knots submerged
Propulsion	
surfaced	Two 6-cylinder, four-stroke MAN S6V35/35 diesel engines = 1,100hp
submerged	Two SSW combined motor/generators = 580kW
Armament	Four 50cm bow and one 50cm stern torpedo tube, plus one 8.8cm (UB 62, UB 64 from 1918: one 10.5cm) gun
Crew	Three officers and 31 men
Fates	
UB 60	Surrendered 26 November 1918; scrapped 1921
UB 61	Sunk with all hands 29 November 1917 by mine in the North Sea
UB 62	Surrendered 21 November 1918; scrapped 1922 at Swansea
UB 63	Missing, believed sunk with all hands some time after 4 January 1918
UB 64	Surrendered 21 November 1918; scrapped 1921 at Fareham
UB 65	Sunk with all hands 10 July 1918 following an accidental explosion south of Ireland

Below: General-arrangement drawings of the Type UB III (UB 66–UB 71).

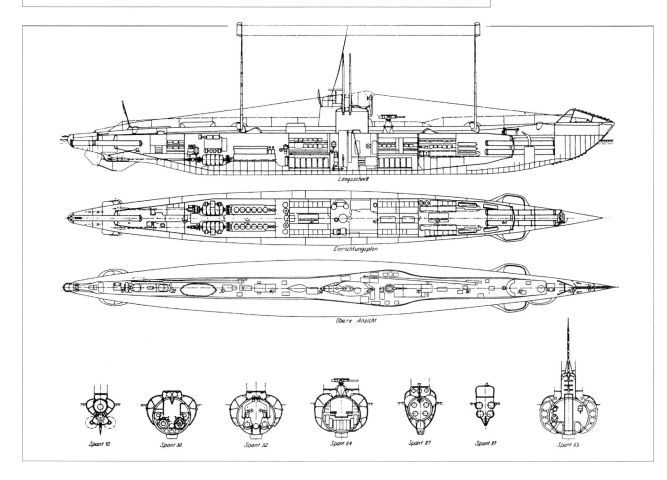

UB 66–UB 71

Type	UB III type coastal (medium) U-boats
Design and development	Ocean-going, double-hull type. Official design (1915–16).
Builders	Germaniawerft, Kiel
In service	1917
Type displacement	513 tonnes surfaced, 647 tonnes submerged
Dimensions	55.83 × 5.8 × 3.67m
Speed	13.2 knots surfaced, 7.6 knots submerged
Range	9,090nm at 6 knots surfaced, 55nm at 4 knots submerged
Propulsion	
surfaced	Two 6-cylinder, four-stroke MAN S6V35/35 diesel engines = 1,100hp
submerged	Two SSW combined motor/generators = 580kW
Armament	Four 50cm bow and two 50cm stern torpedo tubes, plus one 8.8cm (UB 67, UB 68 from 1918: one 10.5cm) gun
Crew	Three officers and 31 men
Fates	
UB 66	Lost with all hands on or after 10 January 1918 in the eastern Mediterranean Sea
UB 67	Surrendered 24 November 1918; scrapped at Swansea
UB 68	Sunk 4 October 1918 off Malta (4 fatalities)
UB 69	Sunk with all hands 9 January 1918 off Sicily
UB 70	Lost with all hands April 1918
UB 71	Sunk with all hands 21 April 1918 off Minorca

UB 72–UB 74

Type	UB III type coastal (medium) U-boats
Design and development	Ocean-going, double-hull type. Official design (1915–16).
Builders	A. G. Vulcan, Hamburg
In service	1917
Type displacement	508 tonnes surfaced, 639 tonnes submerged
Dimensions	55.52 × 5.76 × 3.7m
Speed	13.4 knots surfaced, 7.5 knots submerged
Range	8,420nm at 6 knots surfaced, 55nm at 4 knots submerged
Propulsion	
surfaced	Two 6-cylinder, four-stroke MAN S6V35/35 (UB 73, UB 74: Körting) diesel engines = 1,100hp (UB 73, UB 74: 1,060hp)
submerged	Two SSW combined motor/generators = 580kW
Armament	Four 50cm bow and one 50cm stern torpedo tube, plus one 8.8cm (UB 73 from 1918: one 10.5cm) gun
Crew	Three officers and 31 men
Fates	
UB 72	Sunk 12 May 1918 in the English Channel (34 fatalities)
UB 73	Surrendered 21 November 1918; scrapped 1921 at Brest
UB 74	Sunk with all hands 26 May 1918 in the English Channel

UB 75–UB 79

Type	UB III type coastal (medium) U-boats
Design and development	Ocean-going, double-hull type. Official design (1915–16).
Builders	Blohm & Voss, Hamburg
In service	1917
Type displacement	516 tonnes surfaced, 648 tonnes submerged
Dimensions	55.3 × 5.8 × 3.68m
Speed	13.6 knots surfaced, 7.8 knots submerged
Range	8,680nm at 6 knots surfaced, 55nm at 4 knots submerged
Propulsion	
surfaced	Two 6-cylinder, four-stroke MAN S6V35/35 diesel engines = 1,100hp
submerged	Two SSW combined motor/generators = 580kW
Armament	Four 50cm bow and one 50cm stern torpedo tube, plus one 8.8cm (UB 77, UB 79 from 1918: one 10.5cm) gun
Crew	Three officers and 31 men
Fates	
UB 75	Sunk with all hands 10 December 1917 by mine in the English Channel
UB 76	Surrendered 12 March 1919; scrapped 1922 at Rochester
UB 77	Surrendered 16 January 1919; scrapped 1922 at Swansea
UB 78	Sunk with all hands 9 May 1918 west of Cherbourg
UB 79	Surrendered 26 November 1918; scrapped 1922 at Swansea

Below: UB 80, typifying the medium-sized Type UB III U-boat.

UB 80–UB 87

Type	UB III type coastal (medium) U-boats
Design and development	Ocean-going, double-hull type. Official design (1915–16).
Builders	A. G. Weser, Bremen
In service	1917
Type displacement	516 tonnes surfaced, 647 tonnes submerged
Dimensions	55.85 × 5.8 × 3.72m
Speed	13.4 knots surfaced, 7.5 knots submerged
Range	8,180nm at 6 knots surfaced, 50nm at 4 knots submerged
Propulsion	
surfaced	Two 6-cylinder, four-stroke Körting (UB 82–UB 85: Daimler MU336; UB 86, UB 87: Benz DS375) diesel engines = 1,060hp
submerged	Two SSW combined motor/generators = 580kW
Armament	Four 50cm bow and one 50cm stern torpedo tube, plus one 8.8cm gun
Crew	Three officers and 31 men
Fates	
UB 80	Surrendered 26 November 1918; scrapped 1922 at La Spezia
UB 81	Sunk 2 December 1917 by mine in the English Channel (29 fatalities)
UB 82	Sunk with all hands 17 April 1918 in the Irish Sea
UB 83	Sunk with all hands 10 September 1918 off the Orkney Islands
UB 84	Sunk 7 December 1917 in the Baltic Sea following a collision, raised, surrendered 26 November 1918; scrapped 1921 at Brest
UB 85	Sunk 30 April 1918 in the Irish Sea
UB 86	Surrendered 24 November 1918; scrapped 1921 at Falmouth
UB 87	Surrendered 26 November 1918; scrapped 1921 at Brest

UB 88–UB 102

Type	UB III type coastal (medium) U-boats
Design and development	Ocean-going, double-hull type. Official design (1915–16).
Builders	A. G. Vulcan, Hamburg
In service	1918
Type displacement	510 tonnes surfaced, 640 tonnes submerged
Dimensions	55.52 × 5.76 × 3.73m
Speed	Over 13 knots surfaced, 7.4 knots submerged
Range	7,120nm at 6 knots surfaced, 55nm at 4 knots submerged
Propulsion	
surfaced	Two 6-cylinder, four-stroke MAN-Vulcan S6V35/35 (UB 100–UB 102: AEG) diesel engines = 1,100hp (UB 100– UB 102: 1,060hp)
submerged	Two SSW combined motor/generators = 580kW
Armament	Four 50cm bow and one 50cm stern torpedo tube, plus one 10.5cm gun
Crew	Three officers and 31 men
Fates	
UB 88	Surrendered 26 November 1918; to USA; sunk 3 January 1919 off San Pedro, California
UB 89	Sunk 21 October 1918 off Kiel following a collision with the light cruiser *Frankfurt*; raised, surrendered
UB 90	Sunk with all hands 16 October 1918 in the North Sea
UB 91	Surrendered 21 November 1918; scrapped 1921 at Briton Ferry
UB 92	Surrendered 21 November 1918; scrapped 1921 at Briton Ferry
UB 93	Sunk 30 April 1918 in the Irish Sea
UB 94	Surrendered 24 November 1918; scrapped 1921 at Falmouth
UB 95	Surrendered 21 November 1918; scrapped 1919 at La Spezia
UB 96	Surrendered 21 November 1918; scrapped 1919–20 at Bo'ness
UB 97	Surrendered 21 November 1918; scrapped 1921 at Falmouth
UB 98	Surrendered 21 November 1918; scrapped 1922 at Portmadoc
UB 99	Surrendered 26 November 1918; became French *Carissan*; scrapped 1935
UB 100	Surrendered 22 November 1918; scrapped 1922 at Dordrecht
UB 101	Surrendered 26 November 1918; scrapped 1919–20 at Felixstowe
UB 102	Surrendered 21 November 1918; scrapped 1919 at La Spezia

UB 103–UB 117

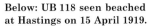

Type	UB III type coastal (medium) U-boats
Design and development	Ocean-going, double-hull type. Official design (1915–16).
Builders	Blohm & Voss, Hamburg
In service	1917–18
Type displacement	Over 519 (UB 103, UB 105, UB 109: 510) tonnes surfaced, 649 (UB 103, UB 105, UB 109: 629) tonnes submerged
Dimensions	55.3 × 5.8 × 3.7m
Speed	13.3 knots surfaced, 7.5 knots submerged
Range	7,420nm at 6 knots surfaced, 55nm at 4 knots submerged
Propulsion	
surfaced engines	Two 6-cylinder, four-stroke MAN-Vulcan S6V35/35 diesel = 1,100hp
submerged	Two SSW (UB 109–UB 114: Maffei; UB 115–UB 118: AEG) combined motor/generators = 580kW
Armament	Four 50cm bow and one 50cm stern torpedo tube, plus one 8.8cm (from 1918: 10.5cm) or (UB 115, UB 117) 10.5cm gun or (UB 106) both
Crew	Three officers and 31 men
Fates	
UB 103	Sunk with all hands 16 September 1918 in the English Channel
UB 104	Sunk with all hands September 1918 in the North Sea
UB 105	Sunk with all hands 16 October 1918 in the North Sea
UB 106	Sunk with all hands 15 March 1918 in the Baltic Sea
UB 107	Sunk with all hands 27 July 1918 in the North Sea
UB 108	Sunk with all hands July 1918 in the English Channel
UB 109	Sunk 29 August 1918 by mine in the English Channel (28 fatalities)
UB 110	Sunk 19 July 1918 in the North Sea; raised 4 October 1918; scrapped in England
UB 111	Surrendered 21 November 1918; scrapped 1919–20 at Bo'ness
UB 112	Surrendered 24 November 1918; scrapped 1921 at Falmouth
UB 113	Sunk with all hands September or October 1918, cause and location unknown
UB 114	Sunk 13 May 1918 in an accident at Kiel (7 fatalities); raised, surrendered 26 November 1918; scrapped 1921 at Toulon
UB 115	Sunk with all hands 29 September 1918 in the North Sea
UB 116	Sunk with all hands 28 October 1918 off the Orkney Islands; raised, scrapped
UB 117	Surrendered 26 November 1918; scrapped 1919–20 at Felixstowe

UB 118–UB 132

Type	UB III type coastal (medium) U-boats
Design and development	Ocean-going, double-hull type. Official design (1915–16).
Builders	A. G. Weser, Bremen
In service	1918
Type displacement	512 tonnes surfaced, 643 tonnes submerged
Dimensions	55.85 × 5.8 × 3.72m
Speed	13.9 knots surfaced, 7.6 knots submerged
Range	7,280nm at 6 knots surfaced, 55nm at 4 knots submerged
Propulsion	
surfaced	Two 6-cylinder, four-stroke Daimler MU336 (UB 121–UB 127: Körting; UB 128–UB 132: Benz DS375) diesel engines = 1,060hp
submerged	Two SSW (UB 128–UB 132: Schiffsunion) combined motor/generators = 580kW
Armament	Four 50cm bow and one 50cm stern torpedo tube, plus one 10.5cm (UB 124: 8.8cm) gun
Crew	Three officers and 31 men
Fates	
UB 118	Surrendered 20 November 1918; sunk 15 April 1919 off Hastings
UB 119	Sunk with all hands May 1918 in the North Sea
UB 120	Surrendered 24 November 1918; scrapped 1922 at Swansea
UB 121	Surrendered 20 November 1918; scrapped 1921 at Toulon
UB 122	Surrendered 24 November 1918; ran aground 1921 off the east coast of Britain
UB 123	Sunk with all hands 19 October 1918 by mine in the North Sea
UB 124	Sunk 20 July 1918 in the Irish Sea (2 fatalities)
UB 125	Surrendered 20 November 1918; became Japanese O 6; scrapped 1921 at Kure
UB 126	Surrendered 24 November 1918; scrapped 1921 at Toulon
UB 127	Sunk with all hands September 1918 (by mine?) in the North Sea
UB 128	Surrendered 3 February 1919; scrapped 1921 at Falmouth
UB 130	Surrendered 26 November 1918; scrapped 1921 at Toulon
UB 131	Surrendered 24 November 1918; beached 9 January 1921 at Hastings
UB 132	Surrendered 22 November 1918; scrapped at Swansea

UB 142, UB 143, UB 148, UB 149

Type	UB III type medium U-boats
Design and development	Ocean-going, double-hull type. Official design (1915–16).
Builders	A. G. Weser, Bremen
In service	1918
Type displacement	523 tonnes surfaced, 653 tonnes submerged
Dimensions	55.85 × 5.8 × 3.75m
Speed	13.5 knots surfaced, 7.5 knots submerged
Range	7,280nm at 6 knots surfaced, 50nm at 4 knots submerged
Propulsion	
surfaced	Two 6-cylinder, four-stroke Benz DS375 (UB 149: Körting) diesel engines = 1,060hp
submerged	Two Schiffsunion (UB 149: SSW) combined motor/generators = 580kW
Armament	Four 50cm bow and one 50cm stern torpedo tube, plus one 10.5cm (UB 124: one 10.5cm and one 8.8cm) gun
Crew	Three officers and 31 men
Fates	
UB 142	Surrendered 22 November 1918; scrapped 1921 at Landerneau
UB 143	Surrendered 1 December 1918; became Japanese O 7; scrapped 1921 at Yokosuka
UB 148	Surrendered 1 December 1918; to USA; sunk with all hands off Cape Charles, Virginia
UB 149	Surrendered 22 November 1918; scrapped 1922 at Swansea

Above: A British propaganda postcard issued after UC 5 had become stranded in the Thames estuary in April 1916.

UC 1–UC 10

Type	UC I type small minelaying U-boats
Design and development	Coastal, single-hull type. Official design (1914).
Builders	A. G. Vulcan, Hamburg
In service	1915
Type displacement	168 tonnes surfaced, 183 tonnes submerged
Dimensions	33.99 × 3.15 × 3.04m
Speed	6.2 knots surfaced, 5.22 knots submerged
Range	780nm at 5 knots surfaced, 50nm at 4 knots submerged
Propulsion	
surfaced	One 4-cylinder, four-stroke Daimler RS166 diesel engine = 90hp
submerged	One SSW combined motor/generator = 130kW
Armament	Six mine chutes (12 mines), plus one machine gun
Crew	One officer and 13 men
Fates	
UC 1	Sunk with all hands July 1917 off the coast of Flanders
UC 2	Sunk with all hands 2 July1915 in the North Sea; raised by the British, scrapped
UC 3	Sunk with all hands 27 May 1916 by mine in the North Sea
UC 4	Scuttled 5 October 1918 off the coast of Flanders
UC 5	Ran aground 27 April 1916 in the Thames estuary; scuttled, raised and scrapped
UC 6	Sunk with all hands 27 September 1917 in the Thames estuary
UC 7	Sunk with all hands 7 July 1916 north of Zeebrugge
UC 8	Ran aground on the Dutch coast; interned, became Dutch M 1 1932
UC 9	Sunk with all hands 21 October 1915 by one of her own mines in the North Sea
UC 10	Sunk with all hands 21 August 1916 in the English Channel

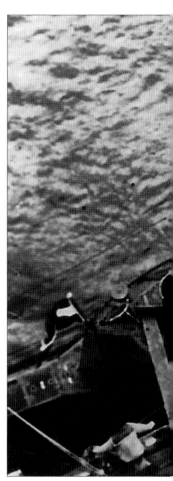

UC 11–UC 15

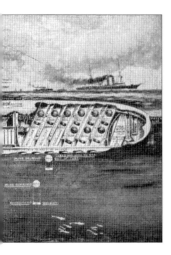

Below: UC 14 as the Austro-Hungarian U 18.

Type	UC I type small minelaying U-boats
Design and development	Coastal, single-hull type. Official design (1914).
Builders	A. G. Weser, Bremen
In service	1915
Type displacement	168 tonnes surfaced, 182 tonnes submerged
Dimensions	33.99 × 3.15 × 3.06m
Speed	6.49 knots surfaced, 5.67 knots submerged
Range	910nm at 5 knots surfaced, 50nm at 4 knots submerged
Propulsion	
surfaced	One 6-cylinder, four-stroke Benz diesel engine = 80hp
submerged	One SSW combined motor/generator = 130kW
Armament	Six mine chutes (12 mines), plus (UC 11 only, from 1916) one 45cm bow torpedo tube, plus one machine gun
Crew	One officer and 13 men
Fates	
UC 11	Sunk 24 July 1917 by mine in the English Channel (18 fatalities)
UC 12	Sunk with all hands 16 June 1916 by one of her own mines off Taranto
UC 13	Ran aground 29 November 1915 in the Black Sea
UC 14	Sunk with all hands 3 October 1917 by mine off the coast of Flanders
UC 15	Lost with all hands November 1916 in the Black Sea

UC 16–UC 24

Type	UC II type minelaying U-boats
Design and development	Official design (1915).
Builders	Blohm & Voss, Hamburg
In service	1916
Type displacement	417 tonnes surfaced, 493 tonnes submerged
Dimensions	52.15 × 5.22 × 3.68m
Speed	11.6 knots surfaced, 7.0 knots submerged
Range	9,430nm at 7 knots surfaced, 55nm at 4 knots submerged
Propulsion	
surfaced	Two 6-cylinder, four-stroke MAN S6V23/34 diesel engines = 500hp
submerged	Two BBC combined motor/generators = 340kW
Armament	Two 50cm bow and one 50cm stern torpedo tubes, plus six mine chutes (18 mines), plus one 8.8cm (some boats, from 1918: one 10.5cm) gun
Crew	Three officers and 23 men
Fates	
UC 16	Sunk with all hands October 1917 by mine off Zeebrugge
UC 17	Surrendered 26 November 1918; scrapped 1920 at Preston
UC 18	Sunk with all hands 19 February 1917 in the English Channel
UC 19	Sunk with all hands 6 December 1916 off the south coast of Ireland
UC 20	Surrendered 16 January 1919; scrapped 1920 at Preston
UC 21	Sunk with all hands September or October 1917, cause and location unknown
UC 22	Surrendered 3 February 1919; scrapped 1921 at Landerneau
UC 23	Surrendered 14 November 1918; scrapped 1921 at Bizerta
UC 24	Sunk 24 May 1917 in the Adriatic Sea (24 fatalities)

UC 25–UC 33

Type	UC II type minelaying U-boats
Design and development	Official design (1915).
Builders	A. G. Vulcan, Hamburg
In service	1916
Type displacement	400 tonnes surfaced, 480 tonnes submerged
Dimensions	51.12 × 5.22 × 3.68m
Speed	11.6 knots surfaced, 6.7 knots submerged
Range	9,260nm (UC 28–UC 30: 9,410nm; UC 31–UC 33: 10,040nm) at 7 knots surfaced, 53nm at 4 knots submerged
Propulsion	
surfaced	Two 6-cylinder, four-stroke MAN S6V23/34 (UC 28–UC 30: Daimler MU256) diesel engines = 500hp (UC 28–UC 30: 660hp)
submerged	Two SSW combined motor/generators = 340kW
Armament	Two 50cm bow and one 50cm stern torpedo tubes, plus six mine chutes (18 mines), plus one 8.8cm (some boats, from 1918: one 10.5cm) gun
Crew	Three officers and 23 men
Fates	
UC 25	Scuttled 29 October 1918 off Pola
UC 26	Sunk 9 May 1917 off Cap Gris Nez (24 fatalities)
UC 27	Surrendered 3 February 1919; scrapped 1921 at Landerneau
UC 28	Surrendered 12 February 1919; scrapped
UC 29	Sunk 7 June 1917 off the south coast of Ireland (23 fatalities)
UC 30	Sunk with all hands September or October 1917, cause and location unknown
UC 31	Surrendered 3 February 1919; scrapped 1921 at Landerneau
UC 32	Surrendered 14 November 1918; scrapped 1921 at Bizerta
UC 33	Sunk 24 May 1917 in the Adriatic Sea (24 fatalities)

UC 34–UC 39

Type	UC II type minelaying U-boats
Design and development	Official design (1915).
Builders	Blohm & Voss, Hamburg
In service	1916
Type displacement	427 tonnes surfaced, 509 tonnes submerged
Dimensions	53.15 × 5.22 × 3.65m
Speed	11.9 knots surfaced, 6.8 knots submerged
Range	10,108nm at 7 knots surfaced, 54nm at 4 knots submerged
Propulsion	
surfaced	Two 6-cylinder, four-stroke MAN S6V23/34 (UC 37–UC 39: S6V26/36) diesel engines = 500hp (UC 37–UC 39: 600hp)
submerged	Two SSW combined motor/generators = 340kW
Armament	Two 50cm bow and one 50cm stern torpedo tubes, plus six mine chutes (18 mines), plus one 8.8cm (some boats, from 1918: one 10.5cm) gun
Crew	Three officers and 23 men
Fates	
UC 34	Scuttled 30 October 1918 off Pola
UC 35	Sunk 16 May 1918 off the south-west coast of Sardinia (20 fatalities)
UC 36	Lost with all hands May 1917 in the English Channel
UC 37	Surrendered 1919; scrapped 1920 in Malta
UC 38	Sunk 13 December 1917 n the Gulf of Corinth (9 fatalities)
UC 39	Sunk 8 February 1817 in the North Sea (7 fatalities)

Left: The bows of a Type UC II minelaying U-boat of the UC 16–UC 24 class.
Below: UC 26 in a glassy sea.
Bottom: UC 34 approaches Pola.

UC 40-UC 45

Type	UC II type minelaying U-boats
Design and development	Official design (1915).
Builders	A. G. Vulcan, Hamburg
In service	1916
Type displacement	400 tonnes surfaced, 480 tonnes submerged
Dimensions	51.11 × 5.22 × 3.68m
Speed	11.7 knots surfaced, 6.7 knots submerged
Range	9,410nm at 7 knots surfaced, 60nm at 4 knots submerged
Propulsion	
surfaced	Two 6-cylinder, four-stroke Körting diesel engines = 520hp
submerged	Two SSW combined motor/generators = 340kW
Armament	Two 50cm bow and one 50cm stern torpedo tubes, plus six mine chutes (18 mines), plus one 8.8cm (some boats, from 1918: one 10.5cm) gun
Crew	Three officers and 23 men
Fates	
UC 40	Sunk 21 December 1919 in an accident in the North Sea (1 fatality)
UC 41	Sunk with all hands 21 August 1917 in the North Sea following the detonation of her own mines
UC 42	Sunk with all hands 10 September 1917 by mine off the south coast of Ireland
UC 43	Sunk withall hands 11 March 1917 in the Atlantic Ocean
UC 44	Sunk 4 August 1917 by mine off the south coast of Ireland (28 fatalities); raised, scrapped
UC 45	Sunk 17 September 1917 in the North Sea in a diving accident; raised; surrendered 1918; scrapped 1920 at Preston

UC 46-UC 48

Type	UC II type minelaying U-boats
Design and development	Official design (1915).
Builders	A. G. Weser, Hamburg
In service	1916
Type displacement	420 tonnes surfaced, 502 tonnes submerged
Dimensions	51.85 × 5.22 × 3.67m
Speed	11.7 knots surfaced, 6.9 knots submerged
Range	7,280nm at 7 knots surfaced, 54nm at 4 knots submerged
Propulsion	
surfaced	Two 6-cylinder, four-stroke MAN S6V26/36 diesel engines = 600hp
submerged	Two SSW combined motor/generators = 340kW
Armament	Two 50cm bow and one 50cm stern torpedo tubes, plus six mine chutes (18 mines), plus one 8.8cm (some boats, from 1918: one 10.5cm) gun
Crew	Three officers and 23 men
Fates	
UC 46	Sunk with all hands 8 February 1917 in the English Channel
UC 47	Sunk with all hands 18 November 1917 in the North Sea
UC 48	Interned in Spain, scuttled 15 March 1919 en route to hand-over

UC 49–UC 54

Below: General arrangement of the UC 49 class U-boat.

Type	UC II type minelaying U-boats
Design and development	Official design (1915).
Builders	Germaniawerft, Kiel
In service	1916–17
Type displacement	434 tonnes surfaced, 511 tonnes submerged
Dimensions	52.69 × 5.22 × 3.64m
Speed	11.8 knots surfaced, 7.2 knots submerged
Range	8,820nm at 7 knots surfaced, 56nm at 4 knots submerged
Propulsion	
surfaced	Two 6-cylinder, four-stroke Körting (UC 51–UC 54: Daimler MU526) diesel engines = 600hp (UC 51–UC 54: 660hp)
submerged	Two BBC combined motor/generators = 460kW
Armament	Two 50cm bow and one 50cm stern torpedo tubes, plus six mine chutes (18 mines), plus one 8.8cm (some boats, from 1918: one 10.5cm) gun
Crew	Three officers and 23 men
Fates	
UC 49	Sunk with all hands 8 August 1918 south-west of Berry Head
UC 50	Sunk with all hands 4 February 1918 in the Bay of Biscay
UC 51	Sunk with all hands 17 November 1917 by mine in the English Channel
UC 52	Surrendered 16 January 1919; scrapped 1920 at Morecambe
UC 53	Scuttled 28 October 1918 off Pola
UC 54	Scuttled 28 october 1918 at Trieste

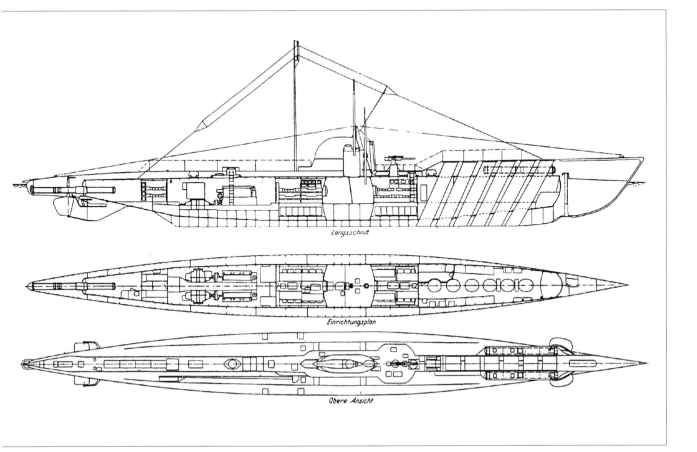

Langsschnitt

Einrichtungsplan

Obere Ansicht

UC 55–UC 60

Type	UC II type minelaying U-boats
Design and development	Official design (1915).
Builders	Kaiserliche Werft, Danzig
In service	1916–17
Type displacement	415 tonnes surfaced, 498 tonnes submerged
Dimensions	52.67 × 5.22 × 3.61m
Speed	11.6 knots surfaced, 7.3 knots submerged
Range	8,660–9,450nm at 7 knots surfaced, 52nm at 4 knots submerged
Propulsion	
surfaced	Two 6-cylinder, four-stroke Körting (UC 58–UC 60: Daimler MU526) diesel engines = 600hp (UC 58–UC 60: 660hp)
submerged	Two BBC combined motor/generators = 460kW
Armament	Two 50cm bow and one 50cm stern torpedo tubes, plus six mine chutes (18 mines), plus one 8.8cm (some boats, from 1918: one 10.5cm) gun
Crew	Three officers and 23 men
Fates	
UC 55	Sunk 28 September 1918 off Lerwick (10 fatalities)
UC 56	Surrendered 26 March 1919; scrapped 1923 at Rochefort
UC 57	Lost with all hands some time after 17 November 1917
UC 58	Surrendered 24 November 1918; scrapped 1921 at Cherbourg
UC 59	Surrendered 21 November 1918; scrapped 1919–20 at Bo'ness
UC 60	Surrendered 23 February 1919; scrapped 1921 at Rainham

Below left: UC 56 at the Spanish port of Santander in 1918.

UC 61–UC 64

Below: UC 61, beached off Calais after her crew had scuttled her on 26 July 1917.

Type	UC II type minelaying U-boats
Design and development	Official design (1915).
Builders	A. G. Weser, Bremen
In service	1916–17
Type displacement	422 tonnes surfaced, 504 tonnes submerged
Dimensions	51.85 × 5.22 × 3.67m
Speed	11.9 knots surfaced, 7.2 knots submerged
Range	8,000nm at 7 knots surfaced, 59nm at 4 knots submerged
Propulsion	
surfaced	Two 6-cylinder, four-stroke MAN S6V26/36 diesel engines = 600hp
submerged	Two SSW combined motor/generators = 460kW
Armament	Two 50cm bow and one 50cm stern torpedo tubes, plus six mine chutes (18 mines), plus one 8.8cm (some boats, from 1918: one 10.5cm) gun
Crew	Three officers and 23 men
Fates	
UC 61	Ran aground 26 July 1917 in the English Channel; scuttled
UC 62	Lost with all hands mid-October 1917 (by mine?) in the English Channel
UC 63	Sunk 1 November 1917 in the English Channel (26 fatalities)
UC 64	Sunk with all hands 20 June 1918 by mine in the English Channel

UC 65-UC 73

Type	UC II type minelaying U-boats
Design and development	Official design (1915).
Builders	Blohm & Voss, Hamburg
In service	1916
Type displacement	427 tonnes surfaced, 508 tonnes submerged
Dimensions	53.15 × 5.22 × 3.64m
Speed	12.0 knots surfaced, 7.4 knots submerged
Range	8,660–10,420nm at 7 knots surfaced, 52nm at 4 knots submerged
Propulsion	
surfaced	Two 6-cylinder, four-stroke MAN S6V26/36 diesel engines = 600hp
submerged	Two SSW combined motor/generators = 460kW
Armament	Two 50cm bow and one 50cm stern torpedo tubes, plus six mine chutes (18 mines), plus one 8.8cm (some boats, from 1918: one 10.5cm) gun
Crew	Three officers and 23 men
Fates	
UC 65	Sunk 3 November 1917 in the English Channel (22 fatalities)
UC 66	Sunk with all hands 12 June 1917 in the English Channel
UC 67	Surrendered 16 January 1919; scrapped 1919–20 at Briton Ferry
UC 68	Sunk with all hands 13 March 1917 off Start Point following the detonation of her own mines
UC 69	Sunk 6 December 1917 in the English Channel following a collision with U 96 (11 fatalities)
UC 70	Sunk with all hands 28 August 1918 in the North Sea
UC 71	Sunk 20 January 1919 in an accident en route to hand-over
UC 72	Sunk with all hands 20 August 1918 in the Bay of Biscay
UC 73	Surrendered 16 January 1919; scrapped 1920 at Briton Ferry

UC 74-UC 79

Type	UC II type minelaying U-boats
Design and development	Official design (1915).
Builders	A. G. Vulcan, Hamburg
In service	1916–17
Type displacement	410 tonnes surfaced, 493 tonnes submerged
Dimensions	52.11 × 5.22 × 3.65m
Speed	11.8 knots surfaced, 7.3 knots submerged
Range	8,660–10,230nm at 7 knots surfaced, 52nm at 4 knots submerged
Propulsion	
surfaced	Two 6-cylinder, four-stroke Körting (UC 76–UC 79: Daimler MU256) diesel engines = 600hp (UC 76–UC 79: 660hp)
submerged	Two SSW combined motor/generators = 460kW
Armament	Two 50cm bow and one 50cm stern torpedo tubes, plus six mine chutes (18 mines), plus one 8.8cm gun
Crew	Three officers and 23 men
Fates	
UC 74	Surrendered 26 March 1919; scrapped 1921 at Toulon
UC 75	Sunk 31 May 1918 in the North Sea (19 fatalities)
UC 76	Surrendered 1 December 1918; scrapped 1919–20 at Briton Ferry
UC 77	Sunk with all hands July 1918 in the English Channel, cause and exact location unknown
UC 78	Sunk with all hands 2 May 1918 by mine in the English Channel
UC 79	Sunk with all hands 19 April 1918 by mine in the English Channel

Right: UC 97 was transferred to the United States after World War I and was sunk in Lake Michigan in 1921.

UC 90–UC 105

Type	UC III type minelaying U-boats
Design and development	Ocean-going, double-hull type.Official design.
Builders	Blohm & Voss, Hamburg
In service	1918
Type displacement	491 tonnes surfaced, 571 tonnes submerged
Dimensions	56.51 × 5.54 × 3.77m
Speed	11.5 knots surfaced, 6.6 knots submerged
Range	9,850nm at 7 knots surfaced, 40nm at 4.5 knots submerged
Propulsion	
surfaced	Two 6-cylinder, four-stroke MAN S6V26/36 diesel engines = 600hp
submerged	Two SSW combined motor/generators = 570kW
Armament	Two 50cm bow and one 50cm stern torpedo tubes, plus six mine chutes (14 mines), plus one 10.5cm or 8.8cm gun
Crew	Three officers and 29 men
Fates	
UC 90	Surrendered 1 December 1918; became Japanese O 4; scrapped 1921 at Kure
UC 91	Sunk 5 September 1918 following a collision with *Alexandra Woermann* (17 fatalities); raised; sunk 10 February 1919 in an accident en route to hand-over
UC 92	Surrendered 24 November 1918; scrapped 1921 at Falmouth
UC 93	Surrendered 26 November 1918; scrapped 1919 at La Spezia
UC 94	Surrendered 26 November 1918; scrapped 1919 at Taranto
UC 95	Surrendered 22 November 1918; scrapped 1922 at Fareham
UC 96	Surrendered 24 November 1918; scrapped 1919–20 at Morecambe
UC 97	Surrendered 22 November 1918; to USA; sunk February 1921 in Lake Michigan
UC 98	Surrendered 24 November 1918; scrapped 1919 at La Spezia
UC 99	Surrendered 22 November 1918; became Japanese O 5; scrapped 1921 at Sasebo
UC 100	Surrendered 22 November 1918; scrapped 1921 at Cherbourg
UC 101	Surrendered 24 November 1918; scrapped 1922 at Dordrecht
UC 102	Surrendered 22 November 1918; scrapped 1922 at Dordrecht
UC 103	Surrendered 22 November 1918; scrapped 1921 at Cherbourg
UC 104	Surrendered 24 November 1918; scrapped 1921 at Brest
UC 105	Surrendered 22 November 1918; scrapped 1922 at Swansea

KRIEGSMARINE

U A

Type	U A
Design and development	Ocean-going, double-hull type. Ordered by, and built for, Turkey; ready for delivery 28 September 1938 (named *Batiray*) but requisitioned and redesignated U A.
Builder	Germaniawerft, Kiel
In service	21 September 1939
Type displacement	1,128 tonnes surfaced, 1,284 tonnes submerged
Dimensions	86.65 × 6.8 × 4.12m
Speed	18.0 knots surfaced, 8.4 knots submerged
Range	13,100nm at 10 knots surfaced, 75nm at 4 knots submerged
Propulsion	
surfaced	Two two-stroke Burmeister & Wain diesel engines = 4,200hp
submerged	Two BBC GB UB721/8 combined motor/generators = 960kW
Armament	Four 53.3cm bow and two 53.3cm stern torpedo tubes, plus one 10.5cm and two 2cm guns
Crew	Four officers and 41 men
Fate	Decommissioned at Neustadt May 1944; scuttled 2 May 1945 at Kiel

Below: The submarine *Batiray*, built for Turkey but taken over by the Kriegsmarine in 1939 and redesignated U A.

U 25, U 26

Type	IA (2 boats)
Design and development	Ocean-going, double-hull type. Derived from the German-designed E 1, which was built in Spain for the Turkish Navy and entered service in 1934.
Builder	Deschimag A. G. Weser, Bremen
In service	1936
Type displacement	862 tonnes surfaced, 983 tonnes submerged
Dimensions	72.39 × 6.21 × 4.3m
Speed	17.75–18.6 knots surfaced, 8.3 knots submerged
Range	7,900nm at 10 knots surfaced, 78nm at 4 knots submerged
Propulsion	
surfaced	Two 8-cylinder, four-stroke MAN M8V40/46 diesel engines = 2,800hp
submerged	Two BBC GG UB720/8 double-acting motors = 780kW
Armament	Four 53.3cm bow and two 53.3cm stern torpedo tubes (14 torpedoes or 42 mines), plus one 10.5cm and one 2cm gun
Crew	Four officers and 39 men
Fates	
U 25	Sunk with all hands 30 August 1940 near Terschelling following the detonation of one of her mines
U 26	Sunk 1 July 1940 in the North Atlantic Ocean

U 1–U 6

Type	IIA (6 boats)
Design and development	Coastal, single-hull type. Derived from the World War I-era Type U F and the later, German-designed Finnish submarine *Vessiko*. Prototype for the Type II series of U-boats.
Builder	Deutsche Werke, Kiel
In service	1935
Type displacement	254 tonnes surfaced, 303 tonnes submerged
Dimensions	40.9 × 4.08 × 3.83m
Speed	13.0 knots surfaced, 6.9 knots submerged
Range	1,600nm at 8 knots surfaced, 35nm at 4 knots submerged
Propulsion	
surfaced	Two 6-cylinder, four-stroke MWM RS127S diesel engines = 700hp
submerged	Two SSW PG VV322/36 double-acting motors = 300kW
Armament	Three 53.3cm bow torpedo tubes (5 torpedoes or 18 mines), plus one single 2cm or (from 1942) two twin 2cm Flak
Crew	Three officers and 22 men
Fates	
U 1	Sunk with all hands 8 April 1940 by mine off Terschelling
U 2	Sunk 8 April 1944 west of Pillau following a collision with the fishing vessel *Helmi Söhle* (17 fatalities)
U 3	Decommissioned 1 August 1944 at Gotenhafen (Gdynia)
U 4	Decommissioned 1 August 1944 at Gotenhafen
U 5	Sunk 19 March 1943 in a diving accident west of Pillau (21 fatalities)
U 6	Decommissioned 7 August 1944 at Gotenhafen

Left: The Type IA U-boat U 26.

U 7–U 24, U 120, U 121

Type	IIB (20 boats)
Design and development	Coastal, single-hull type, developed from Type IIA
Builder	Germaniawerft, Kiel (U 13–U 16: Deutsche Werke, Kiel; U 120, U 121: Flender Werke, Lübeck)
In service	1935–36 (U 120, U 121: 1940)
Type displacement	279 tonnes surfaced, 328 tonnes submerged
Dimensions	42.7 × 4.08 × 3.9m
Speed	13.0 knots surfaced, 7 knots submerged
Range	3,100nm at 8 knots surfaced, 35–43nm at 4 knots submerged
Propulsion	
surfaced	Two 6-cylinder, four-stroke MWM RS127S diesel engines = 700hp
submerged	Two SSW PG VV322/36 double-acting motors = 300kW
Armament	Three 53.3cm bow torpedo tubes (5 torpedoes or 18 mines), plus one single 2cm or (from 1942) two twin 2cm Flak
Crew	Three officers and 22 men
Fates	
U 7	Sunk with all hands 18 February 1944 in a diving accident in the Baltic Sea
U 8	Scuttled 4 May 1945 at Wilhelmshaven
U 9	Sunk 20 September 1844 in the Black Sea
U 10	Decommissioned 1 August 1944 at Danzig
U 11	Scuttled 3 May 1945 at Kiel
U 12	Sunk with all hands 5 October 1939 by mine in the English Channel
U 13	Sunk 31 May 1940 north-west of Newcastle-upon-Tyne
U 14	Scuttled 4 May 1945 at Wilhelmshaven
U 15	Sunk with all hands 30 January 1940 west of Heligoland following a collision with the torpedo-boat *Iltis*
U 16	Sunk with all hands 25 October 1939 in the English Channel
U 17	Scuttled 5 May 1945 at Wilhelmshaven
U 18	Collided with the torpedo-boat T 156 20 November 1936 in Lübeck Bay (8 fatalities); recommissioned 1937; scuttled 25 August 1944 in the Black Sea
U 19	Scuttled 10 September 1944 in the Black Sea
U 20	Scuttled 10 September 1944 in the Black Sea
U 21	Decommissioned 10 September 1944 at Pillau
U 22	Sunk with all hands prior to 23 March 1940 by mine
U 23	Scuttled 10 September 1944 in the Black Sea
U 24	Scuttled 25 August 1944 in the Black Sea
U 120	Scuttled 4 May 1945 at Bremerhaven
U 121	Scuttled 4 May 1945 at Bremerhaven

Above: The Type IIA boat U 1.

U 56–U 63

Above: The Type IIB boat U 23.

Type	IIC (8 boats)
Design and development	Coastal, single-hull type. Developed from Type IIB.
Builder	Deutsche Werke, Kiel
In service	1938–40
Type displacement	291 tonnes surfaced, 341 tonnes submerged
Dimensions	43.9 × 4.08 × 3.82m
Speed	12.0 knots surfaced, 7.0 knots submerged
Range	3,800nm at 8 knots surfaced, 35–42nm at 4 knots submerged
Propulsion	
surfaced	Two 6-cylinder, four-stroke MWM RS127S diesel engines = 700hp
submerged	Two SSW PG VV322/36 double-acting motors = 300kW
Armament	Three 53.3cm bow torpedo tubes (5 torpedoes or 18 mines), plus one single 2cm or (from 1942) four 2cm Flak
Crew	Three officers and 22 men
Fates	
U 56	Decommissioned 28 April 1945 at Kiel; scuttled 3 May 1945
U 57	Scuttled 3 May 1945 at Kiel
U 58	Scuttled 3 May 1945 at Kiel
U 59	Scuttled 3 May 1945 at Kiel
U 60	Scuttled 5 May 1945 at Wilhelmshaven
U 61	Scuttled 5 May 1945 at Wilhelmshaven
U 62	Scuttled 5 May 1945 at Wilhelmshaven
U 63	Sunk 25 February 1940 off the Shetland Islands (1 fatality)

Below: U 59, a Type IIC U-boat.

U 137–U 152

Type	IID (16 boats)
Design and development	Coastal, single-hull type with saddle tanks. Developed from Type IIC.
Builder	Deutsche Werke, Kiel
In service	1940–41
Type displacement	314 tonnes surfaced, 364 tonnes submerged
Dimensions	43.97 × 4.92 × 3.93m
Speed	12.7 knots surfaced, 7.4 knots submerged
Range	5,650nm at 8 knots surfaced, 56nm at 4 knots submerged
Propulsion	
surfaced	Two 6-cylinder, four-stroke MWM RS127S diesel engines = 700hp
submerged	Two SSW PG VV322/36 double-acting motors = 300kW
Armament	Three 53.3cm bow torpedo tubes (5 torpedoes or 18 mines), plus one single 2cm or (from 1942) four 2cm Flak
Crew	Three officers and 22 men
Fates	
U 137	Scuttled 5 May 1945 at Wilhelmshaven
U 138	Sunk 18 June 1941 off Cadiz
U 139	Scuttled 5 May 1945 at Wilhelmshaven
U 140	Scuttled 5 May 1945 at Wilhelmshaven
U 141	Scuttled 5 May 1945 at Wilhelmshaven
U 142	Scuttled 5 May 1945 at Wilhelmshaven
U 143	Surrendered 30 June 1945 at Wilhelmshaven
U 144	Sunk with all hands 10 August 1941 north-west of Dagö
U 145	Surrendered 30 June 1945 at Wilhelmshaven
U 146	Scuttled 5 May 1945 at Wilhelmshaven
U 147	Sunk with all hands 2 June 1941 off north-west Ireland
U 148	Scuttled 5 May 1945 at Wilhelmshaven
U 149	Surrendered 30 June 1945 at Wilhelmshaven
U 150	Surrendered 30 June 1945 at Wilhelmshaven
U 151	Scuttled 5 May 1945 at Wilhelmshaven
U 152	Scuttled 5 May 1945 at Wilhelmshaven

U 27–U 36

Type	VIIA (10 boats)
Design and development	Ocean-going (medium), single-hull type. Derived from the Type UB III of World War I and developed from the Turkish *Brinci Inönü* and Finnish *Vetehinen*.
Builder	Deschimag A. G. Weser, Hamburg (U 33–U 36: Germaniawerft, Kiel)
In service	1936–37
Type displacement	626 tonnes surfaced, 745 tonnes submerged
Dimensions	64.51 × 5.85 × 4.37m
Speed	16–17 knots surfaced, 8.0 knots submerged
Range	6,200nm at 10 knots surfaced, 73–94nm at 4 knots submerged
Propulsion	
surfaced	Two 6-cylinder, four-stroke MAN M6V40/46 diesel engines (without supercharging) = 2,300hp
submerged	Two BBC GG UB720/8 double-acting motors = 560kW
Armament	Four 53.3cm bow and one 53.3cm stern torpedo tube (11 torpedoes or 33 mines), plus one 8.8cm and one 2cm Flak or (from 1944) one 3.7cm and four twin 2cm Flak
Crew	Four officers and 40–56 men
Fates	
U 27	Sunk 20 September 1939 west of Scotland
U 28	Sunk 17 March 1944 at Neustadt as a result of an operational error
U 29	Scuttled 4 May 1945 at Flensburg
U 30	Scuttled 4 May 1945 outside Flensburg
U 31	Sunk 2 November 1940 north-west of Ireland (2 fatalities)
U 32	Sunk 30 October 1940 north-west of Ireland (9 fatalities)
U 33	Sunk 12 February 1940 in the Firth of Clyde (25 fatalities)
U 34	Sunk 5 August 1943 off Memel following a collision with the U-boat tender *Lech* (4 fatalities); raised 24 August 1943; decommissioned 8 September 1943; sunk (?) off Warnemünde 2 February 1944
U 35	Sunk 29 November 1939 north-west of Bergen
U 36	Sunk with all hands 4 December 1939 south-west of Kristiansand

Above: U 141's conning tower, seen in a photograph taken at Lorient.
Left: U 28, a Type VIIA boat.

U 45–U 55

Type	VIIB (11 boats)
Design and development	Ocean-going (medium), single-hull type. As Type VIIA, but possessing greater range.
Builder	Germaniawerft, Kiel
In service	1938–39
Type displacement	753 tonnes surfaced, 857 tonnes submerged
Dimensions	66.5 × 6.2 × 4.74m
Speed	17.2–17.9 knots surfaced, 8.0 knots submerged
Range	8,700nm at 10 knots surfaced, 90nm at 4 knots submerged
Propulsion	
surfaced	Two 6-cylinder, four-stroke Germaniawerft F46 (U 51–U 55: MAN M6V40/46) diesel engines (with supercharging) = 3,200hp (U 51–U 55: 2,800hp)
submerged	Two BBC GG UB720/8 (U 47, U 48, U 50, U 53, U 55: AEG GU460/8-276) double-acting motors = 560kW
Armament	Four 53.3cm bow and one 53.3cm stern torpedo tube (14 torpedoes or 39 mines), plus one 8.8cm and one 2cm Flak or (from 1944) one 3.7cm and four twin 2cm Flak

(continued overleaf)

U 45–U 55 (continued)	
Crew	Four officers and 40–56 men
Fates	
U 45	Sunk with all hands 14 October 1939 south-west of Ireland
U 46	Scuttled 5 May 1945 in Kupfermühlen Bay
U 47	Sunk with all hands 7 March 1941 south-east of Ireland
U 48	Scuttled 3 May 1945 at Neustadt
U 49	Sunk 15 April 1940 off Narvik (1 fatality)
U 50	Sunk with all hands 7 April 1940 off Terschelling
U 51	Sunk with all hands 20 August 1940 west of Nantes
U 52	Scuttled 3 May 1945 at Neustadt
U 53	Sunk with all hands 23 February 1940 west of the Orkney Islands
U 54	Lost with all hands 14 February 1940 in the North Sea
U 55	Sunk 30 January 1940 south-west of the Scilly Isles (1 fatality)

U 73–U 76

Type	VIIB (4 boats)
Design and development	Ocean-going (medium), single-hull type. As Type VIIA, but possessing greater range.
Builder	Vegesacker Werft, Kiel
In service	1940
Type displacement	753 tonnes surfaced, 857 tonnes submerged
Dimensions	66.5 × 6.2 × 4.74m
Speed	17.2–17.9 knots surfaced, 8.0 knots submerged
Range	8,700nm at 10 knots surfaced, 90nm at 4 knots submerged
Propulsion	
surfaced	Two 6-cylinder, four-stroke MAN M6V40/46 diesel engines (with supercharging) = 2,800hp
submerged	Two BBC GG UB720/8 double-acting motors = 560kW
Armament	Four 53.3cm bow and one 53.3cm stern torpedo tube (14 torpedoes or 39 mines), plus one 8.8cm and one 2cm Flak or (later) one 3.7cm and four twin 2cm Flak
Crew	Four officers and 40–56 men
Fates	
U 73	Sunk 16 December 1943 off Oran (16 fatalities)
U 74	Sunk with all hands 2 May 1942 east of Cartagena
U 75	Sunk 28 December 1942 off Mersa Matruh (14 fatalities)
U 76	Sunk 5 April 1941 south of Iceland (1 fatality)

Below left: Only 24 Type VIIB U-boats were built, eleven of them by Germaniawerft at Kiel. This is U 45, lost off Ireland in October 1939.
Right: U 73, one of four Type VIIB boats built by Vegesacker Werft.

U 83–U 87

Type	VIIB (5 boats)
Design and development	Ocean-going (medium), single-hull type. As Type VIIA, but possessing greater range.
Builder	Flenderwerke, Lübeck
In service	1941
Type displacement	753 tonnes surfaced, 857 tonnes submerged
Dimensions	66.5 × 6.2 × 4.74m
Speed	17.2–17.9 knots surfaced, 8.0 knots submerged
Range	8,700nm at 10 knots surfaced, 90nm at 4 knots submerged
Propulsion	
surfaced	Two 6-cylinder, four-stroke Germaniawerft F46 (U 85, U 86: MAN M6V40/46) diesel engines (with supercharging) = 3,200hp (U 85, U 86: 2,800hp)
submerged	Two AEG GU460/8-276 (U 85, U 86: BBC GG UB720/8) double-acting motors = 560kW
Armament	Four 53.3cm bow and one 53.3cm stern (not U 83) torpedo tube (14 torpedoes or 39 mines), plus one 8.8cm and one 2cm Flak or (later) one 3.7cm and four twin 2cm Flak
Crew	Four officers and 40–56 men
Fates	
U 83	Sunk with all hands 4 March 1943 south-east of Cartagena
U 84	Lost with all hands 7 August 1943 in the Western Atlantic Ocean
U 85	Sunk with all hands 14 April 1942 off Cape Hatteras
U 86	Lost with all hands 28 November 1943 in the Atlantic Ocean
U 87	Sunk with all hands 4 March 1943 in the Atlantic Ocean west of Laoighise

U 99–U 102

Type	VIIB (4 boats)
Design and development	Ocean-going (medium), single-hull type. As Type VIIA, but possessing greater range.
Builder	Germaniawerft, Kiel
In service	1940
Type displacement	753 tonnes surfaced, 857 tonnes submerged
Dimensions	66.5 × 6.2 × 4.74m
Speed	17.2–17.9 knots surfaced, 8.0 knots submerged
Range	8,700nm at 10 knots surfaced, 90nm at 4 knots submerged
Propulsion	
surfaced	Two 6-cylinder, four-stroke Germaniawerft F46 (U 101: MAN M6V40/46) diesel engines (with supercharging) = 3,200hp (U 101: 2,800hp)
submerged	Two BBC GG UB720/8 (U 101, U 102: AEG GU460/8-276) double-acting motors = 560kW
Armament	Four 53.3cm bow and one 53.3cm stern torpedo tube (14 torpedoes or 39 mines), plus one 8.8cm and one 2cm Flak or (later) one 3.7cm and four twin 2cm Flak
Crew	Four officers and 40–56 men
Fates	
U 99	Sunk 17 March 1941 south-east of Iceland (3 fatalities)
U 100	Sunk 17 March 1941 south-east of Iceland (38 fatalities)
U 101	Scuttled 3 May 1945 at Neustadt
U 102	Sunk with all hands 1 July 1940 in the Bay of Biscay

Left: U 83, one of a batch of five Type VIIB boats laid down at the Flenderwerke in Lübeck, is seen here outside one of the U-boat bunkers built by the Germans at Brest, in France. U 83 was lost in the Atlantic in August 1943. Below: U 99, the boat commanded by Otto Kretschmer, the most successful U-boat captain of World War II. U 99 accounted for 245,000grt of enemy merchant shipping.

U 69–U 72, U 77–82, U 88–89, U 132–136, U 201–212, U 221–458, U 465–U 486, U 551–U 683, U 701–U 722, U 731–U 768, U 771– U 779, U 821, U 822, U 825–U 828, U 901, U 903–U 905, U 907, U 921–930, U 951–U 1010, U 1013–U 1025, U 1051– U 1058, U 1063–U 1065, U 1101–U 1110, U 1131, U 1132, U 1161–U 1172, U 1191– U 1210, U 1271–U 1275, U 1277–U 1279, U 1303–U 1308

Type	VIIC and VIIC/41 (659 boats)
Design and development	Ocean-going (medium), single-hull type. Similar to Type VIIB. The most numerous—and the most successful—submarine design of all time.
Builders	Blohm & Voss, Hamburg: U 551–U 650, U 951–U 995, U 997–U 1010, U 1013–U 1025
	Danziger Werft: U 401–U 430, U 1166–U 1176
	Deutsche Werke, Kiel: U 451–U 458, U 465–U 473, U 475–U 486
	Flenderwerke, Lübeck: U 88–U 92, U 301–U 308, U 903, U 904
	Flensburger Schiffahrt-Gesellschaft: U 351–U 370, U 1301–U 1308
	Germaniawerft, Kiel: U 69–U 72, U 93–U 98, U 201–U 212, U 221–U 232, U 235–U 250, U 1051–U 1058, U 1063–U 1065
	Howaldtswerke, Kiel: U 371–U 394, U 396–U 400, U 651–U 683, U 1131, U 1132
	Kriegsmarinewerft, Wilhelmshaven: U 751–U 768, U 771–U 779
	Neptunwerft, Rostock: U 921–U 930
	Nordseewerke, Emden: U 331–U 350, U 1101–U 1110
	Schichau, Danzig: U 431–U 450, U 731–U 750, U 825–U 828, U 1191–U 1210
	Stettiner Oderwerke: U 821, U 822
	Stettiner Vulcan: U 901
	Stülcken & Sohn, Hamburg: U 701–U 722, U 905–U 907
	Vegesacker Werft: U 77–U 82, U 132–U 136, U 251–U 300, U 1271–U 1279
In service	1940–45
Type displacement	769 tonnes surfaced, 871 tonnes submerged
Dimensions	67.1 × 6.2 × 4.74m
Speed	17.0–17.7 knots surfaced, 7.6 knots submerged
Range	8,500nm at 10 knots surfaced, 80nm at 4 knots submerged
Propulsion	
surfaced	Two 6-cylinder, four-stroke Germaniawerft F46 (U 88, U 90, U 132–U 136: MAN M6V40/46) diesel engines (with supercharging) = 3,200hp (U 88, U 90, U 132–U 136: 2,800hp)
submerged	Two AEG GU460/8-276 double-acting motors = 560kW: U 69–U 72, U 89, U 93–U 98, U 201–U 212, U 221–U 232, U 235–U 300, U 331–U 348, U 351–U 374, U 431–U 450, U 731–U 750, U 1051–U 1058, U 1063–U 1065, U 1191–U 1210, U 1271–U 1279, U 1301–U 1308

(continued overleaf)

U 69 etc. (continued)

	Two BBC GG UB720/8 double-acting motors = 560kW: U 77– U 82, U 88, U 90–U 92, U 132–U 136, U 401, U 451, U 551– U 650, U 751, U 821, U 822, U 825–U 828, U 929, U 930, U 951–U 995, U 997–U 1010, U 1013–U 1025
	Two Garbe & Lahmeyer RP137c double-acting motors = 560kW: U 301–U 328, U 375–U 394, U 396–U 400, U 701–U 722, U 752–U 768, U 771–U 779, U 1131, U 1132
	Two SSW GU343/38-8 double-acting motors = 560kW: U 349, U 350, U 402–U 430, U 453–U 458, U 465–U 473, U 475– U 486, U 651–U 683, U 901, U 903–U 907, U 921–U 928, U 1101–U 1110, U 1161–U 1172
Armament	Four 53.3cm bow and one 53.3cm stern torpedo tube (14 torpedoes or 39 mines), plus one 8.8cm and one 2cm Flak, with the following variations:
	Two bow torpedo tubes: U 72, U 80, U 554, U 555
	No stern torpedo tube: U 203, U 331, U 351, U 401, U 431, U 651
	From 1943, the following had their Flak armament increased and their minelaying equipment removed: U 88–U 92, U 333– U 350, U 352–U 370, U 374–U 394, U 396–U 401, U 404– U 430, U 435–U 450, U 454–U 458, U 657–U 683, U 702– U 722, U 731–U 750, U 754–U 768, U 771–U 779, U 1271– U 1279, U 1301–U 1308
Crew	Four officers and 40–56 men
Fates	
U 69	Sunk with all hands 12 February 1943 in the western North Atlantic Ocean
U 70	Sunk 7 March 1941 south-east of Iceland (20 fatalities)
U 71	Scuttled 5 May 1945 at Wilhelmshaven
U 72	Sunk 30 March 1945 at Bremen
U 77	Sunk 29 March 1943 east of Cartagena (38 fatalities)
U 78	Sunk 26 April 1945 at Pillau
U 79	Sunk 23 December 1941 north of Sollu
U 80	Sunk 28 November 1944 west of Pillau as a result of a diving malfunction (52 fatalities)
U 81	Sunk 9 January 1944 at Pola (2 fatalities)
U 82	Sunk with all hands 6 February 1942 north-east of the Azores
U 88	Sunk with all hands 12 September 1942 south of Spitzbergen
U 89	Sunk with all hands 12 May 1943 in the North Atlantic Ocean
U 90	Sunk with all hands 24 July 1942 east of Newfoundland
U 91	Sunk 26 February 1944 in the central North Atlantic Ocean (36 fatalities)
U 92	Decommissioned 12 October 1944 following bomb damage; scrapped in Norway after the war
U 93	Sunk 15 January 1942 north-east of Madeira (6 fatalities)
U 94	Sunk 28 August 1942 east of Kingston (19 fatalities)
U 95	Sunk 28 November 1941 south-west of Almeria (35 fatalities)
U 96	Sunk 30 March 1945 at Wilhelmshaven; scrapped
U 97	Sunk 16 June 1943 west of Haifa (27 fatalities)
U 98	Sunk with all hands 15 November 1942 west of Gibraltar
U 132	Sunk with all hands 4 November 1942 south-east of Cape Farewell
U 133	Sunk with all hands 14 March 1942 by mine off Salamis
U 134	Sunk with all hands 24 August 1943 in the Bay of Biscay
U 135	Sunk 15 July 1943 off Cape Juby (5 fatalities)
U 136	Sunk with all hands 11 July 1942 west of Madeira
U 201	Sunk with all hands 17 February 1943 east of Newfoundland
U 202	Sunk 2 June 1943 south-east of Cape Farewell (18 fatalities)
U 203	Sunk 24 April 1943 south of Cape Farewell (10 fatalities)
U 204	Sunk with all hands 19 October 1941 off Tangier
U 205	Sunk 17 February 1943 off Cyrenaica
U 206	Sunk with all hands 29 November 1941 west of Nantes

(continued overleaf)

Right: U 132 at La Pallice. In the foreground is an MG 34; periscope and flagstaff are also apparent.

Far right, upper: The conning tower of U 135, showing the fixed (and in this instance unshielded) FuMB 29 'Bali' passive radar array.

Far right, lower: Personnel crowd the conning tower of U 201, under Kapitän-leutnant Adalbert Schnee ('Schneemann'), after a successful sortie.

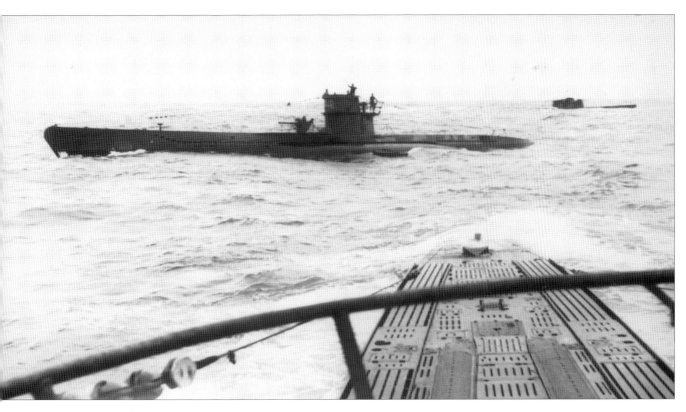

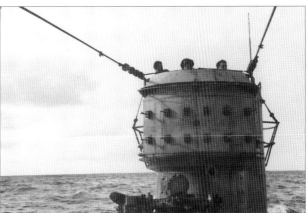

U 69 etc. (continued)

U 207	Sunk with all hands 11 September 1941 in the Denmark Strait, south-east of Angmagssali
U 208	Sunk with all hands 7 December 1941 west of Gibraltar
U 209	Sunk with all hands 7 May 1943 south-east of Cape Farewell
U 210	Sunk 6 August 1942 south of Cape Farewell (6 fatalities)
U 211	Sunk with all hands 19 November 1943 east of the Azores
U 212	Sunk with all hands 21 July 1944 in the English Channel south-east of Brighton
U 221	Sunk with all hands 27 September 1943 south-west of Ireland
U 222	Sunk 2 September 1942 west of Pillau following a collision with U 626 (42 fatalities)
U 223	Sunk 30 March 1944 north of Palermo (23 fatalities)
U 224	Sunk 13 January 1943 west of Algiers (45 fatalities)
U 225	Sunk with all hands 15 February 1943 in the North Atlantic Ocean
U 226	Sunk 6 November 1943 east of Newfoundland
U 227	Sunk with all hands 30 April 1943 north of the Faeroe Islands
U 228	Decommissioned 16 January 1945 at Bergen
U 229	Sunk with all hands 22 September 1943 south-east of Cape Farewell
U 230	Ran aground 21 August 1944 in the roads off Toulon; scuttled
U 231	Sunk 13 January 1944 north-east of the Azores (7 fatalities)
U 232	Sunk with all hands 8 July 1943 west of Oporto
U 235	Sunk 14 April 1945 by depth charges from the German torpedo-boat T 17 north-west of Skagenshorn
U 236	Sunk 6 May 1945 at Schliemünde
U 237	Sunk 4 April 1945 at Kiel
U 238	Sunk with all hands 9 February 1944 south-west of Ireland
U 239	Decommissioned 4 August 1944 at Kiel
U 240	Sunk with all hands 14 May 1944 in the North Atlantic Ocean
U 241	Sunk with all hands 18 May 1944 north-east of the Faeroe Islands
U 242	Sunk with all hands 5 April 1945 by mine in St George's Channel
U 243	Sunk 8 July 1944 west of Nantes (11 fatalities)
U 244	Surrendered 14 May 1945
U 245	Surrendered 30 May 1945 at Bergen
U 246	Sunk with all hands 29 March 1945 in the English Channel off Land's End
U 247	Sunk with all hands 1 September 1944 in the English Channel off Land's End
U 248	Sunk with all hands 16 January 1945 in the central North Atlantic Ocean

(continued on next page)

Far left: U 204 at Brest, September 1941,
Left: Close-up view of U 208's conning tower, with the coat of arms of the boat's 'adopted' city, Cologne, prominent.

Above and below right: U 255 photographed at Tromsø during Operation 'Wunderland II'.

U 69 etc. (continued)

U 249	At Portland 8 May 1945 at the time of the German surrender
U 250	Sunk 30 July 1944 in the Koivisto Strait, Baltic Sea (46 fatalities)
U 251	Sunk 19 April 1945 south of Göteborg (39 fatalities)
U 252	Sunk with all hands 14 April 1942 south-west of Iceland
U 253	Sunk with all hands 25 September 1942 north-west of Iceland
U 254	Sunk 8 December 1942 south-east of Cape Farewell following a collision with U 221 (41 fatalities)
U 255	Surrendered 8 May 1945
U 256	Decommissioned 23 October 1944 at Bergen
U 257	Sunk 24 February 1944 in the central North Atlantic Ocean (30 fatalities)
U 258	Sunk with all hands 20 May 1943 in the North Atlantic Ocean
U 259	Sunk with all hands 15 November 1942 north of Algiers
U 260	Scuttled 12 March 1945 south of Ireland after striking a mine
U 261	Sunk with all hands 15 September 1942 west of the Shetland Islands
U 262	Decommissioned 2 April 1945 at Kiel
U 263	Sunk with all hands 20 January 1944 by mine (?) off La Rochelle
U 264	Sunk 19 February 1944 in the central North Atlantic Ocean
U 265	Sunk with all hands 3 February 1943 south of Iceland
U 266	Sunk with all hands 14 May 1943 in the North Atlantic Ocean
U 267	Scuttled 5 May 1945 in Geltinger Bay
U 268	Sunk with all hands 19 February 1943 west of Nantes
U 269	Sunk 25 June 1944 in the English Channel off Torquay (13 fatalities)
U 270	Sunk 13 August 1944 off La Rochelle
U 271	Sunk with all hands 28 January 1944 west of Limerick
U 272	Sunk 12 November 1942 off Hela (Hel) following a collision with U 634 (29 fatalities)
U 273	Sunk with all hands 19 May 1943 south-west of Iceland
U 274	Sunk with all hands 23 October 1943 south-west of Iceland
U 275	Sunk with all hands 10 March 1945 by mine south of Newhaven
U 276	Scuttled 3 May 1945 at Neustadt
U 277	Sunk with all hands 1 May 1944 south-west of Bear Island
U 278	Surrendered 16 May 1945 at Narvik
U 279	Sunk with all hands 4 October 1943 south-west of Iceland
U 280	Sunk with all hands 16 November 1943 south-west of Iceland
U 281	Surrendered 29 May 1945 at Kristiansand
U 282	Sunk with all hands 29 October 1943 south-east of Greenland
U 283	Sunk with all hands 11 February 1944 south-west of the Faeroe Islands

(continued overleaf)

U 284	Scuttled 21 December 1943 south-east of Greenland following sea water ingress
U 285	Sunk with all hands 15 April 1045 south-west of Ireland
U 286	Sunk with all hands 29 April 1945 off Murmansk
U 287	Scuttled 16 May 1945 in the roads at Altenbruch
U 288	Sunk with all hands 3 April 1944 south of Bear Island
U 289	Sunk with all hands 31 May 1944 south-west of Bear Island
U 290	Scuttled 5 May 1945 in Kupfermühlen Bay
U 291	Surrendered 24 June 1945 at Wilhelmshaven
U 292	Sunk with all hands 27 May 1944 west of Trondheim
U 293	Surrendered 11 May 1945
U 294	At Narvik 16 May 1945 at the time of the German surrender
U 295	At Narvik 16 May 1945 at the time of the German surrender
U 296	Lost with all hands 22 March 1945 in the North Channel
U 297	Lost with all hands on or after 26 November 1944 in the Pentland Firth
U 298	Surrendered 30 May 1945 at Bergen
U 299	Surrendered 29 May 1945 at Kristiansand
U 300	Sunk 22 February 1945 west of Cadiz (9 fatalities)
U 301	Sunk 21 January 1943 in the Mediterranean Sea west of Bonifacio (45 fatalities)
U 302	Sunk with all hands 6 April 1944 south-west of the Azores
U 303	Sunk 21 May 1943 south of Toulon (21 fatalities)
U 304	Sunk with all hands 28 May 1943 south-east of Cape Farewell
U 305	Sunk with all hands 17 January 1944 south-west of Ireland
U 306	Sunk with all hands 31 October 1943 north-east of the Azores
U 307	Sunk 29 April 1945 off Murmansk (37 fatalities)
U 308	Sunk with all hands 4 June 1943 north-east of the Faeroe Islands
U 309	Sunk with all hands 16 February 1945 in the North Sea east of the Moray Firth
U 310	Decommissioned 29 May 1945 at Trondheim; scrapped 1947
U 311	Sunk with all hands 24 April 1944 south-west of Ireland
U 312	At Narvik 19 May 1945 at the time of the German surrender
U 313	At Narvik 19 May 1945 at the time of the German surrender
U 314	Sunk with all hands 3 January 1944 south-east of Bear Island
U 315	Decommissioned 1 May 1945 at Trondheim; scrapped 1947
U 316	Scuttled 2 May 1945 at Travemünde
U 317	Sunk with all hands 26 June 1944 north-east of the Shetland Islands
U 318	At Narvik 19 May 1945 at the time of the German surrender
U 319	Sunk with all hands 15 July 1944 south-west of Lindesnes, Norway

(continued on next page)

Left: U 302 at a rendezvous with U 354 off Spitzbergen during the second half of August 1943.

Clockwise from top left:
U 305; U 307 off Spitzbergen,
August 1944, with the
commander, Oberleutnant
Herrle, at right, in con-
versation with Leutnant
Koehl, head of the Spitz-
bergen weather station
garrison; U 307 in Isfjord,
Spitzbergen; and the same
boat under way in Isfjord.

U 69 etc. (continued)	
U 320	Scuttled 8 May 1945 north-west of Bergen
U 321	Sunk with all hands 2 April 1944 south-west of Ireland
U 322	Sunk with all hands 25 November 1944 west of the Shetland Islands
U 323	Scuttled 3 May 1945 off Nordenham
U 324	Surrendered 30 May 1945 at Bergen; scuttled
U 325	Lost with all hands April 1945 in the English Channel
U 326	Sunk with all hands 25 April 1945 in the Bay of Biscay
U 327	Lost with all hands February 1945 north-west of the British Isles
U 328	Surrendered 30 May 1945 at Bergen
U 331	Sunk 17 November 1942 north-west of Algiers (32 fatalities)
U 333	Sunk with all hands 31 July 1944 west of the Scilly Isles
U 334	Sunk with all hands 14 June 1943 south-west of Iceland
U 335	Sunk 3 August 1942 north-east of the Faeroe Islands (43 fatalities)
U 336	Sunk with all hands 4 October 1943 south-west of Iceland
U 337	Lost with all hands on or after 3 January 1943 in the North Atlantic Ocean
U 338	Lost with all hands on or after 20 September 1943 in the North Atlantic Ocean
U 339	Scuttled 5 May 1945 at Wilhelmshaven
U 340	Sunk 2 November 1943 off Tangier (1 fatality)
U 341	Sunk with all hands 19 September 1943 south-west of Iceland
U 342	Sunk with all hands 17 April 1944 south-west of Iceland
U 343	Sunk with all hands 10 March 1944 south of Sardinia
U 344	Sunk with all hands 22 August 1944 north-east of the North Cape
U 345	Scrapped 1944 at Kiel

(continued on next page)

U 69 etc. (continued)

U 346	Sunk 20 September 1943 off Hela (Hel) as a result of a diving malfunction
U 347	Sunk with all hands 17 July 1944 west of Narvik
U 348	Sunk 30 March 1945 at Hamburg (2 fatalities)
U 349	Scuttled 5 May 1945 in Geltinger Bay (1 fatality)
U 350	Sunk 30 March 1945 at Hamburg
U 351	Scuttled 5 May 1945 at Hörup Haff
U 352	Scuttled 9 May 1942 south of Cape Hatteras following a depth-charge attack (14 fatalities)
U 353	Sunk 16 October 1942 in the North Atlantic Ocean (6 fatalities)
U 354	Sunk with all hands 24 August 1944 north-west of Bear Island
U 355	Lost with all hands on or after 1 April 1944 south-west of Bear Island
U 356	Sunk with all hands 27 December 1942 north of the Azores
U 357	Sunk 26 December 1942 north-west of Ireland (36 fatalities)
U 358	Sunk 1 March 1944 north of the Azores (50 fatalities)
U 359	Sunk with all hands 26 July 1943 south of San Domingo
U 360	Sunk with all hands 2 April 1944 north-west of Hammerfest
U 361	Sunk with all hands 17 July 1944 west of Narvik
U 362	Sunk with all hands 3 September 1944 in the Kara Sea
U 363	At Narvik 16 May 1945 at the time of the German surrender
U 364	Sunk with all hands 29 January 1944 west of Bordeaux
U 365	Sunk with all hands 13 December 1944 east of Jan Mayen
U 366	Sunk with all hands 5 March 1944 north-west of Hammerfest
U 367	Sunk 16 March 1945 by mine off Hela (Hel) (43 fatalities)
U 368	Surrendered 23 June 1945 at Wilhelmshaven
U 369	Surrendered 29 May 1945 at Kristiansand
U 370	Scuttled 5 May 1945 in Geltinger Bay
U 371	Sunk 4 May 1944 north of Constantine in the Mediterranean Sea
U 372	Sunk 4 August 1942 in the Mediterranean Sea off Jaffa
U 373	Sunk 8 June 1944 west of Brest (4 fatalities)
U 374	Sunk 12 January 1942 in the Mediterranean Sea north-east of Catania (43 fatalities)
U 375	Sunk with all hands 30 July 1942 in the Mediterranean Sea north-west of Malta
U 376	Lost with all hands on or after 6 April 1943 in the Bay of Biscay
U 377	Sunk with all hands 15 January 1944 in the Atlantic Ocean
U 378	Sunk with all hands 20 October 1943 in the central North Atlantic Ocean
U 379	Sunk 9 August 1942 south-east of Cape Farewell (40 fatalities)

(continued on next page)

Above: U 371 in the Corinth Canal.
Below left: U 355 at Spitzbergen, seen from the transport *Wolsum*.

U 69 etc. (continued)

U 380	Sunk 11 March 1944 at Toulon (1 fatality)
U 381	Lost with all hands some time after 9 May 1943 in the North Atlantic Ocean
U 382	Scuttled 3 May 1945 at Wilhelmshaven
U 383	Sunk with all hands 1 August 1943 west of Brest
U 384	Sunk with all hands 19 March 1943 south-west of Iceland
U 385	Sunk 11 August 1944 north-west of La Rochelle (1 fatality)
U 386	Sunk 19 February 1944 in the central North Atlantic Ocean (33 fatalities)
U 387	Sunk with all hands 9 December 1944 off Murmansk
U 388	Sunk with all hands 20 June 1943 south-east of Cape Farewell
U 389	Sunk with all hands 5 October 1943 in the Denmark Strait south of Angmagssalik
U 390	Sunk 5 July 1944 in Seine Bay (48 fatalities)
U 391	Sunk with all hands 13 December 1943 north-west of Cape Ortegal
U 392	Sunk with all hands 16 March 1944 in the Strait of Gibraltar
U 393	Sunk 4 May 1945 at Holnis (near Flensburg) (2 fatalities)
U 394	Sunk with all hands 2 September 1944 west of Harstad
U 396	Sunk with all hands 23 April 1945 south-west of the Shetland Islands
U 397	Scuttled 5 May 1945 in Geltinger Bay
U 398	Lost with all hands on or after 17 April 1945 in the North Sea
U 399	Sunk 26 March 1945 in the English Channel off Land's End (46 fatalities)
U 400	Sunk with all hands 17 December 1944 south of Cork
U 401	Sunk with all hands 3 August 1941 south-west of Ireland
U 402	Sunk with all hands 13 October 1943 in the central North Atlantic Ocean
U 403	Sunk with all hands 17 August 1943 off Dakar
U 404	Sunk with all hands 28 July 1943 north-west of Cape Ortegal
U 405	Sunk with all hands 1 November 1943 in the central North Atlantic Ocean
U 406	Sunk 18 February 1944 in the central North Atlantic Ocean (12 fatalities)
U 407	Sunk 19 September 1944 in the Mediterranean Sea south of Milos (5 fatalities)
U 408	Sunk with all hands 5 November 1943 north of Iceland
U 409	Sunk 12 July 1943 in the Mediterranean Sea north of Algiers (11 fatalities)

(continued on next page)

Below: Crew members aboard U 377 at Spitzbergen, October 1942. Below right: U 407's conning tower, La Spezia, 1942.

U 410	Sunk 11 March 1943 at Toulon
U 411	Sunk with all hands 13 November 1942 west of Gibraltar
U 412	Sunk with all hands 22 October 1942 north-east of the Faeroe Islands
U 413	Sunk 20 August 1944 in the English Channel south of Brighton (45 fatalities)
U 414	Sunk with all hands 25 May 1943 in the Mediterranean Sea north-west of Ténès
U 415	Sunk 14 July 1944 at Brest (2 fatalities)
U 416	Sunk 12 December 1944 north-west of Pillau following a collision with the minesweeper M 203 (37 fatalities)
U 417	Sunk with all hands 11 June 1943 south-east of Iceland
U 418	Sunk with all hands 1 June 1943 north-west of Cape Ortegal
U 419	Sunk 8 October 1943 in the North Atlantic Ocean (48 fatalities)
U 420	Lost with all hands some time after 20 October 1943 in the North Atlantic Ocean
U 421	Sunk 29 April 1944 at Toulon
U 422	Sunk with all hands 4 October 1943 north of the Azores
U 423	Sunk with all hands 17 June 1944 north-west of the Faeroe Islands
U 424	Sunk with all hands 11 February 1944 south-west of Ireland
U 425	Sunk 17 February 1945 off Murmansk (52 fatalities)
U 426	Sunk with all hands 8 January 1944 west of Nantes
U 427	At Narvik 16 May 1845 following the German surrender
U 428	Scuttled 3 May 1945 in the Kiel Canal near Audorf
U 429	Sunk 30 March 1945 at Wilhelmshaven
U 430	Sunk 7 April 1945 at Bremen (2 fatalities)
U 431	Sunk with hands 21 October 1943 off Algiers
U 432	Sunk 11 March 1932 in the central North Atlantic Ocean (26 fatalities)
U 433	Sunk 17 November 1941 in the Mediterranean Sea south of Malaga (6 fatalities)
U 434	Sunk 18 December 1941 north of Madeira (2 fatalities)
U 435	Sunk with all hands 9 July 1943 in the North Atlantic Ocean west of Figueira
U 436	Sunk with all hands 26 May 1943 west of Cape Ortegal
U 437	Decommissioned 5 October 1944 at Bergen
U 438	Sunk with all hands 6 May 1943 north-east of Newfoundland
U 439	Sunk 4 May 1943 west of Cape Ortegal following a collision with U 659 (40 fatalities)
U 440	Sunk with all hands 31 May 1943 north-west of Cape Ortegal
U 441	Sunk with all hands 18 June 1944 west of Brest
U 442	Sunk with all hands 12 February 1943 west of Cape St Vincent

(continued on next page)

Left: U 435 at Narvik in August 1942, having collected 'Knospe' meteorological personnel from Spitzbergen.
Below left: The 2cm Flak-vierling (quad 2cm anti-aircraft mounting) aboard U 441—the Kriegsmarine's first 'Flak boat'—in July 1943. On the right is Kapitän Götz von Hartmann, a friend of the author.
Below: U 442 in the North Atlantic, hove-to beside the burning tanker *Empire Litton*, 9 January 1943. Just over a month later, this U-boat went to the bottom off Cape St Vincent.
Right: U 451 at Pillau in 1941.

U 69 etc. (continued)

U 443	Sunk with all hands 23 February 1943 off Algiers
U 444	Sunk 11 March 1943 in the central North Atlantic (41 fatalities)
U 445	Sunk with all hands 24 August 1944 west of St-Nazaire
U 446	Scuttled 3 May 1945 at Kiel
U 447	Sunk with all hands 7 May 1943 west of Gibraltar
U 448	Sunk 14 April 1944 north-east of the Azores (9 fatalities)
U 449	Sunk with all hands 24 June 1943 north-west of Cape Ortegal
U 450	Sunk 10 March 1944 in the Mediterranean Sea south of Ostia
U 451	Sunk 21 December 1941 off Tangier (44 fatalities)
U 452	Sunk with all hands 25 August 1941 south-east of Iceland
U 453	Sunk 21 May in the Ionian Sea north-east of Cape Spartivento (1 fatality)
U 454	Sunk 1 August 1943 north-west of Cape Ortegal (32 fatalities)
U 455	Sunk with all hands some time after 2 April 1944 by mine in the Ligurian Sea
U 456	Sunk with all hands 12 May 1943 in the North Atlantic Ocean
U 457	Sunk with all hands 16 September 1942 in the Barents Sea north-east of Murmansk
U 458	Sunk 22 August 1943 in the Mediterranean Sea south-east of Pantellaria (8 fatalities)
U 465	Sunk with all hands 2 May 1943 in the Bay of Biscay west of St-Nazaire
U 466	Scrapped 19 August 1944 at Toulon
U 467	Sunk with all hands 25 May 1943 south-east of Iceland
U 468	Sunk 11 August 1943 south-west of Dakar (44 fatalities)
U 469	Sunk with all hands 25 March 1943 south of Iceland
U 470	Sunk 16 October 1943 south-west of Iceland (46 fatalities)
U 471	Sunk 6 August 1944 at Toulon
U 472	Sunk 4 March 1944 south-east of Bear Island (22 fatalities)
U 473	Sunk 6 May 1944 south-west of Iceland (23 fatalities)
U 475	Scuttled 3 May 1945 at Kiel
U 476	Sunk 25 May 1944 north-west of Trondheim (33 fatalities)
U 477	Sunk with all hands 3 June 1944 west of Trondheim
U 478	Sunk with all hands 30 June 1944 north-east of the Faeroe Islands
U 479	Lost with hands some time after 15 November 1944 in the Gulf of Finland
U 480	Sunk with all hands 24 February 1945 in the English Channel south-west of Land's End
U 481	At Narvik 16 May 1945 following the German surrender
U 482	Lost with all hands on or after 1 December 1944 in the North Channel
U 483	At Trondheim 29 May 1945 following the German surrender

(continued overleaf)

Above left: U 561 embarking
mines at Augusta, Silesia,
July 1942.
Above: Keeping a lookout
aboard U 561.

U 69 etc. (continued)

U 484	Sunk with all hands 9 September 1944 south of the Hebrides
U 485	At Gibraltar 12 May 1945 following the German surrender
U 486	Sunk with all hands 12 April 1944 north-west of Bergen
U 551	Sunk with all hands 23 March 1941 south-east of Iceland
U 552	Scuttled 5 May 1945 at Wilhelmshaven
U 553	Lost with all hands on or after 20 January 1943 in the central North Atlantic Ocean
U 554	Scuttled 5 May 1945 at Wilhelmshaven
U 555	Decommissioned March 1945 at Hamburg
U 556	Sunk 27 June 1941 south-west of Iceland (5 fatalities)
U 557	Sunk with all hands 16 December 1941 in the Mediterranean Sea off Salamis
U 558	Sunk 20 July 1943 north-west of Cape Ortegal (45 fatalities)
U 559	Sunk 30 October 1942 in the Mediterranean north of Port Said (7 fatalities)
U 560	Scuttled 3 May 1945 at Kiel
U 561	Sunk 12 July 1943 in the Strait of Messina (42 fatalities)
U 562	Sunk with all hands 19 February 1943 north-east of Benghazi
U 563	Sunk with all hands 31 May 1943 south-west of Brest
U 564	Sunk 14 June 1943 north-west of Cape Ortegal (28 fatalities)
U 565	Sunk 30 September 1944 at Skaramanga, Greece (5 fatalities)
U 566	Sunk 24 October 1943 in the eastern North Atlantic Ocean, west of Oporto
U 567	Sunk with all hands 21 December 1941 in the central North Atlantic, north-east of the Azores
U 568	Sunk 29 May 1942 in the Mediterranean Sea, north-east of Tobruk
U 569	Sunk 22 May 1943 in the central North Atlantic Ocean (21 fatalities)
U 570	Captured by the British, commissioned 29 September 1941 as HMS *Graph*; ran aground 20 March 1944 off Islay
U 571	Sunk with all hands 28 January 1944 west of Ireland
U 572	Sunk with all hands 3 August 1943 north-east of Trinidad

(continued on next page)

Above: U 564 takes on supplies—including, foreground, a torpedo—from U 154 in the Caribbean, July 1942.
Below: U 565 off Athens, 6 January 1944. Visible here is the heavy 2cm Flak battery.

U 69 etc. (continued)

U 573	Sold to Spain 2 August 1942; became G 7, then S 1; decommissioned May 1970
U 574	Sunk 19 December 1941 in the Atlantic Ocean off Punta Delgada (28 fatalities)
U 575	Sunk 13 March 1944 north of the Azores (18 fatalities)
U 576	Sunk with all hands 15 July 1942 in the North Atlantic Ocean off Cape Hatteras
U 577	Sunk with all hands 15 January 1942 north-west of Mersa Matruh
U 578	Lost with all hands some time after 9 August 1942 in the Bay of Biscay
U 579	Sunk 5 May 1945 in the Little Belt (24 fatalities)
U 580	Sunk 11 November 1941 off Memel following a collision with the German merchantman *Angelburg* (12 fatalities)
U 581	Sunk 2 February 1942 south-west of the Azores (4 fatalities)
U 582	Sunk with all hands 5 October 1942 south-west of Iceland
U 583	Sunk with all hands 15 November 1941 in the Baltic Sea following a collision with U 153
U 584	Sunk with all hands 31 October 1943 in the central North Atlantic Ocean
U 585	Sunk with all hands 30 March 1942 by mine north of Murmansk
U 586	Sunk 5 July 1944 at Toulon
U 587	Sunk with all hands 27 March 1942 in the central North Atlantic Ocean
U 588	Sunk with all hands 31 July 1942 in the central North Atlantic Ocean
U 589	Sunk with all hands 14 September 1942 south-west of Spitzbergen
U 590	Sunk with all hands 9 July 1943 at the mouth of the River Amazon
U 591	Sunk 30 July 1943 off Pernambuco (Récife) (19 fatalities)
U 592	Sunk with all hands 31 January 1944 south-east of Ireland
U 593	Sunk 13 December 1943 in the Mediterranean Sea north of Constantine

(continued overleaf)

U 69 etc. (continued)

U 594	Sunk with all hands 4 June 1943 west of Gibraltar
U 595	Scuttled 14 November 1943 north-east of Oran
U 596	Sunk by an explosion 24 September 1944 in Skaramanga Bay (1 fatality)
U 597	Sunk with all hands 12 October 1942 south-west of Iceland
U 598	Sunk 23 July 1943 off Natal, Brazil (43 fatalities)
U 599	Sunk with all hands 24 October 1942 north-east of the Azores
U 600	Sunk with all hands 25 November 1943 in the South Atlantic Ocean north of Punta Delgada
U 601	Sunk with all hands 25 February 1944 north-west of Narvik
U 602	Lost with all hands on or after 23 April 1943 in the Mediterranean Sea
U 603	Sunk with all hands 1 March 1944 in the Atlantic Ocean
U 604	Scuttled 11 August 1943 in the central South Atlantic Ocean (16 fatalities)
U 605	Sunk with all hands 14 November 1942 off Algiers
U 606	Sunk 22 February 1943 in the central North Atlantic Ocean (36 fatalities)
U 607	Sunk 13 July 1943 north-west of Cape Ortegal (45 fatalities)
U 609	Sunk with all hands 7 February 1943 in the central North Atlantic Ocean
U 610	Sunk with all hands 8 October 1943 in the North Atlantic Ocean
U 611	Sunk with all hands 8 December 1942 south-west of Iceland
U 612	Scuttled 1 May 1945 at Warnemünde
U 613	Sunk with all hands 23 July 1943 south of the Azores
U 614	Sunk with all hands 29 July 1943 north-west of Cape Finisterre
U 615	Sunk 7 August 1943 in the Caribbean south-east of Curaçao (4 fatalities)
U 617	Sunk 12 September 1943 in the Mediterranean Sea off Melilla; run aground
U 618	Sunk with all hands 14 August 1944 west of St-Nazaire
U 619	Sunk with all hands 5 October 1942 south-west of Ireland
U 620	Sunk with all hands 13 February 1943 north-west of Lisbon
U 621	Sunk with all hands 18 August 1944 off La Rochelle
U 622	Sunk 24 July 1943 at Trondheim
U 623	Sunk with all hands 21 February 1943 in the Atlantic Ocean
U 624	Sunk with all hands 7 February 1943 in the North Atlantic ocean
U 625	Sunk 10 March 1944 west of Ireland
U 626	Sunk with all hands 15 December 1942 in the central North Atlantic Ocean
U 627	Sunk with all hands 27 October 1942 south of Iceland

(continued on next page)

Far left: U 569 at La Spezia.
Left, top: Close-up view of
U 586's conning tower,
Narvik, 1942–43.
Left, centre and bottom:
U 636 at a rendezvous with
U 255 off Novaya Zemlya.
Above: U 590, U 69 and U 584
at St-Nazaire, 25 June 1942.
Right: U 636 again, off
Novaya Zemlya, August
1943.

U 69 etc. (continued)	
U 628	Sunk with all hands 3 July 1943 north-west of Cape Ortegal
U 629	Sunk with all hands 7 June 1944 in the English Channel west of Brest
U 630	Sunk with all hands 6 May 1943 south of Cape Farewell
U 631	Sunk with all hands 17 October 1943 south-east of Cape Farewell
U 632	Sunk with all hands 6 April 1943 south-west of Iceland
U 633	Sunk with all hands 10 March 1943 in the North Atlantic Ocean
U 634	Sunk with all hands 30 August 1944 east of the Azores
U 635	Sunk with all hands 5 April 1943 south-west of Iceland
U 636	Sunk with all hands 21 April 1945 west of Ireland
U 637	Surrendered 27 May 1945 at Stavanger
U 638	Sunk with all hands 5 May 1943 in the North Atlantic Ocean
U 639	Sunk with all hands 28 August 1943 off Mys Zelaniya (Kara Sea)
U 640	Sunk with all hands 14 May 1943 in the North Atlantic Ocean off Cape Farewell

(continued overleaf)

U 69 etc. (continued)

U 641	Sunk with all hands 19 January 1944 south-west of Ireland
U 642	Sunk 5 July 1944 at Toulon
U 643	Sunk 8 October 1943 south of Iceland (30 fatalities)
U 644	Sunk with all hands 7 April 1943 west of Narvik
U 645	Sunk with all hands 24 December 1943 north-east of the Azores
U 646	Sunk with all hands 17 May 1943 south-east of Iceland
U 647	Lost with all hands on or after 28 July 1943 east of the Shetland Islands
U 648	Sunk 23 November 1943 north-east of the Azores
U 649	Sunk 24 February 1943 in the Baltic Sea following a collision with U 232 (35 fatalities)
U 650	Lost with all hands 9 December 1944 in the North Atlantic Ocean
U 651	Sunk 29 June 1941 south of Iceland
U 652	Sunk 2 June 1942 by U 81 after being damaged in the Gulf of Sollum
U 653	Sunk with all hands 15 March 1943 in the North Atlantic Ocean
U 654	Sunk with all hands 22 August 1942 in the Caribbean Sea
U 655	Sunk with all hands 24 March 1942 in the Barents Sea
U 656	Sunk with all hands 1 March 1942 south of Cape Race
U 657	Sunk with all hands 17 May 1943 east of Cape Farewell
U 658	Sunk with all hands 30 October 1942 east of Newfoundland
U 659	Sunk 4 May 1943 west of Cape Finisterre following a collision with U 439 (44 fatalities)
U 660	Sunk 12 November 1942 off Oran (2 fatalities)
U 661	Sunk with all hands 15 October 1942 in the North Atlantic Ocean
U 662	Sunk 21 July 1943 at the mouth of the River Amazon
U 663	Sunk with all hands 7 May 1943 west of Brest
U 664	Sunk 9 August 1943 west of the Azores (7 fatalities)
U 665	Sunk with all hands 22 March 1943 south-west of Ireland
U 666	Lost with all hands some time after 10 February 1944 in the North Atlantic Ocean
U 667	Sunk with all hands 25 August 1944 off La Rochelle
U 668	At Narvik 16 May 1945 following the German surrender
U 669	Lost with all hands some time after 29 August 1943 north-west of Cape Ortegal
U 670	Sunk 20 August 1943 in the Gulf of Danzig following a collision with merchantman *Bolkoburg* (21 fatalities)
U 671	Sunk 4 August 1944 in the English Channel south of Brighton (47 fatalities)
U 672	Scuttled 18 July 1944 in the English Channel north of Guernsey
U 673	Sunk 24 October 1944 north of Stavanger following a collision with U 382
U 674	Sunk with all hands 2 May 1944 north-west of Narvik
U 675	Sunk with all hands 24 May 1944 west of Ålesund
U 676	Lost with all hands on or after 12 February 1945 in the Gulf of Finland
U 677	Sunk 5 April 1945 at Hamburg
U 678	Sunk with all hands 6 July 1944 in the English Channel south-west of Brighton
U 679	Sunk with all hands 9 January 1945 in the Baltic Sea off Baltisch Port
U 680	Surrendered 24 June 1945 at Wilhelmshaven
U 681	Sunk 11 March 1944 west of Bishop's Rock (11 fatalities)
U 682	Sunk 11 March 1945 at Hamburg
U 683	Lost with all hands on or after 20 February 1945 in the North Atlantic Ocean
U 701	Sunk 11 July 1942 off Cape Hatteras (39 fatalities)
U 702	Sunk with all hands 3 April 1942 by mine in the North Sea
U 703	Lost with all hands some time after 22 September 1944 east of Greenland

(continued on next page)

U 69 etc. (continued)

U 704	Scuttled 3 May 1945 at Vegesack
U 705	Sunk with all hands 3 September 1942 west of Brest
U 706	Sunk 2 August 1943 north-west of Cape Ortegal (42 fatalities)
U 707	Sunk with all hands 9 November 1943 east of the Azores
U 708	Scuttled 5 May 1945 at Wilhelmshaven
U 709	Sunk with all hands 1 March 1944 north of the Azores
U 710	Sunk with all hands 24 April 1943 south of Iceland
U 711	Sunk 4 May 1945 at Harstad (32 fatalities)
U 712	Surrendered 29 May 1945 at Kristiansand
U 713	Sunk with all hands 24 February 1944 north-west of Narvik
U 714	Sunk with hands 14 March 1945 off the Firth of Forth
U 715	Sunk 13 June 1944 north-east of the Faeroe Islands (36 fatalities)
U 716	Surrendered 16 May 1945 at Narvik
U 717	Scuttled 5 May 1945 in Flensburger Förde
U 718	Sunk 18 November 1943 north-east of Bornholm following a collision with U 476 (43 fatalities)
U 719	Sunk with all hands 26 June 1944 off north-west Ireland
U 720	Surrendered 24 June 1945 at Wilhelmshaven
U 721	Scuttled 5 May 1945 in Geltinger Bay
U 722	Sunk with all hands 27 March 1945 off the Hebrides
U 731	Sunk with all hands 15 May 1944 in the central Atlantic Ocean
U 732	Sunk 31 October 1943 in the central Atlantic Ocean (31 fatalities)
U 733	Scuttled 5 May 1945 in Flensburger Förde
U 734	Sunk with all hands 9 February 1944 south-west of Ireland
U 735	Sunk 28 December 1944 at Horten (39 fatalities)
U 736	Sunk 6 August 1944 west of St-Nazaire (28 fatalities)
U 737	Sunk 19 December 1944 in Westfjord following a collision with the German minesweeper MRS 25 (31 fatalities)
U 738	Sunk 14 February 1944 off Gotenhafen (Gdynia) following a collision with the merchantman *Erna* (22 fatalities)
U 739	Surrendered 30 June 1945 at Wilhelmshaven
U 740	Lost with all hands on or after 6 June 1944 in the Bay of Biscay
U 741	Sunk 15 August 1944 in the English Channel north-west of Le Havre
U 742	Sunk with all hands 18 July 1944 west of Narvik
U 743	Sunk with all hands on or after 21 August 1944 in the North Sea
U 744	Sunk 6 March 1944 in the central North Atlantic Ocean (12 fatalities)

(continued overleaf)

**Left, top: U 703 transfers
supplies to a BV 138 flying
boat.
Left, centre: U 703 and U 387
at Narvik alongside the
supply ship *Grille*, May
1944.
Left, bottom: U 711 and
U 957 off Sterligora,
Norway, 25–27 September
1944.
Right: Kapitänleutnant
Brasack, commander of
U 737, on board his boat in
Ramsfjord, Spitzbergen.**

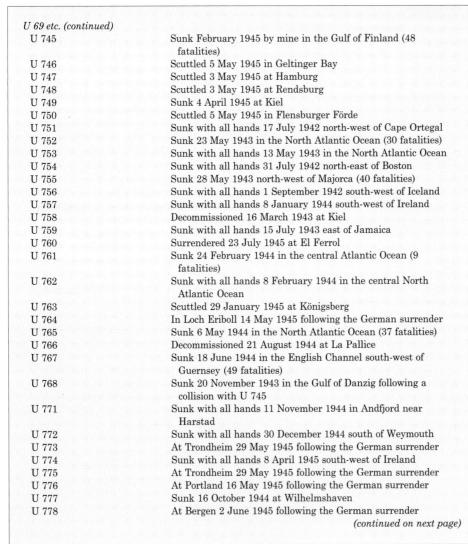

U 69 etc. (continued)

U 745	Sunk February 1945 by mine in the Gulf of Finland (48 fatalities)
U 746	Scuttled 5 May 1945 in Geltinger Bay
U 747	Scuttled 3 May 1945 at Hamburg
U 748	Scuttled 3 May 1945 at Rendsburg
U 749	Sunk 4 April 1945 at Kiel
U 750	Scuttled 5 May 1945 in Flensburger Förde
U 751	Sunk with all hands 17 July 1942 north-west of Cape Ortegal
U 752	Sunk 23 May 1943 in the North Atlantic Ocean (30 fatalities)
U 753	Sunk with all hands 13 May 1943 in the North Atlantic Ocean
U 754	Sunk with all hands 31 July 1942 north-east of Boston
U 755	Sunk 28 May 1943 north-west of Majorca (40 fatalities)
U 756	Sunk with all hands 1 September 1942 south-west of Iceland
U 757	Sunk with all hands 8 January 1944 south-west of Ireland
U 758	Decommissioned 16 March 1943 at Kiel
U 759	Sunk with all hands 15 July 1943 east of Jamaica
U 760	Surrendered 23 July 1945 at El Ferrol
U 761	Sunk 24 February 1944 in the central Atlantic Ocean (9 fatalities)
U 762	Sunk with all hands 8 February 1944 in the central North Atlantic Ocean
U 763	Scuttled 29 January 1945 at Königsberg
U 764	In Loch Eriboll 14 May 1945 following the German surrender
U 765	Sunk 6 May 1944 in the North Atlantic Ocean (37 fatalities)
U 766	Decommissioned 21 August 1944 at La Pallice
U 767	Sunk 18 June 1944 in the English Channel south-west of Guernsey (49 fatalities)
U 768	Sunk 20 November 1943 in the Gulf of Danzig following a collision with U 745
U 771	Sunk with all hands 11 November 1944 in Andfjord near Harstad
U 772	Sunk with all hands 30 December 1944 south of Weymouth
U 773	At Trondheim 29 May 1945 following the German surrender
U 774	Sunk with all hands 8 April 1945 south-west of Ireland
U 775	At Trondheim 29 May 1945 following the German surrender
U 776	At Portland 16 May 1945 following the German surrender
U 777	Sunk 16 October 1944 at Wilhelmshaven
U 778	At Bergen 2 June 1945 following the German surrender

(continued on next page)

**Top left: U 760 in the Baltic, after having rammed the target ship *Venus*.
Top right: U 953's commanding officer, Kommandant H. A. Werner, photographed at Brest in August 1944.**

Above: U 953 in heavy waters in the North Sea.

U 69 etc. (continued)

U 779	At Wilhelmshaven 24 June 1945 following the German surrender
U 821	Sunk 10 June 1944 off Brest (50 fatalities)
U 822	Scuttled 5 May 1945 at Wesermünde
U 825	At Portland 10 May 1945 following the German surrender
U 826	At Durness 10 May 1945 following the German surrender
U 827	Scuttled 5 May 1945 in Flensburger Förde
U 828	Scuttled 5 May 1945 at Wesermünde
U 901	At Stavanger 27 May 1945 following the German surrender
U 903	Scuttled 3 May 1945 at Kiel
U 904	Scuttled 5 May 1945 at Eckernförde
U 905	Sunk with all hands 27 March 1945 south-east of the Faeroe Islands
U 907	At Bergen 2 June 1945 following the German surrender
U 921	Sunk with all hands 30 September 1944 north-west of Hammerfest
U 922	Scuttled 3 May 1945 at Kiel
U 923	Sunk with all hands 9 February 1945 in Kiel Bay
U 924	Scuttled 3 May 1945 at Kiel
U 925	Sunk with all hands some time after 24 August 1944 in the North Atlantic Ocean
U 926	Decommissioned 5 May 1945 at Bergen
U 927	Sunk with all hands 24 February 1945 south-east of Falmouth
U 928	At Bergen 30 May 1945 following the German surrender
U 929	Scuttled 1 May 1945 at Warnemünde
U 930	At Bergen 30 May 1945 following the German surrender
U 951	Sunk with all hands 7 July 1943 north-west of Cape Vincent
U 952	Sunk 29 May 1945 at Toulon
U 953	At Trondheim 29 May 1945 following the German surrender
U 954	Sunk with all hands 19 May 1943 south-east of Cape Farewell
U 955	Sunk with all hands 7 June 1944 north of Cape Ortegal
U 956	In Loch Eriboll 13 May 1945 following the German surrender
U 957	Decommissioned 18 October 1944 at Trondheim
U 958	Scuttled 3 May 1945 at Kiel
U 959	Sunk with all hands 2 May 1944 south-east of Jan Mayen
U 960	Sunk 19 May 1944 north-west of Algiers (31 fatalities)
U 961	Sunk with all hands 29 March 1944 east of Iceland
U 962	Sunk with all hands 8 April 1944 north-west of Cape Finisterre
U 963	Scuttled 20 May off the west coast of Portugal
U 964	Sunk 16 October 1943 south-west of Ireland (47 fatalities)
U 965	Sunk with all hands 30 March 1945 north of Scotland
U 966	Sunk 10 November 1943 off Cape Ortegal (8 fatalities)
U 967	Scuttled 19 August 1944 at Toulon
U 968	In Loch Eriboll 19 May 1945 following the German surrender
U 969	Sunk 6 August 1944 at Toulon
U 970	Sunk 8 June 1944 north of El Ferrol (38 fatalities)
U 971	Sunk 24 June 1944 south of Land's End (1 fatality)
U 972	Lost with all hands on or after 15 December 1943 in the Atlantic Ocean
U 973	Sunk 6 March 1944 north-west of Narvik (51 fatalities)
U 974	Sunk 19 April 1944 off Norway (42 fatalities)
U 975	At Horten 27 May 1945 following the German surrender
U 976	Sunk 25 March 1944 south-west of St-Nazaire (4 fatalities)
U 977	Interned 17 August 1945 at Mar del Plata, Argentina; to USA
U 978	At Trondheim 29 May 1945 following the German surrender
U 979	Scuttled 24 May 1945 north of Amrum, North Frisian Islands
U 980	Sunk with all hands 11 June 1944 north-west of Bergen
U 981	Sunk 12 August 1944 off La Rochelle (12 fatalities)
U 982	Sunk 9 April 1945 at Hamburg (1 fatality)
U 983	Sunk 8 September 1943 in the Baltic Sea north of Leba following a collision with U 988 (5 fatalities)
U 984	Sunk with all hands 20 August 1944 west of Brest

(continued overleaf)

U 69 etc. (continued)

U 985	Decommissioned 15 November 1944 at Kristiansand
U 986	Sunk with all hands 17 April 1944 south-west of Ireland
U 987	Sunk with all hands 15 June 1944 west of Narvik
U 989	Sunk with hands 14 February 1945 off the Faeroe Islands
U 990	Sunk 25 May 1944 west of Bodø
U 991	At Narvik 6 May 1945 following the German surrender
U 993	Sunk 4 October 1944 at Bergen (2 fatalities)
U 994	At Trondheim 29 May 1945 following the German surrender
U 995	Decommissioned 8 May 1945 at Trondheim; now at Laboe as a museum exhibit
U 997	At Narvik 16 May 1945 following the German surrender
U 998	Decommissioned 27 June 1944 at Bergen
U 999	Scuttled 5 May 1945 in Flensburger Förde
U 1000	Decommissioned 29 August 1944 at Königsberg
U 1001	Sunk with all hands 8 April 1945 south-west of Land's End
U 1002	At Bergen 30 May 1945 following the German surrender
U 1003	Sunk 23 March 1945 in the North Channel (17 fatalities)
U 1004	At Bergen 2 June 1945 following the German surrender
U 1005	At Bergen 2 June 1945 following the German surrender
U 1006	Sunk 16 October 1944 south-west of the Faeroe Islands (6 fatalities)
U 1007	Sunk 2 May 1 1945 off Lübeck (2 fatalities)
U 1008	Scuttled 6 May 1945 in the Kattegat off Skagens Horn
U 1009	In Loch Eriboll 10 May 1945 following the German surrender
U 1010	In Loch Eriboll 14 May 1945 following the German surrender
U 1013	Sunk 17 March 1944 in the Baltic Sea east of Rügen following a collision with U 286 (25 fatalities)
U 1014	Sunk with all hands 4 February 1945 in the North Channel
U 1015	Sunk 19 May 1944 west of Pillau following a collision with U 1014 (36 fatalities)
U 1016	Scuttled 9 May 1945 in Lübeck Bay
U 1017	Sunk with all hands 19 April 1945 north-west of Ireland
U 1018	Sunk 27 February 1945 in the English Channel south-west of Penzance (51 fatalities)
U 1019	At Trondheim 29 May 1945 following the German surrender
U 1020	Lost with all hands on or after 31 December 1944 off the east coast of Scotland
U 1021	Lost with all hands some time after 14 March 1945 in the North Atlantic Ocean
U 1022	At Bergen 30 May 1945 following the German surrender
U 1023	At Weymouth 10 May 1945 following the German surrender
U 1024	Sunk 12 April 1945 south of the Isle of Man (9 fatalities)
U 1025	Scuttled 5 May 1945 in Flensburger Förde
U 1051	Sunk with all hands 26 January 1945 south of the Isle of Man
U 1052	At Bergen 30 May 1945 following the German surrender
U 1053	Sunk with all hands 15 February 1945 off Bergen as a result of diving too deeply
U 1054	Decommissioned 15 September 1944 at Kiel
U 1055	Lost with all hands on or after 23 April 1945 in the North Atlantic Ocean
U 1056	Scuttled 5 May 1945 in Geltinger Bay
U 1057	Surrendered 2 June 1945 at Bergen
U 1058	In Loch Eriboll 10 May 1945 following the German surrender
U 1063	Sunk 15 April 1945 west of Land's End (29 fatalities)
U 1064	At Trondheim 29 May 1945 following the German surrender
U 1065	Sunk 9 April 1945 north-west of Göteborg (45 fatalities)
U 1101	Scuttled 5 May 1945 in Geltinger Bay
U 1102	At Kiel 13 May 1945 following the German surrender
U 1103	At Cuxhaven 8 May 1945 following the German surrender
U 1104	At Bergen 30 May 1945 following the German surrender
U 1105	In Loch Eriboll 10 May 1945 following the German surrender

(continued on next page)

Top: A Type VII U-boat rescues a shot-down British bomber crew.

Above: U 1165, a Type VIIC/41 boat, at Danzig, late October 1944.

U 69 etc. (continued)

U 1106	Sunk with all hands 29 March 1945 north-west of the Faeroe Islands
U 1107	Sunk 30 April 1945 west of Brest (37 fatalities)
U 1108	At Horten 27 May 1945 following the German surrender
U 1109	In Loch Eriboll 12 May 1945 following the German surrender
U 1110	At Sylt 15 May 1945 following the German surrender
U 1131	Sunk 9 April 1945 at Hamburg
U 1132	Scuttled 4 May 1945 in Kupfermühlen Bay
U 1161	Scuttled 4 May 1945 in Kupfermühlen Bay
U 1162	Scuttled 5 May 1945 in Geltinger Bay
U 1163	Surrendered 29 May 1945 at Kristiansand
U 1164	Decommissioned 5 August 1944 at Kiel
U 1165	At Narvik 16 May 1945 following the German surrender
U 1166	Scuttled 4 May 1945 at Kiel
U 1167	Sunk 30 March 1945 at Hamburg (1 fatality)
U 1168	Scuttled 4 May 1945 in Geltinger Bay
U 1169	Sunk with all hands 29 March 1945 in the English Channel
U 1170	Scuttled 2 May 1945 at Travemünde
U 1171	At Stavanger 27 May 1945 following the German surrender
U 1172	Sunk with all hands 27 January 1945 in St George's Channel
U 1191	Lost with all hands on or after 12 June 1944 in the North Atlantic Ocean
U 1192	Scuttled 3 May 1945 at Kiel
U 1193	Scuttled 5 May 1945 in Geltinger Bay
U 1194	Surrendered 24 June 1945 at Wilhelmshaven
U 1195	Sunk 6 April 1945 in the English Channel south of Spithead (32 fatalities)
U 1196	Scuttled 3 May 1945 at Travemünde
U 1197	Decommissioned 25 April 1945 at Wesermünde
U 1198	At Cuxhaven 8 May 1945 following the German surrender
U 1199	Sunk 21 January 1945 off the Scilly Isles (48 fatalities)
U 1200	Sunk with all hands 11 November 1944 south of Ireland
U 1201	Scuttled 3 May 1945 at Hamburg
U 1202	Decommissioned 10 May 1945 at Bergen
U 1203	At Trondheim 29 May 1945 following the German surrender
U 1204	Scuttled 5 May 1945 in Geltinger Bay
U 1205	Scuttled 3 May 1945 at Kiel
U 1206	Sunk 14 April 1945 off Peterhead as a result of a diving malfunction (4 fatalities)
U 1207	Scuttled 5 May 1945 in Geltinger Bay
U 1208	Sunk with all hands 27 February 1945 south of Waterford
U 1209	Ran aground 18 December 1944 off the Scilly Isles and scuttled (9 fatalities)
U 1210	Scuttled 3 May 1945 off Eckernförde
U 1271	At Bergen 2 June 1945 following the German surrender
U 1272	At Bergen 30 May 1945 following the German surrender
U 1273	Sunk 17 February 1945 by mine in Ostfjord (43 fatalities)
U 1274	Sunk with all hands 16 April 1945 in the North Sea north of Newcastle-upon-Tyne
U 1275	Scuttled 3 May 1945 in Kieler Förde
U 1277	Scuttled 3 June 1945 west of Oporto
U 1278	Sunk with all hands 17 February 1945 north-west of Bergen
U 1279	Sunk with all hands 3 February 1945 north-west of Bergen
U 1301	At Bergen 2 June 1945 following the German surrender
U 1302	Sunk with all hands 7 March 1945 in St George's Channel
U 1303	Scuttled 5 May 1945 in Kupfermühlen Bay
U 1304	Scuttled 5 May 1945 in Kupfermühlen Bay
U 1305	In Loch Eriboll 10 May 1945 following the German surrender
U 1306	Scuttled 5 May 1945 in Flensburger Förde
U 1307	At Bergen 2 June 1945 following the German surrender
U 1308	Scuttled 1 May 1945 north-west of Warnemünde

U 213–U 218

Type	VIID (6 boats)
Design and development	Ocean-going (medium), single-hull type with saddle tank (1939–40). Similar to Type VIIC, but with an additional (9.8m) section abaft the conning tower to accommodate mine chutes.
Builder	Germaniawerft, Kiel
In service	1941–42
Type displacement	965 tonnes surfaced, 1,080 tonnes submerged
Dimensions	76.9 × 6.38 × 5.01m
Speed	16.7 knots surfaced, 7.3 knots submerged
Range	11,200nm at 10 knots surfaced, 69nm at 4 knots submerged
Propulsion	
surfaced	Two 6-cylinder, four-stroke Germaniawerft F46 diesel engines (with supercharging) = 3,200hp
submerged	Two AEG GU460/8-276 double-acting motors = 560kW
Armament	Four 53.3cm bow and one 53.3cm stern torpedo tube, plus five mine chutes (15 mines), plus one 8.8cm and one 2cm Flak and (from 1943) four twin 2cm Flak
Crew	Four officers and 40 men
Fates	
U 213	Sunk with all hands 31 July 1942 in the North Atlantic Ocean
U 214	Sunk with all hands 26 July 1944 in the English Channel
U 215	Sunk with all hands 3 July 1942 in the North Atlantic Ocean
U 216	Sunk with all hands 20 October 1942 south-west of Ireland
U 217	Sunk with all hands 5 June 1943 in the North Atlantic Ocean
U 218	Surrendered 2 June 1945 at Bergen

U 1059–U 1062

Type	VIIF (4 boats)
Design and development	Ocean-going (medium), single-hull, transport type with saddle tanks. Similar to Type VIIC, but with an additional (10.5m) section to accommodate 24 torpedoes.
Builder	Germaniawerft, Kiel
In service	1943
Type displacement	1,084 tonnes surfaced, 1,181 tonnes submerged
Dimensions	77.63 × 7.3 × 4.91m
Speed	17.6 knots surfaced, 7.9 knots submerged
Range	14,700nm at 10 knots surfaced, 75nm at 4 knots submerged
Propulsion	
surfaced	Two 6-cylinder, four-stroke Germaniawerft F46 diesel engines (with supercharging) = 3,200hp
submerged	Two AEG GU460/8-276 double-acting motors = 560kW
Armament	Four 53.3cm bow and one 53.3cm stern torpedo tube, plus one 3.7cm and two twin 2cm Flak, with 21 torpedoes in the stowage compartment and 5 in pressurised containers on the upper deck
Crew	Four officers and 42 men
Fates	
U 1059	Sunk 19 March 1944 in the Central Atlantic Ocean (47 fatalities)
U 1060	Sunk 27 October 1944 in the North Sea (12 fatalities)
U 1061	Surrendered 30 May 1945 at Bergen
U 1062	Sunk with all hands 30 September 1944 in the central Atlantic Ocean

Above: The Type VIIDs were dedicated minelayers and had additional space for mine stowage: note the faired accommodation immediately aft of the conning tower. This is U 214.
Right: U 1061 stranded on the rocks. She was one of the four Type VIIF transports built for the Kriegsmarine.

U 37–U 44

Type	IX (8 boats)
Design and development	Ocean-going, double-hull type with saddle tank (1939–40). Derived from the large MS type boats of World War I and developed through the Type IA (1934–35)
Builder	Deschimag, Bremen
In service	1938–39
Type displacement	1,032 tonnes surfaced, 1,153 tonnes submerged
Dimensions	76.5 × 6.5 × 4.7m
Speed	18.2 knots surfaced, 7.7 knots submerged
Range	10,500nm at 10 knots surfaced, 65–78nm at 4 knots submerged
Propulsion	
surfaced	Two 9-cylinder, four-stroke MAN M9V40/46 diesel engines (with supercharging) = 4,400hp
submerged	Two SSW GU345/34 double-acting motors = 740kW
Armament	Four 53.3cm bow and two 53.3cm stern torpedo tubes (22 torpedoes or 66 mines), plus one 10.5cm gun, one 3.7cm Flak and one 2cm Flak (from 1943–44: 10.5cm deleted, additional Flak embarked)
Crew	Four officers and 44 men
Fates	
U 37	Scuttled 8 May 1945 in Sønderborg Bay
U 38	Scuttled 5 May 1945 at Wesermünde
U 39	Sunk 14 September 1939 north-west of Ireland
U 40	Sunk 13 October 1939 by mine in the English Channel (45 fatalities)
U 41	Sunk with all hands 5 February 1940 south of Ireland
U 42	Sunk 13 October 1939 south-west of Ireland (26 fatalities)
U 43	Sunk with all hands 30 July 1943 south-west of the Azores
U 44	Sunk with all hands 13 March 1940 by mine off Terschelling

U 64, U 65, U 103–U 111, U 122–U 124

Type	IXB (14 boats)
Design and development	As Type IX
Builder	Deschimag, Bremen
In service	1939–40
Type displacement	1,051 tonnes surfaced, 1,178 tonnes submerged
Dimensions	76.5 × 6.76 × 4.7m
Speed	18.2 knots surfaced, 7.3 knots submerged
Range	12,000nm at 10 knots surfaced, 64nm at 4 knots submerged
Propulsion	
surfaced	Two 9-cylinder, four-stroke MAN M9V40/46 diesel engines (with supercharging) = 4,400hp
submerged	Two SSW GU345/34 double-acting motors = 740kW
Armament	Four 53.3cm bow and two 53.3cm stern torpedo tubes (22 torpedoes or 66 mines), plus one 10.5cm gun, one 3.7cm Flak and one 2cm Flak (from 1943–44: 10.5cm deleted, additional Flak embarked)
Crew	Four officers and 44 men
Fates	
U 64	Sunk 13 April 1940 off Narvik (8 fatalities)
U 65	Sunk with all hands 28 April 1941 south-east of Iceland
U 103	Sunk 15 April 1945 at Kiel (1 fatality)
U 104	Lost with all hands in or after November 1940 north-west of Ireland
U 105	Sunk with all hands 2 June 1943 off Dakar
U 106	Sunk 2 August 1943 north-west of Cape Ortegal (22 fatalities)
U 107	Sunk with all hands 18 August 1944 west of La Rochelle
U 108	Sunk 11 April 1944 at Stettin
U 109	Sunk with all hands 4 May 1943 south of Ireland
U 110	Sunk 9 May 1942 east of Cape Farewell (15 fatalities)
U 111	Sunk 4 October 1941 south-west of Tenerife (8 fatalities)
U 122	Lost with all hands some time after 22 June 1940 on passage between the North Sea and the Bay of Biscay
U 123	Decommissioned 17 June 1944 at Lorient
U 124	Sunk with all hands 2 April 1943 west of Oporto

Left: The Type IX boat U 37.
Right: U 105, a Type IXB.

U 66–U 68, U 125–U 131, U 153–U 166, U 171– U 176, U 501–U 524

Type | IXC (54 boats)
Design and development | As Type IX
Builder | Deschimag, Bremen (U 161–U 166: Deschimag-Seebeck, Bremerhaven; U 501–U 524: Deutsche Werft, Hamburg)
In service | 1941–42
Type displacement | 1,120 tonnes surfaced, 1,232 tonnes submerged
Dimensions | 76.76 × 6.76 × 4.7m
Speed | 18.2 knots surfaced, 7.3 knots submerged
Range | 13,450nm at 10 knots surfaced, 63nm at 4 knots submerged
Propulsion
  surfaced | Two 9-cylinder, four-stroke MAN M9V40/46 diesel engines (with supercharging) = 4,400hp
  submerged | Two SSW GU345/34 double-acting motors = 740kW
Armament | Four 53.3cm bow and two 53.3cm stern torpedo tubes (22 torpedoes or 66 mines), plus one 10.5cm gun, one 3.7cm Flak and one 2cm Flak (from 1943–44: 10.5cm deleted, additional Flak embarked)
Crew | Four officers and 44 men

Fates
U 66 | Sunk 6 May 1944 west of Cape Verde (24 fatalities)
U 67 | Sunk 16 July 1943 in the Sargasso Sea (48 fatalities)
U 68 | Sunk 10 April 1944 north-west of Madeira (56 fatalities)
U 125 | Sunk with all hands 6 May 1943 east of Newfoundland
U 126 | Sunk with all hands 3 July 1943 north-west of Cape Ortegal
U 127 | Sunk with all hands 15 December 1941 west of Gibraltar
U 128 | Sunk 17 May 1943 south of Pernambuco (Recife) (7 fatalities)
U 129 | Decommissioned 4 July 1944 at Lorient
U 130 | Sunk with all hands 12 March 1943 west of the Azores
U 131 | Sunk 17 December 1941 north-east of Madeira
U 153 | Sunk with all hands 13 July 1942 off Colón, Panama
U 154 | Sunk with all hands 3 July 1944 north-west of Madeira
U 156 | Sunk with all hands 8 March 1943 east of Barbados
U 157 | Sunk with all hands 13 June 1942 north-east of Havana
U 158 | Sunk with all hands 30 June 1942 west of Bermuda
U 159 | Sunk with all hands 28 July 1943 south of Haiti
U 160 | Sunk with all hands 14 July 1943 south of the Azores
U 161 | Sunk with all hands 27 September 1943 off Bahia
U 162 | Sunk 3 September 1942 off Trinidad (2 fatalities)
U 163 | Sunk with all hands 13 March 1943 in the Bay of Biscay
U 164 | Sunk 6 January 1943 north-west of Pernambuco (Recife) (54 fatalities)
U 165 | Sunk with all hands 27 September 1942 in the Bay of Biscay
U 166 | Sunk with all hands 1 August 1942 in the Gulf of Mexico
U 171 | Sunk 8 October 1942 off Lorient (22 fatalities)
U 172 | Sunk 13 December 1943 west of the Canary Islands (13 fatalities)
U 173 | Sunk with all hands 16 November 1942 off Casablanca
U 174 | Sunk with all hands 27 April 1943 south of Newfoundland
U 175 | Sunk 17 April 1943 south-west of Ireland (13 fatalities)
U 176 | Sunk with all hands 15 May 1943 north-east of Havana
U 501 | Sunk 10 September 1941 in the Denmark Strait (11 fatalities)
U 502 | Sunk with all hands 5 July 1942 west of La Rochelle
U 503 | Sunk with all hands 15 March 1942 south-east of Newfoundland
U 504 | Sunk with all hands 30 July 1943 north-west of Cape Ortegal
U 505 | Damaged 4 June 1944, captured; commissioned in US Navy; placed on display as a museum exhibit in Chicago
U 506 | Sunk 12 July 1943 west of Vigo (48 fatalities)

(continued on next page)

Above: Two photographs depicting a well-weathered U 505, captured by US naval forces on 4 June 1944 north-west of Dakar. In the lower photograph, the escort carrier *Guadalcanal*, which effected the capture, is seen alongside the U-boat. A Type IXC, U 505 is now displayed at the Museum of Science and Industry in Chicago.

U 167–U 170, U 183–U 194, U 525–U 550, U 801– U 803, U 805, U 806, U 841–U 846, U 853–U 858, U 865–U 870, U 877–U 881, U 889, U 1221–U 1235

Type	IXC/40 (97 boats)
Design and development	As Type IX
Builder	Deschimag, Bremen (U 167–U 170, U 801–U 806: Deschimag-Seebeck, Bremerhaven; U 525–U 550, U 1221–U 1235: Deutsche Werft, Hamburg)
In service	1942–44
Type displacement	1,144 tonnes surfaced, 1,257 tonnes submerged
Dimensions	76.76 × 6.76 × 4.7m
Speed	18.2 knots surfaced, 7.3 knots submerged
Range	13,850nm at 10 knots surfaced, 63nm at 4 knots submerged
Propulsion	
surfaced	Two 9-cylinder, four-stroke MAN M9V40/46 diesel engines (with supercharging) = 4,400hp
submerged	Two SSW GU345/34 double-acting motors = 740kW
Armament	Four 53.3cm bow and two stern torpedo tubes (22 torpedoes or 66 mines), plus one 10.5cm gun, one 3.7cm Flak and one 2cm Flak (from 1943–44: 10.5cm deleted, additional Flak embarked)
Crew	Four officers and 44 men
Fates	
U 167	Sunk 6 April 1943 west of the Canary Islands; raised 1951
U 168	Sunk 6 October 1944 in the Java Sea (23 fatalities)
U 169	Sunk with all hands 27 March 1943 south of Iceland
U 170	Surrendered 27 May 1945 at Horten
U 183	Sunk 23 April 1945 in the Java Sea (54 fatalities)
U 184	Lost with all hands on or after 20 November 1942 in the North Atlantic Ocean
U 185	Sunk 24 August 1943 in the central Atlantic Ocean (43 fatalities)

(continued overleaf)

U 167 etc. (continued)

U 186	Sunk with all hands 12 May 1943 north of the Azores
U 187	Sunk 4 February 1943 in the North Atlantic Ocean (9 fatalities)
U 188	Decommissioned 20 August 1944 at Bordeaux
U 189	Sunk with all hands 23 April 1943 east of Cape Farewell
U 190	At Halifax 12 May 1945 following the German surrender
U 191	Sunk with all hands 23 April 1943 south-east of Cape Farewell
U 192	Sunk with all hands 6 May 1943 south of Cape Farewell
U 193	Lost with all hands during or after April 1944 in the Bay of Biscay
U 194	Sunk with all hands 24 June 1943 south of Iceland
U 525	Sunk 11 August 1943 north-west of the Azores (54 fatalities)
U 526	Sunk 14 April 1943 off Lorient (42 fatalities)
U 527	Sunk 23 July 1943 south of the Azores (40 fatalities)
U 528	Sunk 11 May 1943 south-west of Ireland (11 fatalities)
U 529	Lost with all hands on or after 12 February 1943 in the North Atlantic Ocean
U 530	In Mar del Plata 10 July 1945 following the German surrender
U 531	Sunk with all hands 6 May 1943 north-east of Newfoundland
U 532	In Loch Eriboll 13 May 1945 following the German surrender
U 533	Sunk 16 October 1943 in the Gulf of Oman (52 fatalities)
U 534	Sunk 5 May 1945 north-west of Helsingør (3 fatalities)
U 535	Sunk with all hands 5 July 1943 north-east of Cape Finisterre
U 536	Sunk 20 November 1943 north-east of the Azores (38 fatalities)
U 537	Sunk with all hands 110 November 1944 in the Java Sea
U 538	Sunk with all hands 21 November 1943 south-west of Ireland
U 539	Surrendered 2 June 1945
U 540	Sunk with all hands 17 October 1943 east of Cape Farewell
U 541	At Gibraltar 12 May 1945 following the German surrender
U 542	Sunk with all hands 26 November 1943 north of Madeira

(continued on next page)

U 867, a Type IXC/40 U-boat, foundering off Bergen, 19 September 1944.

U 167 etc. (continued)

U 543	Sunk with all hands 2 July 1944 south-west of Tenerife
U 544	Sunk with all hands 16 January 1944 north-west of the Azores
U 545	Sunk 11 February 1944 west of the Hebrides (2 fatalities)
U 546	Sunk 24 April 1945 north-west of the Azores (24 fatalities)
U 547	Decommissioned 31 December 1944 at Stettin
U 548	Sunk with all hands 30 April 1945 east of Cape Hatteras
U 549	Sunk with all hands 29 May 1944 south-west of Madeira
U 550	Sunk 16 April 1944 east of New York (44 fatalities)
U 801	Sunk 17 March 1944 off Cape Verde (10 fatalities)
U 802	In Loch Eriboll 11 May 1945 following the German surrender
U 803	Sunk 27 April 1944 by mine off Swinemünde (9 fatalities)
U 805	At Portsmouth 14 May 1945 following the German surrender
U 806	At Aarhus 8 May 1945 following the German surrender
U 841	Sunk 17 October 1943 east of Cape Farewell (27 fatalities)
U 842	Sunk with all hands 6 November 1943 in the North Atlantic Ocean
U 843	Sunk 9 April 1945 west of Göteborg (44 fatalities)
U 844	Sunk with all hands 16 October 1943 south-west of Iceland
U 845	Sunk 10 March 1944 in the North Atlantic Ocean (10 fatalities)
U 846	Sunk with all hands 4 May 1944 north of Cape Ortegal
U 853	Sunk with all hands 6 May 1945 south-east of New London
U 854	Sunk with all hands 4 February 1944 by mine north of Swinemünde
U 855	Lost with all hands after 17 September 1944 west of Bergen
U 856	Sunk 7 April 1944 east of New York (27 fatalities)
U 857	Lost with all hands during or after April 1945 off Boston
U 858	At Portsmouth 14 May 1945 following the German surrender
U 865	Lost with all hands on or after 8 September 1944 north-west of Bergen
U 866	Sunk with all hands 18 March 1945 north-east of Boston
U 867	Sunk with all hands 19 September 1944 north-west of Bergen
U 868	Surrendered 30 May 1945 at Bergen
U 869	Sunk with all hands 17 February 1945 off Point Pleasant, New Jersey
U 870	Sunk 30 March 1945 by bombs at Bremen
U 877	Sunk 27 December 1944 north-west of the Azores
U 878	Sunk with all hands 10 April 1945 west of St-Nazaire
U 879	Sunk with all hands 30 April 1945 east of Cape Hatteras
U 880	Sunk with all hands 16 April 1945 in the North Atlantic Ocean
U 881	Sunk with all hands 6 May 1945 south-east of Newfoundland
U 889	At St John's, Newfoundland, 12 May 1945 following the German surrender
U 1221	Sunk 3 April 1945 by bombs in Kieler Förde (7 fatalities)
U 1222	Sunk with all hands 11 July 1944 west of La Rochelle
U 1223	Scuttled 5 May 1945 at Wesermünde
U 1224	Commissioned into the Japanese Navy 14 February 1944 as RO-501
U 1225	Sunk with all hands 24 June 1944 north-west of Bergen
U 1226	Lost with all hands after 23 October 1944 in the North Atlantic Ocean
U 1227	Decommissioned 10 April 1945 at Kiel
U 1228	At Portsmouth 17 May 1945 following the German surrender
U 1229	Sunk 20 August 1944 south-east of Newfoundland (18 fatalities)
U 1230	Surrendered 24 June 1945 at Wilhelmshaven
U 1231	In Loch Foyle 12 May 1945 following the German surrender
U 1232	Decommissioned 27 April 1945 at Wesermünde
U 1233	Surrendered 24 June 1945 at Wilhelmshaven
U 1234	Sunk 15 May 1944 off Gotenhafen (Gdynia) following a collision with the tug *Anton* (13 fatalities); recommissioned 17 October 1944; scuttled 5 May 1945 off Hörup Haff
U 1235	Sunk with all hands 15 April 1945 in the North Atlantic Ocean

U 180, U 195

Type	IXD$_1$ (2 boats)
Design and development	Ocean-going, double-hull type. Designed 1939–40 via Types IX, IXB and IXC. Converted to transports 1943.
Builder	Deschimag, Bremen
In service	1942
Type displacement	1,610 tonnes surfaced, 1,799 tonnes submerged
Dimensions	87.58 × 7.5 × 5.35m
Speed	20.8 knots surfaced, 6.9 knots submerged (16.5 knots surfaced following conversion)
Range	9,500nm at 14 knots surfaced (12,750nm at 10 knots following conversion), 115nm at 4 knots submerged
Propulsion	
surfaced	Six 20-cylinder, four-stroke Mercedes-Benz MB501 'vee' diesel engines = 9,000hp; two 6-cylinder, four-stroke Germaniawerft F46 diesel engines (with supercharging) = 3,200hp following conversion
submerged	Two SSW GU345/34 double-acting motors = 740kW
Armament	Four 53.3cm bow and two 53.3cm stern torpedo tubes (24 torpedoes or 72 mines), plus one 10.5cm gun, one 3.7cm Flak and one 2cm Flak (from 1943–44: torpedo tubes deleted, gun armament one 3.7cm Flak and four 2cm Flak, capacity for 252 tonnes of freight)
Crew	Four officers and 51 men
Fates	
U 180	Lost with all hands on or after 24 August 1944 west of Bordeaux
U 195	Taken over by the Japanese 6 May 1945

Above: Commissioning ceremonial aboard U 180, one of only two Type IXD$_1$ U-boats.

U 177–U 179, U 181, U 182, U 196–200, U 847–U 852, U 859–U 864, U 871–876

Below: The Type IXD₂ U 198 under the command of Fregattenkapitän Hartmann in the Indian Ocean. She went down off the Seychelles on 12 August 1944, the entire crew perishing.

Type	IXD$_2$ (28 boats)
Design and development	Ocean-going, double-hull type ('Monsun' boats). Developed from Types IX, IXB, IXC and IXD.
Builder	Deschimag, Bremen
In service	1942–44
Type displacement	1,616 tonnes surfaced, 1,804 tonnes submerged
Dimensions	87.58 × 7.5 × 5.35m
Speed	19.2 knots surfaced, 6.9 knots submerged
Range	13,450nm at 10 knots surfaced (diesel-electric propulsion), 63nm at 4 knots submerged
Propulsion	
surfaced	Two nine-cylinder, four-stroke MAN M9V40/46 diesel engines (with supercharging) = 4,400hp; plus, for cruising, two 6-cylinder, four-stroke MWM RS34S diesel engines = 1,000hp
submerged	Two SSW GU345/34 double-acting motors = 740kW
Armament	Four 53.3cm bow and two 53.3cm stern torpedo tubes (24 torpedoes or 72 mines), plus one 10.5cm gun, one 3.7cm Flak and one 2cm Flak (from 1943–44: torpedo tubes deleted, gun armament one 3.7cm Flak and four twin 2cm Flak)
Crew	Four to seven officers and 51–57 men
Fates	
U 177	Sunk 6 February 1944 west of Ascension Island (50 fatalities)
U 178	Scuttled 25 August 1944 at Bordeaux
U 179	Sunk with all hands 8 October 1942 off Cape Town
U 181	Taken over by the Japanese 6 May 1945
U 182	Sunk with all hands 16 May 1943 north of Tristan da Cunha
U 196	Lost with all hands on or after 30 September 1942 in the Indian Ocean
U 197	Sunk with all hands 20 August 1942 south of Madagascar
U 198	Sunk with hands 12 August 1944 off the Seychelles
U 199	Sunk 31 July 1943 east of Rio de Janeiro (50 fatalities)
U 200	Sunk with all hands 24 June 1943 south-west of Iceland
U 847	Sunk with all hands 27 August 1942 in the Sargasso Sea
U 848	Sunk with all hands 5 November 1943 south-west of Ascension Island
U 849	Sunk with all hands 25 November 1943 west of the Congo estuary
U 850	Sunk with all hands 20 December 1943 west of Madeira
U 851	Lost with all hands March or April 1944 in the North Atlantic Ocean
U 852	Run aground 3 May 1944 on the coast of Somaliland (7 fatalities)
U 859	Sunk 23 September 1944 in the Strait of Malacca (48 fatalities)
U 860	Sunk 15 June 1944 south of St Helena (45 fatalities)
U 861	Surrendered 29 May 1945 at Trondheim
U 862	Taken over by the Japanese 6 May 1945
U 863	Sunk with all hands 29 September 1944 east of Recife
U 864	Sunk with all hands 9 February 1945 west of Bergen
U 871	Sunk with all hands 26 September 1944 north-west of the Azores
U 872	Decommissioned 10 August 1944 at Bremen following bomb damage
U 873	At Portsmouth 17 May 1945 following the German surrender
U 874	At Horten 28 May 1945 following the German surrender
U 875	Surrendered 2 June 1945
U 876	Scuttled 4 May 1945 off Eckernförde

U 883

Type	IXD/42 (1 boat)
Design and development	As Type IXD$_2$
Builder	Deschimag, Bremen
In service	1945
Type displacement	1,616 tonnes surfaced, 1,804 tonnes submerged
Dimensions	87.58 × 7.5 × 5.35m
Speed	19.2 knots surfaced, 6.9 knots submerged
Range	31,000nm at 10 knots surfaced (diesel-electric propulsion), 57nm at 4 knots submerged
Propulsion	
surfaced	Two 9-cylinder, four-stroke MAN M9V40/46 diesel engines (with supercharging) = 4,400hp; plus, for cruising, two 6-cylinder, four-stroke MWM RS34S diesel engines (without supercharging) = 1,000hp
submerged	Two SSW GU345/34 double-acting motors = 740kW
Armament	Four 53.3cm bow and two 53.3cm stern torpedo tubes (24 torpedoes or 72 mines), plus one 3.7cm Flak and four 2cm Flak
Crew	Seven officers and 57 men
Fate	Surrendered 21 June 1945 at Wilhelmshaven

Below: U 883, the sole example of the Type IXD/42 U-boat. She is seen here at Wilhelmshaven on 16 May 1945 following her handover to British forces after the surrender.

Above: U 119, one of the Type XB minelayers.

U 116–U 119, U 219, U 220, U 233, U 234

Type	Type XB minelayers (8 boats)
Design and development	Ocean-going, double-hull type (1938 design)
Builder	Germaniawerft, Kiel
In service	1941–44
Type displacement	1,763 tonnes surfaced, 2,177 tonnes submerged
Dimensions	89.8 × 9.2 × 4.71m
Speed	17.0 knots surfaced, 7.0 knots submerged
Range	18,450nm at 10 knots surfaced, 93nm at 4 knots submerged
Propulsion	
surfaced	Two 9-cylinder, four-stroke Germaniawerft F46 a 9 pu diesel engines (with supercharging) = 4,200hp
submerged	Two AEG GU720/8-287 double-acting motors = 800kW
Armament	Two 53.3cm stern torpedo tubes and 66 mines, plus one 10.5cm gun, one 3.7cm Flak and one 2cm Flak (later one 3.7cm Flak and four 2cm Flak)
Crew	Five officers and 47 men
Fates	
U 116	Sunk with all hands on or after 6 October 1942 in the North Atlantic Ocean
U 117	Sunk 7 August 1943 in the North Atlantic Ocean (62 fatalities)
U 118	Sunk 12 June 1943 west of the Canary Islands (43 fatalities)
U 119	Sunk with all hands 24 June 1943 north-west of Cape Ortegal
U 219	Taken over by the Japanese 6 May 1945
U 220	Sunk with all hands 28 October 1943 in the North Atlantic Ocean
U 233	Sunk 5 July 1944 east of Halifax (32 fatalities)
U 234	At Portsmouth 17 May 1945 following the German surrender

U 459–U 464, U 487–U 490

Below: An example of a
Type XIV *Milchkuh*—U 464.

Type	Type XIV supply boats (8 boats)
Design and development	Ocean-going, double-hull type (1939–40 design)
Builder	Deutsche Werke, Kiel
In service	1941–43
Type displacement	1,688 tonnes surfaced, 1,932 tonnes submerged
Dimensions	67.1 × 9.35 × 6.51m
Speed	14.9 knots surfaced, 6.2 knots submerged
Range	12,350nm at 10 knots surfaced, 55nm at 4 knots submerged
Propulsion	
surfaced	Two 6-cylinder, four-stroke Germaniawerft F46 diesel engines (with supercharging) = 3,200hp
submerged	Two SSW GU343/38-8 double-acting motors = 560kW
Armament	Two 3.7cm Flak and one 2cm Flak (increased armament from 1943–44)
Cargo	Four torpedoes and 432 tonnes diesel oil
Crew	Six officers and 47 men
Fates	
U 459	Sunk 24 July 1943 north-west of Cape Ortegal (19 fatalities)
U 460	Sunk 4 October 1943 north of the Azores (62 fatalities)
U 461	Sunk 30 July 1943 north-west of Cape Ortegal (53 fatalities)
U 462	Sunk 30 July 1943 north-west of Cape Ortegal (1 fatality)
U 463	Sunk with all hands 16 May 1943 north-west of Spain
U 464	Sunk 20 August 1942 south-east of Iceland (2 fatalities)
U 487	Sunk 13 July 1943 in the central Atlantic ocean (31 fatalities)
U 488	Sunk with all hands 26 April 1944 north-west of Cape Verde
U 489	Sunk 4 August 1943 south-east of Iceland (1 fatality)
U 490	Sunk 12 June 1944 north-west of the Azores

V 80

Type	Type V 80 (1 boat)
Design and development	Single-hull type. Design by Hellmuth Walter GmbH and Germaniawerft, Kiel (1938–39)
Builder	Germaniawerft, Kiel
In service	From April 1940
Type displacement	73 tonnes surfaced, 76 tonnes submerged
Dimensions	22.05 × 2.1 × 3.2m
Speed	28.1 knots submerged
Range	50nm at 28 knots submerged
Propulsion	
surfaced	One Walter turbine = 2,000hp
Armament	None
Crew	Four
Fate	
V 80	Scuttled 29 March 1945 off Hela

Right: V 80 photographed in Germaniawerft's assembly hall.

Below: V 80 under way, in disruptive camouflage. With a designed underwater speed of over 28 knots, she was nothing less than the sensation of her day, her performance unmatched until the advent of nuclear submarines more than ten years later.

U 792, U 793

Type	Type Wa 201 (2 experimental boats)
Design and development	Single-hull type. Design by Hellmuth Walter GmbH and Blohm und Voss, Hamburg (1942)
Builder	Blohm und Voss, Hamburg
In service	1943–44
Type displacement	277 tonnes surfaced, 309 tonnes submerged
Dimensions	39.05 × 4.5 × 4.3m
Speed	9.0 knots surfaced, 25.0 knots submerged
Range	2,910nm at 8.5 knots surfaced, 127nm at 20 knots submerged
Propulsion	
surfaced	One 8-cylinder, four-stroke Deutz SAA 8M517 diesel engine (with supercharging) = 230hp
submerged	Two Walter turbines = 5,000hp plus one AEG-Maschine AWT97 = 57kW
Armament	Two 53.3cm bow torpedo tubes (length 5m)
Crew	Twelve
Fates	
U 792	Scuttled 4 May 1945 off Rendsburg; subsequently raised, transferred to Britain as war booty and employed in experimental work.
U 793	As U 792

Below left: U 793, one of the Type Wa 201 Walter boats. Bottom left: U 793 at Kiel. Above: U 794 is lowered into the water at Kiel.

U 794, U 795

Type	Type Wk 202 (2 experimental boats)
Design and development	Single-hull type. Design by Hellmuth Walter GmbH and Germaniawerft, Kiel (1942)
Builder	Germaniawerft, Kiel
In service	1943–44
Type displacement	236 tonnes surfaced, 259 tonnes submerged
Dimensions	34.6 × 4.5 × 4.55m
Speed	9.0 knots sufaced, 25.0 knots submerged
Range	1,840nm at 9 knots surfaced, 117nm at 20 knots submerged
Propulsion	
surfaced	One 8-cylinder, four-stroke Deutz SAA 8M517 diesel engine (with supercharging) = 230hp
submerged	Two Walter turbines = 5,000hp plus one AEG-Maschine AWT97 = 57kW
Armament	Two 53.3cm bow torpedo tubes (length 5m)
Crew	Twelve
Fates	
U 794	Scuttled 5 May 1945 in Geltinger Bay
U 795	Blown up 3 May 1945 at Germaniawerft

Below: Another view of the Type Wk 202 boat U 794. Below right: U 1407, a Type XVIIB. She became the British *Meteorite* postwar.

U 1405–U 1407

Type	Type XVII B (3 boats)
Design and development	Single-hull type. Design by Hellmuth Walter GmbH and Blohm und Voss, Hamburg (1942–43)
Builder	Blohm und Voss, Hamburg
In service	1944–45
Type displacement	312 tonnes surfaced, 337 tonnes submerged
Dimensions	41.45 × 4.5 × 4.3m
Speed	8.8 knots surfaced, 5.5 or 25.0 knots submerged (depending upon propulsion system activated)
Range	3,000nm at 8 knots surfaced, 123nm at 25 knots submerged
Propulsion	
surfaced	One 8-cylinder, four-stroke Deutz SAA 8M517 diesel engine (with supercharging) = 230hp
submerged	One Walter turbine = 2,500hp (planned: two Walter turbines = 5,000hp) plus one AEG-Maschine AWT98 = 55kW
Armament	Two 53.3cm bow torpedo tubes (length 5m)
Crew	Three officers and 16 men
Fates	
U 1405	Scuttled 5 May 1945 in Eckernförde Bay
U 1406	Scuttled 7 May 1945 at Cuxhaven; raised, transferred to USA
U 1407	Scuttled 7 May 1945 at Cuxhaven; raised, transferred to Great Britain and in service 1944–49 as *Meteorite*.

U 2501–2531, U 2533–U 2536, U 2539– U 2546, U 2548, U 2551, U 2552, U 3001– U 3035, U 3037–3041, U 3044, U 3051– U 3530

Type	Type XXI (118 boats)
Design and development	Double-hull type (8 sections) with streamlined outer casing. Official design (1943). Prefabricated (modular) construction by Deschimag, Bremen, administered by the Ingenieurbüro Glückauf at Blankenburg, Harz
Builder	Sections: 32 steel companies
	Fitting-out: 11 shipyards
	Assembly and final construction: Blohm und Voss, Hamburg (U 3001–U 3041, U 3044, U 3047, U 3050, U 3051: Deschimag, Bremen; U 3501–U 3530: Schichau, Danzig)
In service	1944–45
Type displacement	1,621 tonnes surfaced, 1,819 tonnes submerged
Dimensions	76.7 × 8.0 × 6.32m
Speed	15.6 knots surfaced, 17.2 knots submerged
Range	15,500nm at 10 knots or 5,100nm at 15.6 knots surfaced, 340nm at 5 knots or 110nm at 10 knots or 30nm at 15 knots submerged
Propulsion	
surfaced	Two 6-cylinder, four-stroke MAN M6V40/46KBB diesel engines (with supercharging) = 4,000hp
submerged	Two SSW GU365/30 double-acting motors = 4,100kW plus (for silent running) two SSW GV232/28 motors = 166kW
Armament	Six 53.3cm bow torpedo tubes plus four 2cm Flak
Crew	Five officers and 52 men
Fates	
U 2501	Scuttled 3 May 1945 at Hamburg
U 2502	Surrendered 3 June 1945 at Oslo
U 2503	Sunk 4 May 1945 in the Little Belt and scuttled
U 2504	Scuttled 3 May 1945 off Hamburg
U 2505	Scuttled 3 May 1945 off Hamburg
U 2506	Surrendered 14 June 1945 at Bergen
U 2507	Scuttled 5 May 1945 in Geltinger Bay
U 2508	Scuttled 3 May 1945 at Kiel
U 2509	Sunk 8 April 1945 by aerial bombing
U 2510	Scuttled 2 May 1945 at Travemünde
U 2511	Surrendered 14 June 1945 at Bergen
U 2512	Scuttled 8 May 1945 at Eckernförde

(continued on next page)

Below: The striking, streamlined conning tower of the Type XXI U-boat is evident in this photograph of U 3035.

Above: Type XXI boats lie silently at their moorings following their surrender to the Allies at the end of the war.

U 2501 etc. (continued)

U 2513	Surrendered 18 May 1945 at Horten; transferred to the USA, sunk 8 October 1951 off Key West
U 2514	Sunk 8 April 1945 at Hamburg
U 2515	Sunk 17 January 1945 at Hamburg
U 2516	Sunk 9 April 1945 at Kiel
U 2517	Scuttled 5 May 1945 in Geltinger Bay
U 2518	Surrendered 18 May 1945 at Horten; transferred to French Navy as *Roland Morillot*; scrapped 1969
U 2519	Scuttled 3 May 1945 at Kiel
U 2520	Scuttled 3 May 1945 at Kiel
U 2521	Sunk 4 May 1945 south-east of the Flensburg Lightvessel (41 fatalities)
U 2522	Scuttled 5 May 1945 in Geltinger Bay
U 2523	Sunk 17 January 1945 at Hamburg
U 2524	Sunk 3 May 1945 south-east of Fehmarn, Baltic Sea (2 fatalities), then scuttled
U 2525	Scuttled 5 May 1945 in Geltinger Bay
U 2526	Scuttled 2 May 1945 at Travemünde
U 2527	Scuttled 2 May 1945 at Travemünde
U 2528	Scuttled 2 May 1945 at Travemünde
U 2529	Surrendered 3 June 1945 at Kristiansand; became British N 27; handed over to Soviets 5 November 1945
U 2530	Sunk 31 December 1944 at Hamburg; raised; sunk again 17 January 1945 in dock
U 2531	Scuttled 2 May 1945 at Travemünde
U 2533	Scuttled 2 May 1945 at Travemünde
U 2534	Scuttled 8 May 1945 in Neustadt Bay
U 2535	Scuttled 2 May 1945 at Travemünde
U 2536	Scuttled 2 May 1945 at Travemünde
U 2538	Scuttled 8 May 1945 south-west of Aerö bei Marstal
U 2539	Scuttled 3 May 1945 at Kiel

(continued on next page)

U 2501 etc. (continued)

U 2540	Scuttled 4 May 1945 near the Flensburg Lightvessel; raised in 1957, commissioned into the Bundesmarine 1 September 1960 as *Wilhelm Bauer*; transferred 1984 to Deutsches Schiffahrtsmuseum, Bremerhaven
U 2541	Scuttled 5 May 1945 in Geltinger Bay
U 2542	At Kiel 3 April 1945
U 2543	Scuttled 3 May 1945 at Kiel
U 2544	Scuttled 5 May 1945 south-east of Aarhus
U 2545	Scuttled 3 May 1945 at Kiel
U 2546	Scuttled 3 May 1945 at Kiel
U 2548	Scuttled 3 May 1945 at Kiel
U 2551	Scuttled 5 May 1945 off Flensburg
U 2552	Scuttled 3 May 1945 at Kiel
U 3001	Scuttled 5 May 1945 north-west of Wesermünde
U 3002	Scuttled 2 May 1945 at Travemünde
U 3003	Sunk 4 April 1945 at Kiel
U 3004	Scuttled 3 May 1945 at Hamburg
U 3005	Scuttled 5 May 1945 at Wesermünde
U 3006	Scuttled 5 May 1945 at Wesermünde
U 3007	Sunk 24 February 1945 at Bremen (1 fatality)
U 3008	Surrendered 6 August 1945, transferred to the USA; employed in trials until 1954; scrapped 1955
U 3009	Scuttled 5 May 1945 at Wesermünde
U 3010	Scuttled 3 May 1945 at Kiel
U 3011	Scuttled 3 May 1945 at Travemünde
U 3012	Sunk 3 May 1945 east of the Fehmarn Lightvessel
U 3013	Scuttled 3 May 1945 at Travemünde
U 3014	Scuttled 3 May 1945 off Neustadt
U 3015	Scuttled 5 May 1945 in Geltinger Bay
U 3016	Scuttled 2 May 1945 at Travemünde
U 3017	Surrendered 18 May 1945 at Horten; became British N 41; scrapped 1949 at Newport
U 3018	Scuttled 3 May 1945 at Travemünde
U 3019	Scuttled 3 May 1945 at Travemünde
U 3020	Scuttled 3 May 1945 at Travemünde
U 3021	Scuttled 3 May 1945 at Travemünde
U 3022	Scuttled 3 May 1945 at Kiel
U 3023	Scuttled 3 May 1945 at Travemünde
U 3024	Scuttled 3 May 1945 off Neustadt
U 3025	Scuttled 3 May 1945 at Travemünde
U 3026	Scuttled 3 May 1945 at Travemünde
U 3027	Scuttled 3 May 1945 at Travemünde
U 3028	Scuttled 3 May 1945 at Kiel
U 3029	Scuttled 3 May 1945 in the outer narrows at Kiel
U 3030	Scuttled 9 May 1945 in Eckernförde Bay
U 3031	Scuttled 3 May 1945 at Kiel
U 3032	Scuttled 3 May 1945 in the Fehmarn Belt
U 3033	Scuttled 5 May 1945 in Wasserleben Bay
U 3034	Scuttled 5 May 1945 in Wasserleben Bay
U 3035	Surrendered 31 May 1945 at Stavanger; became British N 28; transferred to Soviet Union 5 November 1945
U 3037	Scuttled 3 May 1945 at Travemünde
U 3038	Scuttled 3 May 1945 at Kiel
U 3039	Scuttled 3 May 1945 at Kiel
U 3040	Scuttled 3 May 1945 at Kiel
U 3041	Surrendered 18 May 1945 at Horten; became British N 29; transferred to Soviet Union 5 November 1945
U 3044	Scuttled 5 May 1945 in Geltinger Bay
U 3501	Scuttled 5 May 1945 west of Wesermünde

(continued on next page)

U 2501 etc. (continued)

U 3502	Scuttled 3 May 1945 at Hamburg
U 3503	Scuttled 8 May 1945 west of Göteborg
U 3504	Scuttled 5 May 1945 at Wilhelmshaven
U 3505	Scuttled 3 May 1945 at Kiel
U 3506	Scuttled 3 May 1945 at Hamburg
U 3507	Scuttled 3 May 1945 at Travemünde
U 3508	Sunk 30 March 1945 at Wilhelmshaven
U 3509	Scuttled 5 May 1945 west of Wesermünde
U 3510	Scuttled 5 May 1945 in Geltinger Bay
U 3511	Scuttled 3 May 1945 at Travemünde
U 3512	Sunk 8 April 1945 at Hamburg
U 3513	Scuttled 3 May 1945 at Travemünde
U 3514	Surrendered 6 June 1945 at Bergen
U 3515	Surrendered 18 May 1945 at Horten; became British N 30; transferred to Soviet Union 5 November 1945
U 3516	Scuttled 2 May 1945 at Travemünde
U 3517	Scuttled 2 May 1945 at Travemünde
U 3518	Scuttled 3 May 1945 at Kiel
U 3519	Sunk 2 March 1945 by mine at Warnemünde (65 fatalities)
U 3520	Sunk with all hands 31 January 1945 by mine north-east of Bülk
U 3521	Scuttled 2 May 1945 at Travemünde
U 3522	Scuttled 2 May 1945 at Travemünde
U 3523	Sunk 6 May 1945 east of Aarhus (58 fatalities)
U 3524	Scuttled 5 May 1945 in Geltinger Bay
U 3525	Scuttled 3 May 1945 at Kiel
U 3526	Scuttled 5 May 1945 in Geltinger Bay
U 3527	Scuttled 5 May 1945 west of Wesermünde
U 3528	Scuttled 5 May 1945 west of Wesermünde
U 3529	Scuttled 5 May 1945 in Geltinger Bay
U 3530	Scuttled 3 May 1945 at Kiel

U 2321–U 2337, U 2340–U 2360, U 2362–U 2371, U 4701–U 4707, U 4709–U 4712

Type	Type XXIII (62 boats)
Design and development	Single-hull type (4 sections). Official design (1943). Prefabricated (modular) construction by Ingenieurbüro Glückauf at Blankenburg, Harz
Builder	Sections: various steel companies
	Assembly and final construction: Deutsche Werft, Hamburg (U 2332, U 2333, U 4701–U 4707, U 4709–U 4712: Germaniawerft, Kiel)
In service	1944–45
Type displacement	234 tonnes surfaced, 258 tonnes submerged
Dimensions	34.68 × 3.02 × 3.66m
Speed	9.7 knots surfaced, 12.5 knots submerged
Range	4,450nm at 6 knots or 2,600nm at 8 knots surfaced, 63nm at 4 knots submerged
Propulsion	
surfaced	One 6-cylinder, four-stroke MWM RS134S diesel engine (without supercharging) = 575hp
submerged	One AEG GU4463-8 double-acting motor = 427kW plus (for silent running) one BBC CCR188 motor = 25.8kW
Armament	Two 53.3cm bow torpedo tubes
Crew	Two officers and 12 men

(continued on next page)

Above: A photograph of
U 2361, showing the
hydrodynamic appearance
of the Type XXIII U-boat.

U 2321 etc. (continued)

Fates

U 2321	Surrendered 29 May 1945 at Kristiansand
U 2322	Surrendered 27 May 1945 at Stavanger
U 2323	Sunk 26 July 1944 by mine west of Möltenort (2 fatalities); scrapped 1946
U 2324	Surrendered 8 May 1945 at Stavanger
U 2325	Surrendered 29 May 1945 at Kristiansand
U 2326	In Loch Foyle 14 May 1945 following the German surrender
U 2327	Scuttled 3 May 1945 at Hamburg
U 2328	Surrendered 2 June 1945 at Bergen
U 2329	Surrendered 27 May 1945 at Stavanger
U 2330	Scuttled 3 May 1945 at Kiel
U 2331	Sunk 10 October 1944 in an accident off Hela (15 fatalities); raised, blown up 3 May 1945
U 2332	Scuttled 3 May 1945 at Hamburg
U 2333	Scuttled 5 May 1945 in Geltinger Bay
U 2334	Surrendered 29 May 1945 at Kristiansand
U 2335	Surrendered 29 May 1945 at Kristiansand
U 2336	Surrendered 21 June 1945 at Wilhelmshaven
U 2337	Surrendered 29 May 1945 at Kristiansand
U 2340	Sunk 30 March 1945 at Hamburg
U 2341	Surrendered 21 June 1945 at Wilhelmshaven
U 2342	Sunk 26 December 1944 off Swinemünde (8 fatalities)
U 2343	Scuttled 5 May 1945 in Geltinger Bay
U 2344	Sunk 18 February 1945 off Heiligendamm following a collision with U 2336 (11 fatalities)
U 2345	Surrendered 27 May 1945 at Stavanger
U 2346	Scuttled 5 May 1945 in Geltinger Bay
U 2347	Scuttled 5 May 1945 in Geltinger Bay
U 2348	Surrendered 27 May 1945 at Stavanger

(continued on next page)

U 2321 etc. (continued)

U 2349	Scuttled 5 May 1945 in Geltinger Bay
U 2350	Surrendered 29 May 1945 at Kristiansand
U 2351	Surrendered 21 June 1945 at Wilhelmshaven
U 2352	Scuttled 5 May 1945 at Hörup Haff
U 2353	Surrendered 29 May 1945 at Kristiansand
U 2354	Surrendered 29 May 1945 at Kristiansand
U 2355	Scuttled 3 May 1945 north-west of Laboe
U 2356	Surrendered 21 June 1945 at Wilhelmshaven
U 2357	Scuttled 5 May 1945 in Geltinger Bay
U 2358	Scuttled 5 May 1945 in Geltinger Bay
U 2359	Sunk 2 May 1945 in the Kattegat (12 fatalities)
U 2360	Scuttled 5 May 1945 in Geltinger Bay
U 2362	Scuttled 5 May 1945 in Geltinger Bay
U 2363	Surrendered 29 May 1945 at Kristiansand
U 2364	Scuttled 5 May 1945 in Geltinger Bay
U 2365	Scuttled 8 May 1945 in the Kattegat; raised June 1956; to the Bundesmarine as *Hai*
U 2366	Scuttled 5 May 1945 in Geltinger Bay
U 2367	Scuttled 9 May 1945 in the Schlei estuary; raised August 1956; to the Bundesmarine as *Hecht*
U 2368	Scuttled 5 May 1945 in Geltinger Bay
U 2369	Scuttled 5 May 1945 in Geltinger Bay
U 2370	Scuttled 2 May 1945 at Hamburg
U 2371	Scuttled 3 May 1945 at Hamburg
U 4701	Scuttled 5 May 1945 at Hörup Haff
U 4702	Scuttled 5 May 1945 in Geltinger Bay
U 4703	Scuttled 5 May 1945 in Geltinger Bay
U 4704	Scuttled 5 May 1945 at Hörup Haff
U 4705	Scuttled 3 May 1945 at Kiel
U 4706	Surrendered 29 May 1945 at Kristiansand
U 4707	Scuttled 5 May 1945 in Geltinger Bay
U 4709	Scuttled 4 May 1945 at Germaniawerft, Kiel
U 4710	Scuttled 5 May 1945 in Geltinger Bay
U 4711	Scuttled 4 May 1945 at Germaniawerft, Kiel
U 4712	Scuttled 4 May 1945 at Germaniawerft, Kiel

BUNDESMARINE

Hai, Hecht

Type	240 Class (2 boats)
Design and development	Former Type XXIII boats salvaged after the war, repaired, modified and re-engined with diesel-electric machinery
Builder	Deutsche Werft, Hamburg
In service	1945 (Kriegsmarine); 1956 (Bundesmarine)
Type displacement	234 tonnes surfaced, 275 tonnes submerged
Dimensions	36.0 × 3.0 × 3.28m
Speed	10.0 knots surfaced, 12.5 knots submerged
Range	1,350nm at 9 knots surfaced
Propulsion	
surfaced	One 12-cylinder 'vee', four-stroke Mercedes-Benz MB820S1 diesel engine (without supercharging) = 600hp
submerged	Output 470kW
Armament	Two 53.3cm bow torpedo tubes
Crew	17
Fates	
Hai	Scuttled (as U 2365) 8 May 1945 in the Kattegat; raised June 1956, recommissioned August 1956; sunk 14 September 1966 in the North Sea following water ingress (19 fatalities); raised 24 September 1966; scrapped 1968
Hecht	Scuttled (as U 2367) in the Schlei estuary 9 May 1945; raised August 1956, recommissioned 1 October 1957; scrapped 1969 at Kiel

Left: The U-boat *Hai* (240 Class), formerly the Type XXIII U 2365.
Below: *Wilhelm Bauer* (241 class), which was a wartime Type XXI. Scuttled at the end of the war, she was raised in the 1950s, converted and refitted, and served the Bundesmarine in the training role. She is now preserved as a museum boat.

Wilhelm Bauer

Type	241 Class (1 boat)
Design and development	Former Type XXI boat salvaged after the war, repaired, modified and re-engined with diesel-electric machinery; used for trials and training
Builder	Blohm und Voss, Hamburg
In service	1945 (Kriegsmarine); 1960 (Bundesmarine)
Type displacement	1,620 tonnes surfaced, 1,820 tonnes submerged
Dimensions	75.4 × 6.6 × 5.77m
Speed	10.0 knots surfaced, 12.5 knots submerged
Range	Not known
Propulsion	
surfaced	Two 12-cylinder 'vee', four-stroke Mercedes-Benz MB820S1 diesel engines (without supercharging) = 1,200hp
submerged	Output not known
Armament	Four 53.3cm bow torpedo tubes
Crew	57
Fates	Scuttled (as U 2540) 4 May 1945 off the Flensburg Lightvessel; raised 1957, refitted by Howaldtswerke, Kiel, and recommissioned 1 September 1960 (with original machinery); later re-engined with diesel-electric drive (decreasing output from 4,000hp to 1,200hp); collided with destroyer *Lütjens* 27 April 1976; laid up 28 November 1982 at Wilhelmshaven, decommissioned 15 March 1983, subsequently transferred to Deutsche Schiffahrtsmuseum, Bremerhaven

U 1–U 3

Type	201 Class (3 boats)
Design and development	Diesel-electric submarines. Design by Ingenieur-Kontor Lübeck and Howaldtswerke-Deutsche Werft (HDW), Kiel
Builder	Howaldtswerke-Deutsche Werft, Kiel
In service	1962–64
Type displacement	395 tonnes surfaced, 433 tonnes submerged
Dimensions	42.4 × 4.59 × 3.8m
Speed	10.0 knots surfaced, 17.0 knots submerged
Range	3,800nm at 6 knots surfaced
Propulsion	
surfaced	Two 12-cylinder 'vee', four-stroke Mercedes-Benz MB820S1 diesel engines (without supercharging) = 1,200hp
submerged	Output 1,100kW
Armament	Eight 53.3cm bow torpedo tubes
Crew	21
Fates	
U 1	Decommissioned 25 March 1966; scrapped 1971
U 2	Decommissioned 15 August 1963; scrapped 1971
U 3	Decommissioned 15 September 1967; scrapped 1971

Hans Techel, Friedrich Schürer

Type	202 Class (2 boats)
Design and development	Conceived as small hunter/killer submarines. Diesel and electric motors installed in parallel but functioning via a single gearbox
Builder	Atlaswerke, Bremen
In service	1965–66
Type displacement	100 tonnes surfaced, 137 tonnes submerged
Dimensions	22.0 × 3.4 × 2.7m
Speed	6.0 knots surfaced, 13.0 knots submerged
Range	400nm at 10 knots surfaced, 270nm at 5 knots submerged
Propulsion	
surfaced	One 12-cylinder, four-stroke Mercedes-Benz MB836 diesel engine = 425hp
submerged	Output 260kW
Armament	Two 53.3cm bow torpedo tubes
Crew	6
Fates	
Hans Techel	Decommissioned 15 December 1966; scrapped
Friedrich Schürer	Decommissioned 15 December 1966; scrapped

Above: U 2 (201 Class).
Below: *Friedrich Schürer* (202 Class) at her launching, 1965.

U 4–U 8

Above: The launch of *Hans Techel* (202 Class).

Above: The launch of *Hans Techel* (202 Class).

Type	205 Class (5 boats)
Design and development	Diesel-electric submarines. Design by Lübeck Ingenieur-Kontor (Engineering Office) and Howaldtswerke-Deutsche Werft (HDW), Kiel
Builder	Howaldtswerke-Deutsche Werft, Kiel
In service	1962–64
Type displacement	419 tonnes surfaced, 455 tonnes submerged
Dimensions	43.04 × 4.59 × 3.8m
Speed	10.0 knots surfaced, 17.0 knots submerged
Range	400nm at 10 knots surfaced
Propulsion	
surfaced	Two 12-cylinder 'vee', four-stroke Mercedes-Benz MB820S1 diesel engines (without supercharging) = 1,200hp
submerged	Output 1,100kW
Armament	Eight 53.3cm bow torpedo tubes
Crew	21
Fates	
U 4	Decommissioned 1 August 1974; scrapped 1977
U 5	Decommissioned 17 May 1974; scrapped
U 6	Decommissioned 23 August 1974; scrapped
U 7	Decommissioned 12 July 1974; scrapped
U 8	Decommissioned 9 October 1974; scrapped

U 9–U 12, U 1 (ii), U 2 (ii)

Type	205 Class (6 boats)
Design and development	Diesel-electric submarines. Design by Lübeck Ingenieur-Kontor (Engineering Office) and Howaldtswerke-Deutsche Werft (HDW), Kiel
Builder	Howaldtswerke-Deutsche Werft, Kiel
In service	1966–69
Type displacement	419 tonnes surfaced, 455 tonnes submerged
Dimensions	43.04 × 4.59 × 3.8m
Speed	10.0 knots surfaced, 17.0 knots submerged
Range	Not known
Propulsion	
surfaced	Two 12-cylinder 'vee', four-stroke Mercedes-Benz MB820S1 diesel engines (without supercharging) = 1,200hp
submerged	Output not known
Armament	Eight 53.3cm bow torpedo tubes
Crew	21
Fates	
U 9	Decommissioned 3 June 1993; transferred to Speyer Technik-Museum
U 10	Decommissioned 6 February 1993; transferred to Marine-Museum, Wilhelmshaven
U 11	Sunk as target
U 12	Sonar trials boat
U 1 (ii)	Decommissioned 29 November 1991; scrapped from 1993
U 2 (ii)	Decommissioned 19 March 1992; scrapped

Above: U 4, of the 205 Class. Below: U 9, a sister-boat of U 4.

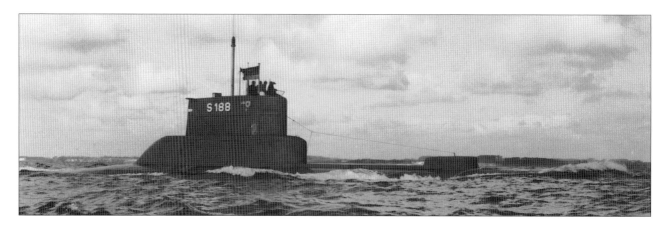

U 13–U 30

Type	206 Class (18 boats)
Builder	Howaldtswerke-Deutsche Werft, Kiel (U 14, U 16, U 18, U 20, U 22, U 23, U 24, U 26, U 28, U 30: Rheinstahl-Nordseewerke, Emden)
In service	1973–75
Type displacement	456 tonnes surfaced, 500 tonnes submerged
Dimensions	48.62 × 4.59 × 4.3m
Speed	10.0 knots surfaced, 17.0 knots submerged
Range	4,500nm at 6 knots
Propulsion	
surfaced	Two 12-cylinder 'vee', four-stroke MTU 12V 493 AZ 80 GA 31L diesel engines = 1,200hp
submerged	Output 1,100 kW
Armament	Eight 53.3cm bow torpedo tubes
Crew	22
Fates	As of 2002, all remain in service following conversion to 206A-Class standard

Right: U 22 (206 Class).

Right: Another view of U 22.

U 31–U 34

Type	212A Class (4 boats)
Builder	Howaldtswerke-Deutsche Werft, Kiel (U 32, U 34: Thyssen Nordseewerke, Emden)
In service	2004
Type displacement	1,450 tonnes surfaced, 1,830 tonnes submerged
Dimensions	56.0 × 7.0 × 6.0m approx.
Speed	
Range	
Propulsion	Diesel-electric propulsion incorporating air-independent propulsion (AIP) system using nine Siemens 34kW hydrogen fuel cells (9 modules)
Armament	Six torpedo tubes (2 × 3) with water ram launch system
Crew	Twenty-seven officers and men
Fates	First boat in service March 2004

Below and right: U 31, the first of the German Navy's new 212A Class submarines. (Photos: HDW/YPS Peter Neumann)

EXPORT SUBMARINES

Type	209/1100	209/1200	209/1400	214
Design	HDW, Kiel	HDW, Kiel	HDW, Kiel	HDW, Kiel
Type	Diesel-electric	Diesel-electric	Diesel-electric	AIP
Diplacement (tonnes)	1,105/1,230	1,180/1,290	1,454/1,586	1,700
Dimensions (m)	54.4 × 6.2 diam.	55.9 × 6.2 diam.	62.0 × 6.2 diam.	65 × ? diam.
Engine output (kW)	1,760	1,760	2,800	
Speed (knots)				
surfaced	11.0	11.0	15.0	
submerged	21.5	21.5	22.0	
Range (nm @ knots)				
surfaced	10,000 @ 10	10,000 @ 10	10,000 @ 10	
submerged	20 @ 20, 400 @ 4	20 @ 20, 400 @ 4	20 @ 20, 400 @ 4	
Armament	Eight 53.3cm TT	Eight 53.3cm TT	Eight 53.3cm TT	Eight 53.3cm TT
Crew	31	33	30	27

The 209 class are based on the 205 and 206 design, and have become the the most ubiquitous class of submarine to have been built in the West postwar. Altogether five versions have been produced, and these are in service with twelve navies—those of Argentina (two 209/1200), Peru (six 209/1200), Colombia (two 209/1200), Venezuela (two 209/1300), Equador (two 209/1200), Indonesia (two 209/1200), Chile (two 209/1400), India (four 209/1500), Brazil (three 209/1400), South Korea (nine 209/1200), Turkey (six 209/1200 and four 209/1400) and Greece (four 209/1100 and four 209/1200). The 214 Class is a further development, incorporating air-independent propulsion (AIP). Examples are scheduled for delivery to Greece (three) and South Korea (three).

Projects

KAISERLICHE MARINE

Type UF

Single-hull type submersible. Official design 1917–18 (Project 48A), War Contract X. Type displacement 364 tonnes surfaced, 410 tonnes submerged; range 3,500nm at 7 knots surfaced, 64nm at 4 knots submerged. UF 1–UF 92 ordered; boats under construction broken up on slipways.

In 1924 the design was developed by the Ingenieurs-Kantoor vor Scheepsbouw (IvS) in The Hague in various submarine projects for Estonia and Finland, Project 179 (1930) and also the Finnish *Vesikko* (commissioned in 1936 and illustrated opposite).

EVOLUTION OF TYPE II U-BOAT

		Kaiserliche Marine	IvS	Kriegsmarine			
		UF design	*Vesikko*	Type IIA	Type IIB	Type IIC	Type IID
Displacement (tonnes)	surfaced	364	250	254	279	291	314
	submerged	410	300	303	328	341	361
Length (m)		44.6	40.9	40.9	42.7	43.9	43.97
Beam (m)		4.44	4.1	4.08	4.08	4.08	4.92
Draught (m)		3.95	4.2	3.83	3.9	3.82	3.93
Engine output (hp)	surfaced	2×300	2×350	2×350	2×350	2×350	2×350
	submerged	2×310	2×180	2×180	2×180	2×205	2×205
Max rpm	surfaced	450		476	476	476	470
	submerged	360		360	375	375	375
Maximum speed (knots)	surfaced	11.0	13.0	13.0	13.0	12.0	12.7
	submerged	7.0	7.0	6.9	7.0	7.0	7.4
Range (nm at knots)	surfaced	3,500/7		1,600/8	3,100/8	3,200/8	5,650/8
	submerged	64/4	61.1/?	35/4	35–43/4	35–42/4	56/4
Oil bunkerage (tonnes)		26		11.61	21.5	22.7	38.3
Diving time (sec)		25		25	25	25	25
Bow torpedo tubes		4	3	3	3	3	3
Stern torpedo tubes		1	2	–	–	–	–
Torpedo stowage		7		5	5	5	5
Gun armament		1×8.8cm					
Crew		30		25	25	25	25
Power factor ($\sqrt[3]{\frac{N_{max}}{\sqrt[3]{D^2}}}$)		2,275	2,603	2,594	2,540	2,517	2,474
		2,239	2,003	1,998	2,033	2,033	2,007

EVOLUTION OF TYPE IA U-BOAT

		Kaiserliche Marine	IvS	Kriegsmarine
		UG design	E 1 ('Spanienboot')	Type IA, U 25, U 26
Displacement (tonnes)	surfaced	640	745	862
	submerged	965	983	
Length (m)		64.0	72.38	72.39
Beam (m)		6.2	6.2	6.21
Draught (m)		4.0	4.0	4.3
Engine output (hp)	surfaced	2 × 850	2 × 1,400	2 × 1,540
	submerged	2 × 550	2 × 500	2 × 500
Max rpm	surfaced			485
	submerged			310
Maximum speed (knots)	surfaced	14.4	17.0	18.6
	submerged	8.0	8.5	8.3
Range (nm at knots)	surfaced	8,000/8	7,000/10	7,900/10
	submerged	90/3	101/4	78/4
Oil bunkerage (tonnes)		75		96
Diving time (sec)				55
Bow torpedo tubes		4	4	4
Stern torpedo tubes		2	2	2
Torpedo stowage		12	14	14
Gun armament		1 × 10.5cm	1 × 10.5	1 × 10.5
Crew		30	32	43
Power factor ($\sqrt[3]{\frac{N_{max}}{\sqrt[3]{D^2}}}$)		2,839	3,242	3,247
		2,337	2,172	2,163

Type UG

Mixed type submersible with saddle tanks. Official design 1918 (Project 51A), War Contract X. Type displacement 640 tonnes surfaced, 410 tonnes submerged; range 8,000nm at 6 knots surfaced, 90nm at 3 knots submerged. No orders were forthcoming.

IvS developed this design into the Spanish E 1, which was built at Cadiz, launched in 1930 but never entered service owing to the political problems then becoming apparent in Spain. The boat was purchased by Turkey and commissioned into that country's navy in 1934 as *Gür*.

The design served as the basis for the Type IA U-boat which later entered service with the Kriegsmarine.

U-Panzerkreuzer

Double-hull type, armoured submersible (long-range commerce raider). Official design (Project 47), War Contract X.

Type displacement 4,100 tonnes; range 13,200nm at 10 knots surfaced, 80nm at 4 knots (?) submerged; ten torpedo tubes (4 bow, 4 side, 2 stern); output 6,000hp surfaced, 2,800kW submerged; crew 10 officers and 90 men plus a prize crew of 2 officers and 25 men.

This was a project only, and no orders were placed.

UD 1

Double-hull type submersible. Official design 1917 (Project 50), War Contract AA, Kaiserliche Werft, Kiel. Type displacement 3,800 tonnes (surfaced), 4,500 tonnes submerged; steam turbines, combined output 24,000hp; four boilers in pressurised tanks; projected speed 25 knots.

Ordered February 1918, not built; materials scrapped November 1918.

REICHSMARINE/KRIEGSMARINE

Type III

1934 design, similar to Type IA but with additional stowage for 21 torpedoes or 21 mines. Not ordered.

Type III mod.

1934 design, similar to Type IA but with additional (exterior) accommodation for 48 mines and pressurised, watertight hangar for two light motor boats. Not ordered.

Type IV

Supply boat, 1934 design, similar to Type IA but with additional stowage for 21 torpedoes or 21 mines; not ordered.

Type V

1934 design project for a fast, closed-cycle, diesel-powered submarine deriving oxygen from H_2O_2 (hydrogen peroxide). Not ordered.

Type VI

1934 design derivative of Type IA with standard steam drive. Not proceeded with.

KRIEGSMARINE

Type VII/42

Ocean-going, single-hull type with saddle tanks, 1942–43 design. As Type VII but with a stengthened pressure hull for a deeper diving capability. Ordered 1943 but cancelled in September of that year in favour of the Type XXI.

Type XA

Ocean-going, double-hull type (1937 design) derived from the First World War I U-Minekreuzer (q.v.) or Project 45 but abandoned in favour of the Type XB.

Type XI

Double-hull type submarine cruiser, 1937–38 design. Eight 12-cylinder, four-stroke MRM RS12 V26/34 diesel engines = 2,000hp each for surface drive; projected maximum speed 23 knots; range 26,600nm at 10 knots. Orders were placed with Deschimag, Bremen, in January 1939 for four boats, but these were cancelled in September that year.

Type XII

Double-hull type fleet boat, 1938 design. Derived from the Type IX. There were plans for boats of this type to be built by Deschimag, Bremen, but no orders were placed.

Type XIII

A 1939 project for a single-hull type developed from the Type II. Not ordered.

Types XV, XVI

Studies only for maintenance/supply boats of, respectively, 2,500 and 5,000 tons, able to accommodate torpedoes, provisions and diesel fuel oil.

V 300

Single-hull type 1940–41 design by Hellmuth Walter and Germaniawerft, Kiel, powered by two Walter turbines of 2,180hp each giving a projected underwater speed of 10 knots. One example (U 791) ordered from Germaniawerft, Kiel, in February 1942 but discarded that summer in favour of the Wk 202.

Type XVIIK

Experimental boat for closed-cycle type machinery. One 20-cylinder, four-stroke Daimler-Benz MB501 diesel

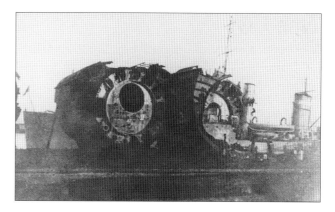

engine = 1,500hp. One boat (U 798) ordered from Germania-werft, Kiel, in February 1944 but still under construction when the slipway was captured in February 1945. Dismantled in May 1945.

Type XVIII

1942–43 design by Walter and Deutsche Werke, Kiel. Two Walter turbines = 7,500hp each for a designed underwater speed of 24 knots; two 12-cylinder, four-stroke MWM RS12 V26/349 diesel engines = 2,000hp each for a designed surfaced speed of 18.5 knots. Orders were placed with Deutsche Werke, Kiel, for U 796 and U 797 in January 1943, but the boats were discarded in favour of the Type XXVIW.

Type XIX

Late 1942 design for a boat developed from the Type XB specifically for transporting rubber and precious metals. Study project for the Type XX.

Type XX

Double-hull type transport to a 1943 OKM/A. G. Weser design for voyages to and from the Far East. Designed surfaced range 18,900nm at 10 knots. Orders placed in March 1943 for a total of 30 boats with Deutsche Werft, Hamburg, and Vegesacker Werft but construction halted in May 1944 in favour of the Type XXI.

Type XXII

Walter design for a boat for deployment in the Mediterranean and coastal use. One Walter turbine = 1,850hp for underwater propulsion and one 12-cylinder, four-stroke Deutz R12 V26/340 diesel engine for surfaced propulsion. Two boats, U 1153 and U 1154, ordered from Howaldtswerke, Kiel, in 1943 but cancelled that autumn in favour of the Type XXIII.

Type XXIV

Double-hull type (1943 design) for an ocean-going boat similar to the Type XVII. Two Walter turbines = 7,500hp each for surfaced propulsion; fourteen torpedo tubes. Not ordered.

Type XXV

1943 design for a true electro-boat for coastal operations. Orders not placed.

Type XXVIW

Walter design in conjunction with Ingenieurburö Glückauf. Designed displacement 842 tonnes surfaced, 926 tonnes submerged; one Walter turbine = 7,500hp; maximum speed 24 knots; 10 torpedo tubes (4 bow, 2 × 3 amidships in a so-called Schneeorgel—literally, 'snow organ'—arrangement, firing aft). Orders placed with Blohm & Voss, Hamburg, for 100 boats in 1944; U 4501–U 4504 sections constructed by the end of the war.

Above: Bow section of a Type XXVI.

Types XXVI–XXVIA

Interim projects dating from late 1943 through to summer 1944.

Captured Submarines

1914-1918

Russian

US 1 (ex *Burevestrik*). Seized 2 May 1918 at Sevastopol. Not commissioned.

US 2 (ex *Orlau*). Seized 2 May 1918 at Sevastopol. Not commissioned.

US 3 (ex *Utka*). Seized 2 May 1918 at Sevastopol. Commissioned 1 August 1918 but not deployed.

US 4 (ex *Gargara*). Seized 3 May 1918 at Sevastopol. Ran trials in May 1918 but not deployed.

1939-1945

British

UB (ex *Seal*). Minelaying submarine captured by German aircraft 5 May 1940 in the Kattegat. Placed into service 30 November 1940 as a training boat; decommissioned 31 July 1941; scuttled in Heikendorfer Bay 3 May 1945.

Norwegian

UC 1 (ex B 5). Captured 9 April 1940, commissioned 20 November 1940 as a training boat but found unsuitable. Broken up 1942.

UC 2 (ex B 6). Captured 4 May 1940, placed in service 20 November as a training submarine. Decommissioned October 1944, scrapped 1945.

Dutch

UD 1 (ex O 8). Captured 14 May 1940 at Den Helder. Placed in service 21 November 1940. Decommissioned at Kiel 23 November 1943, scuttled there 3 May 1945.

UD 2 (ex O 12). Foundered 14 May 1940 at Den Helder, raised, commissioned into the Kriegsmarine 28 January 1941. Decommissioned at Kiel 6 July 1944, scuttled there 3 May 1945.

UD 3 (ex O 25). Seized at Schiedam 14 May 1940. commissioned 1 March 1942. Put out of action at Kiel as a result of an air raid, scuttled there 3 May 1945.

UD 4 (ex O 26). Captured at Rotterdam 14 May 1940, commissioned 28 January 1941. Scuttled at Kiel 3 May 1945.

Below: UB, the former HMS *Seal*.

Left: UC 2, the former Norwegian B 6, undergoing salvage at Bergen in October 1945.

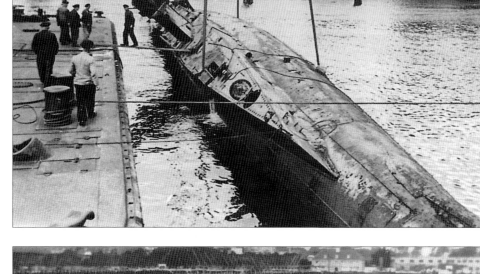

Left: UD 1, the captured Dutch submarine O 8.

Left: UD 4, formerly the Dutch O 26 (right), with a Type VIIC U-boat alongside.

Right, upper: The French submarine *La Favorite* was captured by the Germans and redesignated UF 2. Right, lower: The Italian *Reginaldo Guiliani*, seen in 1941. This boat was designated UIT 23 following her transfer to German service.

UD 5 (ex O 27). Captured at Rotterdam 14 May 1940, placed in service 30 January 1942. Decommissioned at Bergen May 1945.

French

UF 1 (ex *L'Africaine*). Captured on the ways at Le Trait in June 1940; still incomplete at end of war.

UF 2 (ex *La Favorite*). Captured on the ways at Le Trait in June 1940; placed in service 5 November 1940. decommissioned at Gotenhafen 5 July 1944, scuttled there 1945.

UF 3 (ex *L'Astrée*). Captured on the ways at Nantes in June 1940; still incomplete at end of war.

Italian

UIT 1 (ex R 10), **UIT 2** (ex R 11), **UIT 3** (ex R 12), **UIT 4** (ex R 7), **UIT 5** (ex R 8), **UIT 6** (ex R 9). These boats were taken over on 6 March 1943 for completion under German direction, but were destroyed as a result of British bombing in 1944–45.

UIT 7 (ex *Bario*), **UIT 8** (ex *Litio*), **UIT 9** (ex *Sodio*), **UIT 10** (ex *Potassio*), **UIT 11** (ex *Rame*), **UIT 12** (ex *Ferro*), **UIT 13** (ex *Piombo*), **UIT 14** (ex *Zinco*), **UIT 15** (ex *Sparide*), **UIT 16** (ex *Murena*), **UIT 17** (CM 1), **UIT 18** (ex CM 2), **UIT 19** (ex *Nastilo*), **UIT 20** (ex *Grongo*). These boats were incomplete at the time of the Italian capitulation on 8 March 1943. Except for UIT 17, which was sabotaged by Italian partisans in April 1945, they were destroyed by Allied bombing at either Genoa or Monfalcone.

UIT 21 (ex *Giuseppe Finzi*). Seized 9 September 1943 at Bordeaux, scuttled 25 August 1944.

UIT 22 (ex *Alpino Bagnolino*). Taken over 10 September

1943 at Bordeaux; sunk by bombing 1 March 1944 south of the Cape of Good Hope (43 fatalities).

UIT 23 (ex *Reginaldo Giulani*). Taken over 10 September 1943 at Singapore. Torpedoed and sunk 14 February 1944 by the British submarine *Tally Ho!* in the Strait of Malacca (26 fatalities).

UIT 24 (ex *Commandante Capellini*). Seized 10 September 1943 at Sabang. Taken over by the Japanese 10 May 1945 and redesignated I-503.

UIT 25 (ex *Luigi Torelli*). Seized 10 September 1943 at Singapore. Taken over by the Japanese 10 May 1945 and redesignated I-504.

None of the Italian boats, with the exception of UIT 21–UIT 25, which were deployed either at Bordeaux or in the Far East, had yet been commissioned into service at the time of their seizure by the Germans.

Manned Torpedoes and Miniature Submarines

Long before the Kriegsmarine considered the possibility of developing miniature submarines, they already existed in Italy, Great Britain and Japan.

Italy

During the Second World War the Italian Navy commissioned numerous miniature weapons, employing the *Siluro a Lenta Corsa* very successfully. The SLC was a 53.3cm torpedo equipped with an electric motor powered by batteries and armed with an explosive charge in a removable head. Two men, equipped with breathing apparatus, operated the weapon, which was known as *Maiale* (Pig).

The SLC, which was stowed in a watertight container, was transported by submarine to a point near to the target. Passing underneath any anti-submarine netting, it closed the target, and the head containing the explosive charge was removed and attached to the hull or propeller of victim. The SLC and its crew of two then withdrew, the explosive charge being detonated by a time fuse.

Between 1941 and 1943 SLCs sank or damaged some 50,000grt of commercial shipping and 63,000 tons of warships. A major success was achieved during the night 18/19 December 1941 when three SLCs severely damaged the British battleships *Valiant* and *Queen Elizabeth*, together with a tanker and a destroyer, at Alexandria. Concurrent with the SLC, Italy also developed the 'CA' and 'CB' miniature submarines, and these were especially successful in the Black Sea.

Great Britain

During the war the Royal Navy developed a type of mini-submarine designed to attack big ships at their moorings. The most important operations mounted by these so-called 'X-craft' were the attack on the German battleship *Tirpitz* on 22 September 1943 and the sinking of the Japanese heavy cruiser *Takao* on 21 July 1945.

The armament of these submarines comprised two large explosive charges each containing 2 tons of Amatol. These charges could be deposited on the sea bed beneath the target from inside the craft or attached to the keel of the target ship with magnetic clamps by divers, who left their craft through a floodable compartment. The craft were towed to the target area by larger submarines, the temporary crew being replaced by the attack crew before the craft set off. During the attack on *Tirpitz* all six 'X-craft' used were lost, but the German battleship was put out of action for months.

Japan

In Japan, two prototype miniature submarines were built in 1936. They were designed to be transported by ships or large ocean-going submarines, for use in a major surface action; only later was the idea put forward that they might also be employed against large warships whilst the latter were berthed. Thus five miniature submarine, each equipped with two torpedoes, were used during the attack on Pearl Harbor, albeit without success. Other attacks were launched at Sydney and also at Diego Suarez, where damage was caused to the British battleship *Ramillies*.

From the early Type A, further versions—B, C and D—were developed, powered by a diesel motor for surface propulsion and for charging the batteries. The numerous *Kairyu* type miniature submarines, built in 1945, were similar to, though smaller than, their predecessors. Instead of a torpedo, they could be armed with a 600kg warhead and used for suicide attacks. In addition to these submarines, which had a crew of two, three or five men, the Imperial Japanese Navy also commissioned craft of the *Kaiten* type: employed exclusively on suicide missions, these carried a explosive charge of between 1,500 and 1,800kg and were first used in November 1944. However, although *Kaiten* were built in large numbers, their successes were relatively few.

Germany

The Kriegsmarine sponsored the design and construction of various types of manned torpedoes and miniature submarines, as well as various experimental submarines and associated projects, as will be described in the following pages.

Manned Torpedoes

Neger (Negro)

The *Neger*—designed by government surveyor Staff Engineer Richard Mohr (hence the name)[1]—consisted of two vertically connected G 7e torpedoes. The lower carried an armed warhead whereas the 'warhead' of the upper torpedo was empty and could accommodate a pilot.

The disadvantage of the *Neger* was that the pilot's head was only about 50cm (18in) above the surface of the water and he therefore had only a limited range of vision. The window for the pilot was covered by a plastic cap, and the 'cockpit' inside the torpedo offered only sufficient breathable air for one to two hours. With a speed of 4km, the *Neger* therefore had a maximum mission time of seven hours, during which it had to be led to its target and put into action and the carrier torpedo navigated back to its point of origin.

Below: A *Neger* is made ready for sea.

NEGER	
Number built	c.200
Crew	1
Diving depth (m)	–
Length (m)	7.65
Beam (m)	0.53
Maximum hull diameter (m)	0.53
Displacement (armed, m³)	5.0
Output of electric motor (kW)	8.8
Maximum surfaced speed (kt)	4.2
Range (nm @ kt)	30m @ 3
Armament	One 53.3cm torpedo

During the night 20/21 April 1944, thirty *Neger* were used for the first time against enemy ships at the Allied bridgehead of Anzio-Nettuno. Only 17 *Neger* made it into the water in running order, the other 13 capsizing. Three failed to return, with the result that the hitherto secret craft was revealed to the Allies.

The second *Neger* mission took place during the night 5/6 July 1944 at the invasion line in Normandy, 40 being brought to Villers-sur-Mer. Wooden launching ramps were provided, in order to make it easier to put them into the water and to avoid the difficulties that were experienced at Anzio. Several ships, amongst them probably two destroyers, were sunk by the miniature 'submarines', but sixteen craft did not return.

Their next mission resulted in the sinking of the British cruiser HMS *Dragon*, and the final sortie, in the same theatre, took place during the night 16/17 August 1944, which brought about the sinking of the British destroyer *Isis*. *Neger* were thereafter removed from the front line.

Marder (Marten)

Whereas the *Neger* could not dive at all but could only 'cut under' a ship, the *Marder* was equipped with a diving cell in front of the pilot's cabin permitting dives to a depth of 10m.

However, very few *Marder* mission were carried out, owing to a lack of suitable targets. There were plans for U 997 to tow *Marder* from the Narvik area to the seas off Murmansk for a mission against Russian warships, but this mission was called off.

Hai (Shark)

In order to obtain improved range, the *Hai* carrier torpedo featured an additional mid-section with an enhanced battery capacity.

Only one (experimental) unit was built, but this proved difficult to manoeuvre and, because of its excessive length, somewhat unseaworthy.

Miniature Submarines

Molch (Salamander)

A particular advocate of the idea of miniature submarines was Dr Heinrich Dräger, the owner of the Dräger Werke in Lübeck. On 1 October 1941 he presented a series of designs for such craft, which would be propelled by diesel or closed-cycle systems. The Kriegsmarine, however, rejected his proposals.

However, in 1944 Dräger's ideas for a one-man submarine driven exclusively by electric motors were taken up by the Torpedoversuchsanstalt (TVA, or Torpedo Experimental Institute), and the result was the *Molch*. This craft was designed to accommodate two torpedoes, the most important issues in its construction being, first, the use of as many existing torpedo components as possible and, secondly, simplicity of manufacture.

Molche were deployed in the autumn of 1944 at Anzio and at the beginning of 1945 in Dutch waters. There were a few successes, but these were greatly out of proportion to the losses incurred.

Below: A *Marder* is lowered into the water.
Bottom: A British soldier from a Scottish regiment inspects a *Molch*, 1945.

MARDER	
Number built	c.300
Crew	1
Diving depth (m)	–
Length (m)	8.3
Beam (m)	0.53
Maximum hull diameter (m)	0.53
Displacement (armed, m³)	5.5
Output of electric motor (kW)	8.8
Maximum surfaced speed (kt)	4.2
Range (nm @ kt)	30 @ 3
Armament	One 53.3cm torpedo

HAI	
Number built	1
Crew	1
Diving depth (m)	10
Length (m)	11.0
Beam (m)	0.53
Maximum hull diameter (m)	0.53
Displacement (armed, m³)	6.0
Output of electric motor (kW)	8.8
Maximum surfaced speed (kt)	4.2
Range (nm @ kt)	90 @ 3
Armament	One 53.3cm torpedo

MOLCH	
Number built	363
Crew	1
Diving depth (m)	40
Length (m)	10.78
Beam (m)	1.82
Maximum hull diameter (m)	1.16
Displacement (armed, m³)	11.01
Output of electric motor (kW)	10
Maximum surfaced speed (kt)	4.3
Range (nm @ kt)	50 @ 2.9
Armament	Two 53.3cm torpedoes

BIBER	
Number built	324
Crew	1
Diving depth (m)	20
Length (m)	9.03
Beam (m)	1.57
Maximum hull diameter (m)	0.96
Displacement (armed, m³)	6.25
Output of motors (kW/hp)	9.8/3.2
Maximum surfaced speed (kt)	6.5
Range (nm @ kt)	c.100 @ 6.5
Armament	Two 53.3cm torpedoes

A *Biber* on display at the Imperial War Museum, London.

Biber (Beaver)

The *Biber* project featured a streamlined hull, from which, approximately amidships, a small conning tower rose only 52cm above the water. In order to increase the range of vision, a 1.5m periscope was fitted, while the craft was also equipped with a compass and a snorkel to provide fresh air. Two diving cells forward and aft facilitated a diving capability. The pilot was positioned amidships, beneath the superstructure.

The first *Biber* mission took place at Fécamp, France, on 20 August 1944 and resulted in the sinking of a landing craft and a Liberty ship. However, when the Germans were obliged to evacuate Fécamp the next day, all remaining *Biber* had to be blown up.

Newly constructed *Biber* were transferred to Rotterdam in December 1944 with a view to interdicting shipping in the lower Schelde, but these sustained heavy losses and achieved negligible success.

A later project was for a *Biber* with a strengthened hull in order to provide greater rigidity and to make it possible for the craft to reach greater depths. The crew was to have consisted of two men taking turns of duty. However, this project proved stillborn because the craft was too big and too difficult to transport.

Finally, the *Biber III* was to have had a closed-cycle benzene engine, but this project was also not pursued, experience with this form of propulsion being considered insufficient.

Hecht (Type XXVII A) (Pike)

The *Hecht* was a miniature submarine for close-support missions. It was originally assigned to sorties requiring the placing of mines on enemy ships, but subsequent missions would require its employment as an attack submarine.

On 18 January 1944 Grossadmiral Dönitz submitted a plan to Hitler to build 50 submarines of this type, and on 9 March that year Germaniawerft, Kiel, was given a contract for three prototype craft, the residue of the order being placed nine days later. However, construction was halted when it became apparent that a more capable version could be produced.

Seehund (Type XXVIIB) (Seal)

Whereas the *Molch*, *Hecht* and *Biber* have to be considered rather as experimental craft, the way in which the war developed demonstrated that the use of miniature submarines made sense for undertaking missions in waters near coasts vulnerable to air attack and against landing operations.

A *Hecht* and its two-man crew are lowered into the water.

HECHT (Type XXVII A)	
Number built	3 (53 planned)
Crew	2
Diving depth (m)	50
Length (m)	10.39
Beam (m)	1.7
Maximum hull diameter (m)	1.3
Displacement (armed, m^3)	11.83
Output of electric motor (kW)	8.8
Maximum surfaced speed (kt)	5.7
Range (nm @ kt)	c.25 @ 5.7
Armament	One torpedo or one mine

SEEHUND (Type XXVIIB)	
Number built	285
Crew	2–3
Diving depth (m)	30
Length (m)	11.85
Beam (m)	1.7
Maximum hull diameter (m)	1.28
Displacement (armed, m^3)	14.9
Output of motors (kW/hp)	18.4/60
Maximum surfaced speed (kt)	7.7
Range (nm @ kt)	300 @ 7
Armament	Two 53.3cm torpedoes

Technical perfection was eventually achieved with the Type XXVIIB (*Seehund*), designed by the K-Amt, inasmuch as it was the first German miniature submarine to incorporate all the technical equipment of the larger U-boats.

The bases for development were:

1. Suitability for missions above and below water;
2. An armament of two G7e torpedoes;
3. Submarine propulsion by diesel or electric motor;
4. A mission endurance for the two-man crew of about 48 hours (a figure which was, in the event, often considerably surpassed);
5. A sustained high surfaced speed; and
6. An average underwater speed of 4 knots.

Above: A *Seehund* in the 'Konrad' bunker at Kiel, May 1945.

Under a July 1944 programme, 1,000 of these craft were to be built, in part by companies from southern Germany; by the end of the war 285 had been completed, with a further 93 unfinished at the manufacturing sites.

Plans for a slightly larger *Seehund*, in order to increase the craft's endurance at sea, were not pursued.

Following successful trials with closed-circulation Daimler Benz engines by the Forschungsinstitut für Kraftfahrwesen und Fahrzeugmotoren at the Technische Universität Stuttgart (FKFS), plans were developed for a Type XXVIIK. Three prototype craft were ordered from Germaniawerft at Kiel, but they were never completed.

Experimental Submarines; Projects

Kleiner Delphin (Little Dolphin)

Experiments with scale models of the *Biber* and *Seehund* revealed that torpedoes carried on the exterior of the hull considerably increased drag in the water, and a quest for improved designs resulted in the *Delphin* (Dolphin). However, the concept did not progress further than the experimental stage, and three completed craft were blown up near Travemünde on 1 May 1945 together with all plans, spare parts and design papers.

Grosser Delphin (Great Dolphin)

The basic concept of this experimental submarine—of light weight and quick to build; incorporating trimming and diving equipment, a direction finder, a compass and steering and operating equipment; and of a hydrodynamically efficient form—was to have been similar to that of the *Kleiner Delphin* but differed in having a crew of two and being constructed of stronger material.

One example was under construction at the end of the war.

Seeteufel/Elefant (Monkfish/Elephant)

The *Seeteufel* was an amphibious miniature submarine with a 'crawler' drive, the theory being that this latter would solve all the transport and launching problems of miniature weapons.

Serial production was to have taken place at the Borgward factory in Bremen. Three units were ordered as the '0' series, then twenty more, but no production craft were actually completed. After being tested in Eckenförde, one example was brought to Lübeck at the end of the war and destroyed by explosive charges.

KLEINER DELPHIN	
Number built	3
Crew	1
Diving depth (m)	?
Length (m)	5.48
Beam (m)	1.01
Maximum hull diameter (m)	1.01
Displacement (armed, m³)	2.66
Output of electric motor (kW)	9.6
Maximum surfaced speed (kt)	7.0
Range (nm @ kt)	3 @ 10
Armament	One 53.3cm torpedo or one towed mine

GROSSER DELPHIN	
Number built	–
Crew	?
Diving depth (m)	?
Length (m)	8.68
Beam (m)	?
Maximum hull diameter (m)	1.01
Displacement (armed, m³)	8.0
Output of motors (kW/hp)	18/60 (closed-cycle propulsion envisaged)
Maximum surfaced speed (kt)	17.0
Range (nm @ kt)	3 @ 10
Armament	One 53.3cm torpedo or one towed mine

Grundhai (Bull Shark)

Fitted with three searchlights at the bow and with radar, and propelled by twin electric motors, one on each side, this deep-sea, unarmed salvage vessel—never produced—was to have been capable of diving to a depth of 1,000m. On top of the vehicle was to have been an electromagnetic claw, while crawler drive would have enabled the vehicle to proceed along the sea bed.

Left: A Dolphin photographed in the winter of 1944/45.

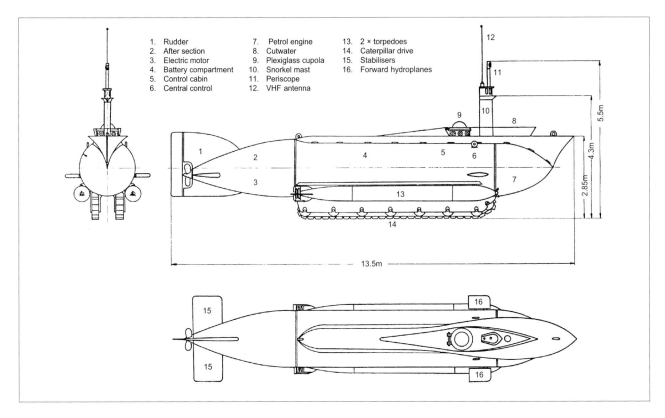

1. Rudder
2. After section
3. Electric motor
4. Battery compartment
5. Control cabin
6. Central control
7. Petrol engine
8. Cutwater
9. Plexiglass cupola
10. Snorkel mast
11. Periscope
12. VHF antenna
13. 2 × torpedoes
14. Caterpillar drive
15. Stabilisers
16. Forward hydroplanes

Above: General-arrangement drawing of the *Seeteufel*, showing the tracked drive for mobility over land.

Below: General arrangement of the *Grundhai*.

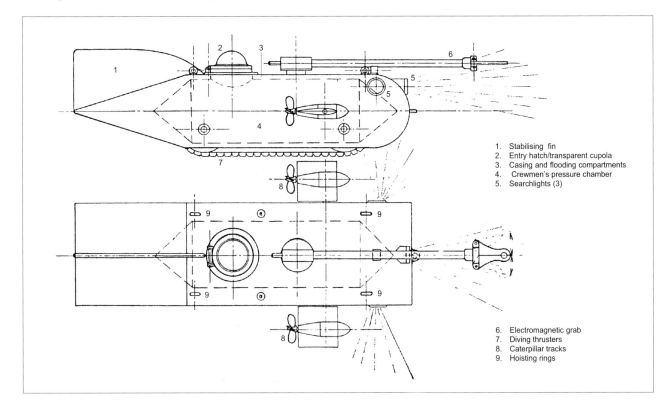

1. Stabilising fin
2. Entry hatch/transparent cupola
3. Casing and flooding compartments
4. Crewmen's pressure chamber
5. Searchlights (3)

6. Electromagnetic grab
7. Diving thrusters
8. Caterpillar tracks
9. Hoisting rings

SEETEUFEL	
Number built	1
Crew	2
Diving depth (m)	100
Length (m)	14.2
Beam (m)	2.0
Maximum hull diameter (m)	1.8
Displacement (armed, m³)	20.0
Output of motors (kW/hp)	8.8/80
Maximum surfaced speed (kt)	10.0
Range (nm @ kt)	300 @ 10 surfaced, 80 @ 8 submerged
Armament	Two torpedoes

GRUNDHAI	
Number built	–
Crew	2
Diving depth (m)	1,000
Length (m)	3.6
Beam (m)	2.0
Maximum hull diameter (m)	?
Displacement (armed, m³)	?
Output of electric motors (kW)	45
Maximum speed (kt)	3.0
Range (nm @ t)	?
Armament	None

Schwertwal (Killer Whale)

In view of some encouraging results from trials involving a Walter turbine system using sea-water injection, the development of a similar propulsion system for long-range torpedoes was only a matter of time, thus making the turbine interesting as a viable propulsion system for miniature submarines.

By July 1944 it was too late to change the outcome of the naval war in favour of the Kriegsmarine by means of new technical developments, but, on the orders of the commander of the Kleinkampfverbände (Small Weapons Units), Vizeadmiral Hellmuth Heye, Versuchskommando 456 (Experimental Unit 456) was nevertheless established. Situated in close proximity to the Walter factory, its task was to develop efficient miniature submarines—and new weapons with which they might be armed—in close co-operation with Professor Walter. The staff of this military command consisted of naval and mechanical engineers, design engineers and designers, as well as skilled labourers, notably welders, coppersmiths and electricians working with the civil engineers and specialists of the Walter company.

On 1 July 1944 work began on a fast, two-man submarine with a length of 11.2m, a diameter of 1.26m and a displacement of 11.25m³. The project was allocated the codename 'Schwertwal'.

Above left: A *Seeteufel* at Eckernförde in 1944.
Above right: A model of the *Grundhai* deep-sea salvage vessel.
Below: *Schwertwal I* at the Walter facility's experimental works.

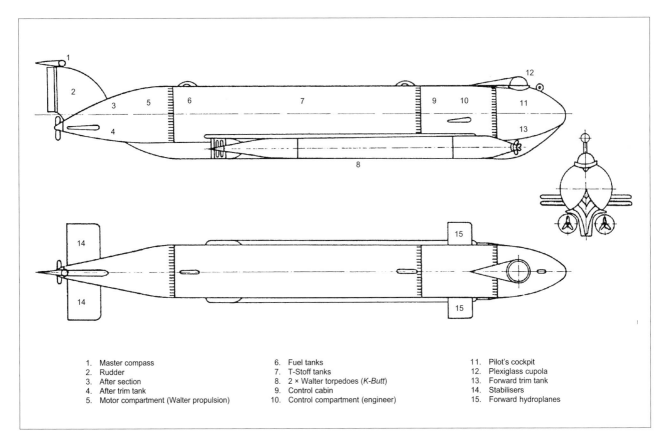

1. Master compass
2. Rudder
3. After section
4. After trim tank
5. Motor compartment (Walter propulsion)
6. Fuel tanks
7. T-Stoff tanks
8. 2 × Walter torpedoes (*K-Butt*)
9. Control cabin
10. Control compartment (engineer)
11. Pilot's cockpit
12. Plexiglass cupola
13. Forward trim tank
14. Stabilisers
15. Forward hydroplanes

Above: General-arrangement drawing of the *Schwertwal I* underwater attack craft.

Below: General arrangement of the *Schwertwal II*, showing the hydrodynamic hull form.

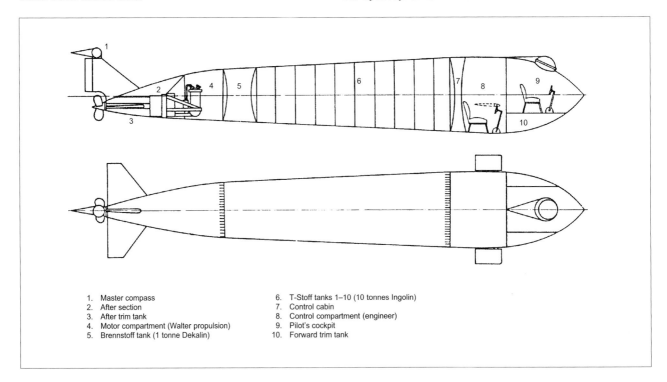

1. Master compass
2. After section
3. After trim tank
4. Motor compartment (Walter propulsion)
5. Brennstoff tank (1 tonne Dekalin)
6. T-Stoff tanks 1–10 (10 tonnes Ingolin)
7. Control cabin
8. Control compartment (engineer)
9. Pilot's cockpit
10. Forward trim tank

SCHWERTWAL I	
Number built	1
Crew	2
Diving depth (m)	100
Length (m)	13.8
Beam (m)	?
Maximum hull diameter (m)	1.5
Displacement (tonnes)	17.5
Output of turbine (hp)	800
Speed (kt)	10.0–30.0
Surfaced range (nm @ kt)	100 @ 30; 500 @ 0
Armament	Two 53.3cm *K-Butt* torpedoes

SCHWERTWAL II	
Number built	–
Crew	2
Diving depth (m)	?
Length (m)	13.5
Beam (m)	?
Maximum hull diameter (m)	2.0
Displacement (tonnes)	18
Output of motor/turbine (kW/hp)	18/80
Maximum submerged speed (kt)	30.0
Range (nm @ kt)	100 @ 30; 500/10
Armament	Two 53.3cm *K-Butt* torpedoes

The first design, *Schwertwal I*, was not intended to be the finished article but a vehicle to test the 800hp engine developed from the Walter sea-water-injection torpedo engine and to test the performance of the craft at high underwater speeds.

The streamlined, torpedo-shaped hull, 13m in length, had a diameter of 1.5m and was equipped with a pilot's cabin at the bow, the propulsion system being installed at the stern. A tail unit comprising rigid stabilisers, built in the light of experience with aerodynamics, was added at the stern, and the hydrovane was at the bow. The hull was tested in the wind tunnel of the Luftfahrtforschungsanstalt (Aviation Research Institute) in Brunswick and observed and measured in the towing channel at the HSVA in Hamburg in order to eliminate the effects of drag. Thus the design evolved into the V 10 fast submarine, designed to reach a maximum speed of 30 knots. The weightiest part of the craft was the 'Ingolin' (hydrogen peroxide) filling of 10-tonne Mipolam containers necessary, it was believed, to ensure that a range of 100nm could be achieved at 30 knots.

It was planned that *Schwertwal* should be as fast and as manoeuvrable under water as was a fighter plane in the air. It was therefore also called an Unterwasserjäger (Underwater Fighter) and was intended for use against submerged enemy submarines, for which purpose small Rückstoss (rocket-propelled) torpedoes were being developed by the Walter company. The main armament would have comprised two K-Butt torpedoes which, however, when attached to the hull would reduce speed and range a good deal. As further weapons, the Grimmsche Schleppmine as well as floating mines and underwater rockets for use against pursuers were under discussion.

As a periscope was out of the question because of the high speed required of the vessel, but a detection device to locate the enemy under water was under development. For orientation the submarine would have had a stabilised aircraft compass designed by the Patin company of Berlin; this had automatic side and depth steering and had func-

tioned perfectly in tests. The main compass was located in a streamlined attachment on the tail unit.

Construction of *Schwertwal I* had been completed by the beginning of 1945, although the craft had yet to be tested. Test-bench trials of the engine had been concluded, and had demonstrated the required performance of 800hp.

The craft was scuttled at the end of the war in the Plön Lake, where the final trials were supposed to have been run. Some two months later it was discovered by the British and raised, but it was quickly scrapped at Kiel on their instructions.

Based on the experience accumulated from the *Schwertwal I*, an improved, even more streamlined *Schwertwal II* was mooted early in 1945. This foresaw an increase in the size of the cabin and included a small, 25hp electric motor without no detriment to the craft's overall performance, enabling the craft to carry out an 8-kilometre clandestine voyage. However, *Schwertwal II* was never built.

Manta (Manta Ray)

Another project stemming from the co-operation between the Walter facility and Versuchskommando 456 was the Untersee-Gleitflächen-Schnellboot Manta (USG submarine). The idea behind its construction was to bring together all the progressive ideas from the various miniature submarine designs in one new project, particularly the necessity to obviate the drag caused by external torpedoes and the need to launch the vehicles into the water easily and successfully.

The *Manta* had a catamaran-like hull comprising three torpedo-like cylinders linked by one wing surface. The central cylinder contained a diesel generator and a cabin for the two-man crew; the rest of the craft, as well as the two other cylinders was given over principally to fuel (Ingolin) stowage. In addition, there were trim tanks and compensating tanks.

The propulsion system was installed within two keels beneath the outer cylinders and consisted of one

SUMMARY OF GERMAN MINIATURE SUBMARINES AND MANNED TORPEDOES

	No built	Crew	Diving depth (m)	Length (m)	Beam (m)	Max. hull diameter (m)	Displacement (m³)	Drive (electric) (kW)	Drive (petrol) (hp)	Drive (diesel) (hp)	Drive (turbine) (hp)	Maximum speed (kt)	Armament
Manned torpedoes													
Neger	c.200	1	–	7.65	?	0.53	?	1 × 9	–	–	–	4–6	1 torpedo
Marder	c.300	1	10	8.3	?	0.53	?	1 × 9	–	–	–	4–6	1 torpedo
Hai	1	1	10	?	?	0.53	?	1 × 9	–	–	–	4–6	1 torpedo
Miniature submarines													
Molch	383	?	40	10.78	1.82	1.16	11.01	1 ×	–	–	–	4.3–5.0	2 torpedoes
Biber	324	1	20	9.03	1.57	0.96	6.25	1	32	–	–	5.3–6.5	2 torpedoes
Hecht	5	2	50	10.39	1.70	1.30	11.83	1 × 9	–	–	–	5.7–6.0	1 torpedo or 1 mine
Seehund	285	3	30	11.7	1.68	1.28	14.9	1	–	60	–	6.0–7.7	2 torpedoes
Experimental boats and projects													
Engelmann-Boot	1	?	?	40.84	?	2.82	?	–	–	–	4 × 1,500	?	?
Seeteufel	–	?	1,000	13.5	2.0	1.8	?	1 × 18	1 × 80	–	–	8–10	2 torpedoes
Grundhai	–	?	?	?	?	?	?	?	?	?	?	?	?
Delphin	–	1	?	5.48	?	1.0	2.5	?	?	?	?	?	Explosive charge
Schwertwal I	1	2	?	13.0	?	1.5	11.25	–	–	–	1 × 800	10–30	2 torpedoes
Schwertwal II	–	2	?	13.5	?	2.0	?	1 × 18	–	–	800	10–30	2 torpedoes
Manta	–	2	50–60	c.15	c.6	1.5	?	2 × 440	–	2	–	40–50	4 standard or 8 homing torpedoes or 8–12 mines or 4 'projectiles'

Schwertwal I-like unit in each. As well as the diesel-electric propulsion system, a diesel-hydraulic transmission installation was also considered. At the sides were to have been located two large aircraft wheels, to enable the craft to roll into the water. Movable gliding surfaces between the side keels would have enabled the craft to hydroplane on the surface of the water.

The wing area between the two outer cylinders was to have been filled with four launching tubes for torpedoes or mines. Navigation equipment was similar to that of the *Schwertwal*.

As with all the Versuchskommando 456 projects, the *Manta* designers paid close attention to crew survivability by providing, for example, a marker buoy with an antenna, a self-inflating dinghy and special diving suits. For an acute emergency there was the option of jettisoning the two electric batteries—which acted also as ballast—from beneath the side keels in order to give the craft added buoyancy and assist it to the surface.

The Kleinst-U-Bootwaffe (Miniature-Submarine Command) gave its blessing to this project, not least because it fulfilled a determination to achieve the maximum concentration of weapons whilst employing the minimum number of men. However, *Manta* did not progress beyond the stage of a model, and at the end of the war all the design documents were destroyed.

Right: A model of the *Manta* fast hydroplane, with a selection of the proposed armament.

MANTA	
Number built	–
Crew	2
Diving depth (m)	50–60
Length (m)	c.15
Beam (m)	c.6
Maximum hull diameter (m)	1.5
Displacement (tonnes)	c.15
with weapons and fuel (tonnes)	c.50
Output of electric motor (kW)	2 × 440
diesel engine (hp)	2 × 600
of Walter turbine (hp)	2 × 800
Maximum surfaced speed (kt)	50.0
Maximum submerged speed (kt)	30.0
Surfaced range (nm @ kt)	200 @ 50; 600 @ 20
Submerged range (nm @ kt)	120 @ 30; 500 @ 10
Armament	Two standard or eight homing torpedoes or 8–12 mines or four 'projectiles'

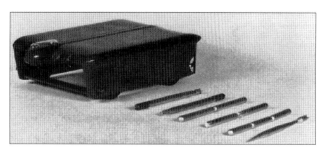

Machinery, Sensors and Weapons

Introduction

Berlin, 5 December 1899: At the first annual conference of the Schiffbautechnische Gesellschaft (Naval Engineering Society)—and in the presence of Kaiser Wilhelm II—its first chairman, Carl Busley, delivered a lecture on the subject 'Modern Submarines' and concluded thus:

> The significant technical inferiority of underwater vehicles existing today . . . does not bode well for any future prospects . . . One cannot but agree with the German naval authorities' decision not to get involved, as yet, in lengthy experiments with submarines, restricting themselves to the construction of conventional warships, cruisers and ocean-going torpedo-boats.[1]

Busley later wrote to Berling[2] explaining that he only gave this lecture, with its devastating criticism of the concept of submarines, at Tirpitz's instigation, in order to assist the latter in his argument with members of the Reichstag who were pressing for the construction of submarines.

Unlike the Staatssekretär (Secretary of State) in the Reichsmarineamt (Imperial Naval Office), other navies had been thinking and acting differently for years. In 1899, the year Busley gave his lecture, the navies of the following countries had begun to commission or order submarines:

United States: *Holland*, launched 17 May 1897 (benzene engine for surfaced drive/electric motor for submerged drive);

France: *Narval*, launched 21 October 1899 (steam/electric); and

Great Britain: No 1, launched 2 October 1901, (benzene/electric).

From the smaller navies:

Turkey: *Abdul Hamid*, launched 1886 (Nordenfeldt-type, steam);

Greece: Nordenfeldt-type ship constructed in 1887, (steam);

Italy: *Delfino*, launched 1895 (benzene/electric); and

Russia: *Delfin*, launched 1903 (benzene/electric).

The German Navy ordered its first submarine, U 1, from Germaniawerft, Kiel, on 4 December 1904. Steam propulsion did not appear to hold promise for this type of craft, the handling of benzene on board submarines was considered too dangerous and diesel engines were apparently too heavy, the choice of machinery for U 1–U 18 was petrol motors—which, however, had a number of disadvantages compared to diesel powerplants:

1. The performance of each individual cylinder could only with difficulty be increased beyond 40hp.
2. The motors were very susceptible to breakdown; indeed, only rarely did all the cylinders function at once. Changes to the number of revolutions could be varied only to a limited degree.
3. The engines could not be steered.
4. Fuel consumption, at 400–500g/hp/hour, was high.
5. There was a highly visible smoke trail by day.
6. Highly visible light was emitted at night.

In view of the foregoing, the Kaiserliche Marine, like the navies of the other major powers, quickly switched to the diesel engine for powering its submarines:

France: Z, launched 28 March 1904;

Great Britain: D 1, launched 16 May 1908;

United States: E 1, launched 27 May 1911; and

Germany: U 19, launched 10 October 1912.

Conventional Powerplants

The equation K = f (A, O, B) proposes that the fighting strength (K) of a ship depends on its propulsion system (A), its weapons (B) and its chances of locating the enemy while avoiding—as far as possible—detection by the enemy (O). It is valid for both submarines and ships, except that for submarines one has to consider the machinery for surfaced and underwater drive separately.

As mentioned in the Introduction, before the First World War diesel motors and, for underwater propulsion, electric motors prevailed. This classical propulsion system has remained the same the world over to the present day.

Diesel Engines

On 4 December 1908 the Kaiserliche Marine invited Germaniawerft in Kiel, Körting in Hanover, MAN in Augsburg, MAN in Nuremberg and Fiat in Turin each to build an experimental 850hp motor. The specification called for a maximum weight of 20,000kg and a tolerance of only 10 per cent (i.e., about 26kg/hp).

MAN in Augsburg settled for an eight-cylinder, four-stroke engine which achieved an output of 900hp at a weight of 22.3kg/hp during a trial run on 31 May 1910. It was designated SM 6 × 400. MAN Nuremberg produced an eight-cylinder, two-stroke engine which, however, was beset with so many problems that in 1910 it was decided not to proceed with it.[3] In 1912 Germaniawerft produced a six-cylinder, two-stroke unit delivering 850hp. Körting failed to complete the development of its engine.

The two Fiat powerplants—ten-cylinder, four-stroke engines each delivering 1,300hp—were destined for the German submarine U 42, which had been under construction at La Spezia since August 1913. The boat was launched on 8 December 1915, but, following Italy's declaration of war on Austria-Hungary on 23 May 1915, she was seized and, after completion, put into service as the Italian *Balilla*. She was sunk on 14 July 1916 by the Austrian torpedo-boats T 65 and T 66.

Making its selection from amongst the submissions, the Kaiserliche Marine then invited MAN Augsburg and Germaniawerft to produce powerplants for, respectively, U 19–U 22 and U 23–U 26. Seven companies were involved with further deliveries of diesel engines for U-boats constructed during the First World War, as follows:

AEG, Berlin:
Six-cylinder, four-stroke engine (530hp) for UB III.

Benz & Cie, Mannheim:
Six-cylinder, four-stroke OS25u (135hp) for Type UB II boats;
Six-cylinder, four-stroke OS32 (300hp) for Type UC II boats;
Six-cylinder, four-stroke S6Ln (450hp) for Type UE I boats;
Six-cylinder, four-stroke OS375 (530hp) for Type UB III boats.

Daimler-Motoren-Gesellschaft, Berlin:
Four-cylinder, four-stroke RS164 (60hp) for Type UB I boats;
Four-cylinder, four-stroke RS166 (90hp) for Type UC I boats;
Six-cylinder, four-stroke RS206 (142hp) for Type UB II boats;
Six-cylinder, four-stroke MU256 (330hp) for Type UC II boats;
Six-cylinder, four-stroke MU336 (530hp) for Type UB III boats;
Six-cylinder, four-stroke MU536 (1,700hp) for large U-boats.

Körting, Hanover:
Six-cylinder, two-stroke engine (450hp) for Type UE I boats;

Four-cylinder, four-stroke engine (60hp) for Type UB I boats;
Six-cylinder, four-stroke engine (142hp) for Type UB II boats;
Six-cylinder, four-stroke engine (260hp) for Type UC II boats;
Six-cylinder, four-stroke engine (300hp) for Type UC III boats;
Six-cylinder, four-stroke engine (530hp) for Type UB III boats;
Six-cylinder, four-stroke engine (1,200hp) for War Mobilisation boats;
Six-cylinder, four-stroke engine (1,800hp) for large U-boats.

Krupp-Germaniawerft, Kiel:
Six-cylinder, two-stroke engine (320hp) for U A;
Six-cylinder, two-stroke engine (850hp) for U 23–U 26;
Six-cylinder, two-stroke engine (925hp) for the pre-war U 31–U 41;
Six-cylinder, two-stroke engine (1,100hp) for the War Mobilisation boats U 63–U 65;
Six-cylinder, two-stroke engine (1,150hp) for the War Mobilisation boats U 66–U 70, U 96–U 98 and U 112–U 114;

The S6Ln, built by Benz & Cie, and (bottom) the MU336 by Daimler.

Six-cylinder, two-stroke engine (1,650hp) for the U-cruiser U 139;

Six-cylinder, four-stroke engine (400hp) for the unbuilt commercial U-boats;

Six-cylinder, four-stroke engine (1,200hp) for the War Mobilisation boat U 172;

Six-cylinder, four-stroke engine (1,700hp) for the large U 129 and U 130.

MAN Augsburg:

Six-cylinder, four-stroke SM 6 × 400 (900hp) for the prewar U 19–U 22;

Six-cylinder, four-stroke S6V41/42 (1,000hp) for the prewar U 27–U 30 and War Mobilisation boats;

Six-cylinder, four-stroke S6V53/53 (1,750hp) for U-cruisers;

Ten-cylinder, four-stroke S10V53/53 (3,030hp) for U-cruisers;

Six-cylinder, four-stroke S6V35/35 (550hp) for UB III type boats;

Six-cylinder, four-stroke S6V23/34 (250hp) for UC II type boats;

Six-cylinder, four-stroke S6V26/36 (300hp) for UC II and UC III type boats;

Six-cylinder, four-stroke S6V45/42 (1,200hp) for War Mobilisation boats and minelaying cruisers.

MAN Nuremberg:

Six-cylinder, two-stroke 8SS35 (850hp) for the War Mobilisation boats U 57–U 59.

Four companies were involved with deliveries of U-boat engines during the Second World War, as follows:

Daimler-Benz, Stuttgart:

Twenty-cylinder, four-stroke MB501 'vee' (1,500hp) for Type IXD$_1$ U 180 and U 195 and the experimental U 798.

Krupp-Germaniawerft, Kiel:

Six-cylinder, four-stroke F46 (1,600hp) for virtually all type VIIs;

Nine-cylinder, four-stroke F46a9pu (2,100hp) for Type X boats.

MAN Augsburg:

Six-cylinder, four-stroke M6V40/46 (1,400hp) for some Type VIIs;

Six-cylinder, four-stroke M6V40/46KBB (2,000hp and upwards) for Type XXI boats;

Clockwise from top left: The Körting 1,200hp engine for War Mobilisation boats; the Krupp-Germaniawerft 1,650hp engine for U 139; the Krupp-Germaniawerft 1,200hp engine for the War Mobilisation boat U 172; the 900hp MAN SM 6×400; the Krupp-Germaniawerft 1,150hp engine for War Mobilisation boats; and the Krupp-Germaniawerft 850hp engine for U 23–U 26.

Far left (top to bottom): First World War diesel engines from MAN—the S6V53/53, S10V53/53 and S6V26/36.

Left (top to bottom): the First World War MAN 8SS35; the 20-cylinder MB501 'vee' for the Type IXD boat of the Second World War; and the Krupp-Germaniawerft F46, the typical powerplant for the ubiquitous Type VII U-boat.

This column: The Krupp-Germaniawerft F46a9pu as fitted to the Type X (top); and the 6-cylinder M6V40/46KBB undergoing installation in a Type XXI U-boat section.

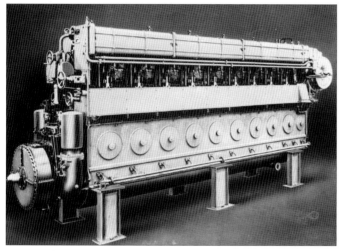

Eight-cylinder, four-stroke M8V40/46 (1,400hp) for Type IA boats and the Turkish *Gür*.

Nine-cylinder, four-stroke M9V40/46 (2,200hp) for Type IX boats.

MWM, Mannheim:

Six-cylinder, four-stroke RS127S (350hp) for Type II U-boats;

Six-cylinder, four-stroke RS135S (350hp) for the experimental V 300 (U 791);

Six-cylinder, four-stroke RS134S (575hp) for Type XXIII boats;

Six-cylinder, four-stroke RS345Su (750hp) for Type IXD$_2$ boats;

Twelve-cylinder, four-stroke RS12V26/34 (2,000hp) for Type XI U-boats.

Two companies have been associated with the production of diesel engines for the Bundesmarine:

Mercedes-Benz, Stuttgart:

Twelve-cylinder, four-stroke MB820S1 'vee' (600hp)—one engine each for *Hai* and *Hecht* and two each for *Wilhelm Bauer*, and for the Types 201, 205 and 206;

Eight-cylinder, four-stroke MB836 (475hp) for the two Type 202 boats.

MTU, Friedrichshafen:

Twelve-cylinder, four-stroke 12V493 AZ80 GA31L for the Type 206 U 13–U 30 (the same motor as that built by Mercedes-Benz under the designation MB 820 81 before the company was taken over).

From the first, the U-boat diesel engine had to fulfil the following requirements:

1. Low volume.
2. Low weight per horsepower. For example, MAN succeeded in reducing the output ratio from 25kg/hp for the large, ten-cylinder 810V53/53 (3,030hp), built during the First World War and designed for cruisers, to 9kg/hp for the final design of the Second World War, the six-cylinder M6V40/46KKB (2,200hp) for Type XXI U-boats.
3. Low specific fuel consumption.
4. Suitable for extended service.
5. High operating safety.
6. Long maintenance intervals.
7. The capability to use the exhaust to blow out the diving tanks.
8. Impact strength.

The introduction of the snorkel during the Second World War brought additional requirements:

The MAN M6V40/46KBB diesel (top), the MAN M9V40/46, and the MWM RS134S, which powered, respectively, the Type XXI, Type IX and Type XXIII U-boats.

A Mercedes-Benz MB820S1 twin installation (top) and an MB836 from the same manufacturer.

9. Extended service at increased negative pressures.
10. Start and drive under high counter-pressures.
11. Chargers suitable for a large range of counter-pressures.

Finally, in the light of modern sensor technology, the engine nowadays has also to be:

12. Part non-magnetic in construction or having magnetic compensation.
13. Soundproofed and flexibly positioned.

All these requirements have been best met by the seemingly simple four-stroke motor.

Whereas historically construction has consisted mainly of suction engines or engines with mechanical chargers, it is now possible to build powerplants with exhaust-gas turbochargers that are better suited to different requirements in the snorkelling mode.

Batteries

In the classical (conventional) submarine propulsion system, all the energy requirements for underwater drive are supplied by electric energy stored in batteries which, while the boat is at sea, are charged by generators during periods above water or during the snorkelling mode.

When, at the beginning of the twentieth century, the Kaiserliche Marine began to build U-boats, it decided in favour of the lead accumulator—already in widespread use the world over—in preference to the alkaline accumulator.

The process of charging and discharging

In its original state, the two lead plates on the surface of the battery are covered with lead sulphate ($PbSO_4$). The electrolyte consists of dilute sulphuric acid.

During charging, electrons are added to the negative plate and taken away from the positive plate. To balance the charge, the negative plate releases negative sulphate (SO_4) ions into the electrolyte; on the positive plate, sulphate ions and lead dioxide (PbO_2) are formed from $PbSO_4$. In its charged state, the negative plate consists of metallic, porous lead and the positive plate is covered with lead dioxide. The concentration of sulphuric acid in the electrolytes has increased, and the acid density rises.

During discharging, electrons flow from the negative plate through the load to the positive plate. To compensate for this, SO_4 ions move into the surface of the negative plate, forming $PbSO_4$ there. Both plates use up sulphuric acid, and acid density decreases.

The chemical procedure in a lead accumulator, for both charging and discharging, is shown in the following equation:

$$PbO_2 + 2H_2SO_4 + Pb \xrightarrow{\text{Discharging}} \xleftarrow{\text{Charging}} PbSO_4 + 2H_2O + PbSO_4$$

The discharge might be continued until the entire effective mass has been converted into lead sulphate, thereby using the highest theoretical capacity of the accumulator.

This capacity is determined by Faraday's laws, which, in electrolysis, describe the connection between the running of the current and the amount of compounds discharged at the electrodes:

$$m = \frac{M \times Q}{Z \times F} \quad g$$

where

m is the mass of the compounds discharged from an electrolyte (in g);

M is the molar mass (in g/mol), the figure corresponding to the relative atomic mass or the relative molecular mass;

Q is the amount of electricity passed during the discharge;

Z is the valency of the chemical element; and

F is the Faraday constant—the amount of charge necessary to discharge 1 mol of a compound with a valency of 1 (96485As/mol)

Lead has a relative atomic mass of 207.21 and a valency of 2. Thus 1As converts:

$$\frac{207.21 \times 1}{2 \times 96485} = 0.0010738g \text{ Pb}$$

This means that 1 As(Amp-second) deposits 0.0010738g of lead. Therefore 1Ah (Amp-hour) deposits 3.866g of lead. Through the same passage of electricity, lead dioxide is converted at the other electrode. Its relative molar mass is calculated as follows:

Pb	207.21
O_2 (2 × 15.9994)	31.99
	239.20

At the same valency (2), 1Ah deposits

$$m = \frac{239.20 \times 3600}{2 \times 96485} = 4.462g \text{ PbO}_2 \text{ (lead oxide)}$$

The only thing remaining is to calculate the amount of sulphuric acid necessary.

Relative molar mass of H_2SO_4:

H_2 (2 × 1.0079)	2.0158
S	32.06
O_4 (4 × 15.9994)	63.9976
	98.074

At a valency of 2, the result is according to the equation

$$PbO_2 + Pb + H_2SO_4 = 2\ PbSO_4 + H_2O$$

$$\frac{2 \times 98.074 \times 3600}{2 \times 96485} = 3.659g \text{ SO}_4$$

The mass turnover for 1Ah = 2Wh (Watt-hours) at a rated voltage of the cells of 2 is as follows:

Pb	3.866g
PbO_2	4.462g
H_2SO_4	3.659g
	11.987g

From this, the specific possible maximum energy density of 1kg of active material can be calculated:

$$\frac{1000(g) \times 2Wh}{11.987(g)} = 166.85Wh$$

If the cell consisted entirely of active material, and if this could be used completely, 166.8Wh per kilogram of cell weight could be produced, although in practice this is of course not possible.

As the voltage is almost the same with all lead accumulators, the achievable energy density depends upon the a number of factors:

1. Non-active component parts are indispensable. A container, a grid for conducting the electrons and links are necessary, and the attention of every battery designer is focused on reducing the weight and size (volume) of these parts.

2. In theory, the discharging process could be continued until all the lead and lead dioxide is converted into lead sulphate. In practice, however, this is not achievable. On the one hand, $PbSO_4$ is virtually a non-conductor, and on the other hand the diffusion between 'inner' acid (between the pores of the active mass) and 'outer' acid (between, under and on top of the plates) would drop so much that a complete discharge would not take place because the pores are clogged up by the formation of $PbSO_4$.

The way forward is, obviously, towards thinner plates, which have the following advantages:

(a) a reduction of the diffusion resistance by shortening the distance of the diffusion path;

(b) improved conduction of electricity through the grid of the plates; and

(c) a reduction of that part of the active mass inside the plates, which is less closely involved in the chemical process.

Nowadays, it is estimated that the active material involved in the process (Pb and PbO_2) is at 50 per cent maximum strength.

3. It is impossible to work with pure sulphuric acid; even highly concentrated sulphuric acid is unusable. It would reduce the life-span, increase the inner cell resistance and cause self-discharge and the development of gas in the dormant cell.

It is therefore essential to dilute the sulphuric acid to an extent that the electrolyte weight is three times that of pure sulphuric acid. German U-boat batteries work with a specific gravity of about 1.26 (g/cm³), which means that one litre of electrolyte contains 346 grams of H_2SO_4. Thus, here also, a percentage of not much more than 30 is involved, compared to the theoretical figures.

Compared with a maximum energy density of 166.8Wh/kg, 50Wh/kg is achieved nowadays and 70Wh/kg is considered possible.

The Lead Battery in German U-Boats

The Watt-Akkumulatoren-Werke in Zehnedick, near Berlin, constructed an accumulator between the active plates of which were thin plates of washed peat fibres. These were supposed to prevent the mass from breaking down and thus short-circuiting. In addition, they would absorb most of the sulphuric acid and prevent any overflow when the U-boat was inclined (for example, during dives).

The first submarine produced by Germaniawerft, *Forelle* (Trout), was provided with such a battery from the Watt factory, and, as the shipyard also required peat batteries for further boats, the Akkumulatoren-Fabrik Aktiengesellschaft (AFA) in Hagen acquired the patents for these to be built in Kiel, i.e. for the Russian *Karp*, *Karas* and *Kambala*, the Norwegian *Kobben*, the Austrian U 3 and U 4 and the German U 1. The cells, made of hard rubber, measured 555 by 250 by 400mm and had a capacity of 715Ah with a ten-hour discharge.

Peat batteries, however, proved to be a failure. Because of their limited acid mobility there were differences in the acid density, which led to the plates being used at a different rate and thus reduced their life. The high internal electric resistance slowed the discharge at high currents (necessary for maximum drive) and resulted in overheating. As a result, and with the consent of Germaniawerft, AFA abandoned the construction of such batteries.

From U 2 onwards, cells with large surface areas were employed. The positive plate was a plate with a narrow grid of soft lead, the negative plate a grid made from hard lead and filled with lead compounds. Thin boards made from fine-grained wood (abutting the negative plate) and corrugated, hard-rubber separators (between the wooden boards and the positive plates) were used for isolation. The positive plates were 6mm thick, the negative plates 5mm. The battery type actually used (24A 215) had, a capacity of 3,000Ah and a lifespan of 300–400 charging and discharging cycles.

From U 1 onwards, the Imperial Navy decided to co-operate fully and exclusively with AFA Hagen, the most efficient supplier of lead batteries—at least, in Europe—and this company, in the event, provided all the batteries for all German U-boats until 1945.

At the suggestion of Berlin, an accumulator testing station was established at Germaniawerft, where, until 1918, all types of proposed U-boat installations were tested.

From U 17 (launched 16 April 1912), AFA and the Kaiserliche Marine began to fit batteries in which the positive plates were also mass plates (MAS type), with an indicated peacetime life of four years and 250 cycles.

After 1918 AFA expanded considerably, setting up branches all over the world. The battery types developed were:

MAD series (1925)
> Positive plates 5.4mm thick
> Negative plates 4.8mm thick
> Separation by undulating and corrugated, hard-rubber plates and wooden boards
> Life: 4 years/250 cycles

POR series (1930)
> Plates as for MAD
> Separation (positive plate)
> Plate made from glass wool; corrugated, hard-rubber plate; ribbed Mipor-separator (made from latex) (negative plate)
> Life: 8–10 years/800–1000 cycles

MAK series (1933)
> Thickness of plates 4.5mm
> Separation: hard-rubber plates 0.3mm thick and ribbed Mipor separators.

MAL series (1940)
> Thickness of plates 4.0mm
> Separation: corrugated, perforated rubber or separator made from synthetic material together with wooden boards 1mm thick
> Life: About 21 months (under combat conditions)

It became obvious at the end of the war that the limits had been reached as far as ever thinner plates and ever smaller distances between the plates were concerned. No further increases in capacity or performance per volume unit could be expected to any significant degree.

After 1945, development work on modern submarine batteries in Germany was halted, but in 1953 Aktiebolaget Tudor in Sweden developed tube plates in which the active mass of the positive plate was held by small tubes made from synthetic material or glass fibre. In addition, they replaced the hard-rubber containers with containers made from polyester strengthened by glass fibre, which had thinner sides. Compared to the batteries of the MAK and MAL series, specific capacity, life expectancy and shock-resistance were improved. Wilhelm Hagen, in Soest-Kassel, Berlin, at first used this technique under licence, but then Varta (the former AFA) in Hagen developed a similar type of cell.

The next evolutionary step may be described as gaining voltage by reducing resistance, and this subject was tackled in different ways. Varta built a cell following a 'tier' system wherein two almost square sets of plates were placed on top of each other and connected in parallel. Hagen built a stretched copper cell (CMS) wherein the conductor resistance of the negative plate was much reduced by inserting in a copper grid. These second-generation batteries were incorporated into submarines built in Germany for export from 1972 onwards. From 1978, the Type 206 submarines of the Bundesmarine were fitted with these batteries, which, at the time, had the highest specifications available in respect of energy density, energy weight, life expectancy, shock resistance, ease of maintenance and minimum gas release.

Wilhelm Hagen A. G. then developed a CMS cell in a 'tier' design and, in 1983, announced that its third-generation batteries had been improved further in terms of energy density and in addition featured modifications designed to improve their efficiency and temperature regulation.

Today, in the development of the lead battery:

There are batteries specifically for long, low-speed sorties and have the highest possible content of active mass (electrochemically effective mass and electrolytes), and batteries in which the plates are especially conductive and have a low inner resistance, for sorties which require a high consumption of electricity. Optimising these two characteristics would be desirable.

The proportion of antimony in the two-component alloy Pb/Sb of the positive mass carrier could be reduced. This results in the following advantages:

(a) The generation of hydrogen in the 'off' position is reduced by a factor of 2 to 2.5;

(b) The charging potential during a charge while snorkelling can be improved by 10 per cent;

(c) The charge voltage during this procedure can be increased to about 2.4V; and

(d) Full-charge and compensation-charge periods can be shortened.

The requirements for every submarine battery—and the challenge for the battery designer—remain:

High-energy density in the discharge range 1–100 hours;

Good acceptance of charge during snorkelling periods;

High shock-resistance;

Low production of hydrogen;

High reliability and long life expectancy;

Low maintenance requirements;

Continuous monitoring regarding the state of the drive battery; and

Reliable predictions for the next phase of the sortie.

There will probably be further progress over the next few years and decades, but no doubt only in small steps and as a result of intensive research.

Nowadays the two German companies guarantee a life of five years at 1,250 charge/discharge cycles for submarine batteries.

Electric Motors

The requirements for a submarine electric (E-Maschine) motor are:

Low weight;

Minimum volume;

Good isolation;

High operational safety and the facility to correct faults occurring during a sortie by means available on board;

Ease of access; and

Ready replaceability of all vulnerable parts.

The first motors, built by Garbe & Lahmeyer for U 1, were similar to those used in land-based machinery and had a completely open design. However, when SSW were awarded the contract for electric motors destined for installation aboard U 2 in 1906, the conditions concerning the volume were very strict, especially the demand that the diameter be as small as possible. As a result, a six-pole double motor designated SGM 310/25 and 310/25, offering 2 × 170kW at 900rpm, and an eight-pole propeller motor, SGM 330/34, with an output of 228kW at 685rpm, were built. However, these motors were also completely open, having no protection against drip or bilge water, still less against mechanical damage. Thus they were first protected with sheet metal from above, then made waterproof up to the centre. Finally, from U 17 onwards, motors that were hitherto completely open, to save weight, were entirely encased in cast shields. To operate them, lockable openings were incorporated into the linings, which were later equipped with inspection holes.

The requirement to be able to change defective spools led to the development of the revolving yoke, wherein the motor casing and magnetic yoke are built separately. In order to achieve a stable drive even at high capacity and a weak field, the rotatability of the yoke was also used to facilitate brush movement.

As both petrol engines and electric motors emit heat, extremely high temperatures were generated in the engine rooms. The greater part of the heat—emitted from the surface of the motor—remained uncooled and merged with the ambient air, and, apart from reducing the efficiency of the crew, these temperatures in current collectors, windings and bearings became far too high. Initially, air was blown into the motors by ventilators, then ventilation wheels were added to the shafts. Finally, after a great deal of experimentation, a sea-water cooling system was introduced from U 16 onwards, whereby cooled air was blown into the motors and the warm air—after being passed through the cooler once more—was fed to the engine room.

In an attempt to overcome these problems, SSW produced a motor designed to emit no heat, or, at least, very little: the magnetic yoke as well as the bearing shield were given vents through which cooling water was passed, and the armature was equipped with a hub through which water ran. The Kaiserliche Marine showed interest in this

Right: Garbe & Lahmeyer
'open' electric motor.
Below: Garbe & Lahmeyer
double electric motor.

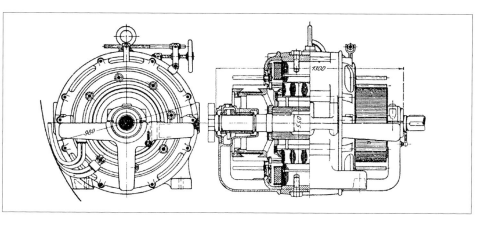

motor but negotiations with SSW were protracted, and by the time agreement had finally been reached the First World War had broken out and the project could not be developed further.

The largest motors built during the First World War were earmarked for the Project 346 U-cruisers: the first three boats, U 139–U 141, were fitted with two AEG double motors of 655kW each and U 142 onwards with SSW double-motors of 965kW each.

As for the AEG motor, the equipment incorporated for silent running was remarkable and consisted of additional winding with fine wire and a second short commutator for each armature. Minimum rpm was achieved by connecting all the commutators of a double motor in series. The unit was 5,395mm in length and 1,750mm high.

The SSW motor for the U-cruiser was designated ZG450/50 + GU450/23 and differed from other motors built hitherto in that between the two 14-pole main motors was a 22-pole 'silent' motor on the same shaft. The output of the two main motors was 775kW at a constant 250rpm and 210V, or 956kW per hour at 268rpm and 205V. The silent motor performed consistently at 33kW at 90rpm and 240V, and by field amplification the rpm could be reduced by up to 50.

During the First World War, SSW remained the main provider of these propulsion systems, accounting for 85–90 per cent of the total, although other companies—AEG, BBG, Maffei-Schwartzkopff and Schiffsunion—were also involved.

When U-boat construction resumed after 1933, little had changed in the world as far as electric propulsion systems were concerned, and the boats for the Reichsmarine were once more equipped with twin electric motors for each of the two propellers, and a two-part battery (see tables overleaf). All the non-Walter craft were of course, strictly speaking, submersibles, with a short underwater range and a low maximum underwater speed (some 7 knots).

The cooling system for the boats of the Second World War had also hardly changed compared to that for boats of the First World War, the cooling air given off resulting in ambient temperatures inside the motor rooms of up to 50°C.

With the introduction by the Allies of improved submarine detection systems at the beginning of 1943, U-boats were driven from the surface, but a relatively quick remedy was found in the snorkel, which could be used to recharge their batteries at periscope depth. However, the low snorkelling speeds (compared to surfaced speeds) and

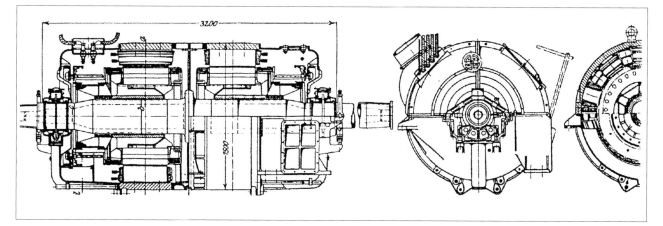

SUMMARY OF ELECTRIC MOTOR INSTALLATIONS IN U-BOATS OF WORLD WAR II		
	Installation	Output (ea) (kW)
Type IA	2 × BBC GG UB720/8	390
Type II	2 × SSW PG W322/36	150
Type VII	2 × AEG GU460/8-276 or	280
	BBC GG UB720/8 or	280
	GL RP137c or	280
	SSW GU343/38-8	280
Type IX	2 × SSW GU345/34	370
Type X (project)	2 × AEG GU720/8-287	400
Type XI	2 × BBC GG UB1200/8	800
Type XIV	2 × SSW GG343/38-8	280
Walter boats		
V 300	1 × Garbe-Lahmeyer RP813	110
Wa 201/202	1 × AEG AWT97	55
Type XVIIB	1 × AEG AT98	55
Type XVIII	2 × SSW GU355/22	150
Type XXVI	1 × SSW	400

the reduced opportunities for sighting enemy ships (i.e., now generally only by periscope) rendered the U-boat a much less effective weapon. It was therefore vital to try to imbue U-boats with a much greater underwater speed and range—and quickly—and at the time, and since the Walter submarine was still under development, this could only be achieved only by installing batteries of greater capacity and enhancing the performance of electric motors.

In Germany, the ocean-going Type XXI U-boat, with a displacement of 1,595/1,790 tonnes, and the coastal Type XXIII, with a displacement of 230/254 tonnes, were under development at this stage of the war, but it was decided to phase out, in due course, the electric Type XXI in favour of the big Walter Type XXVI.

Electric Motors in the Type XXI

The Type XXI completed the transition from submersible to true submarine. Key developments in this development were as follows:

30 April 1943	Appointment of the Befehlshaber der U-Boote (BdU, or Submarine Commander) Karl Dönitz as Oberbfehlshaber der Marine (ObdM, or Supreme Commander of the Navy).
18 June 1943	Type XXI construction methods finalised.
8 July 1943	Presentation to Dönitz and decision by Hitler to start building U-boats in sections.
1 August 1943	'Ingenieurbüro Glückauf' established, under Oelfken.
28 June 1944	Launch of the first true submarine (U 2501) at Blohm & Voss, Hamburg.

Planned   33 submarines per month from autumn 1944.

The submarines were designed for an underwater speed of 18 knots for 1½ hours and 6 knots for 48 hours. In order to achieve this performance, the accumulator batteries had to be enlarged and thus their voltage was raised to 360.

At the beginning of July 1943 a request for tenders for new, efficient electric motors was issued, and by the end of the month SSW had proposed a completely new unit designated 2 GU 365/30 (and codenamed 'Hertha') with the following specifications:

Fast-running;
Transmission gear reduction to propeller shaft 5.079:1;
Test-bench performance (1 hour) at 360V of 1,840kW at 1,675rpm and 5,500amp charge; and
Continuous test-bench performance at 360V of 1,510kW at 1,570rpm and 4,500amp charge.

The unit had a diameter of 1.3m, a length of 3.0m (shaft 3.26m), a weight of 10,330kg and a weight/performance ratio of 5.6kg/kW.

Production of this unit commenced on 1 October 1943 at Dynamowerk Siemensstadt, further production plants being set up in Vienna and Nuremberg. Licence-building was to take place by AEG, BBC and Garbe & Lahmeyer, with a unit production time of five months. SSW began the delivery of the first motors in March 1944.

Onboard trials, however, demonstrated that the batteries—even when fully charged—could not maintain the designed 360V at maximum performance, but, showing a performance of 2 × 1,550kW, U 3507 attained 17.2 knots on 21 November 1944; with full performance, 18 knots would certainly have been possible.

For full power while submerged and for silent running, the Type XXIs were equipped with an additional 'silent'

Below: Siemens 2 GU365/20 ('Hertha'), 1,556kW.

motor per shaft, connected to the latter through a system of twelve V-belts with a gear reduction of 2.68:1.

These motors were also developed by SSW (with production under licence by AEG and BBC).

Type GV 232/28

The features of this motor were as follows:

Eight-pole, separate shunt motor with auxiliary end coil and reversing poles;

Voltage 120 or 360V;

Performance 22 or 83kW;

Speed 91–190rpm and 285–350rpm;

Diameter 1.1m; and

Length 1.42m.

Electric Motors in the Type XXIII

This U-boat was the first and only single-shaft submarine to see service in the German Navy. The main motor was built by AEG.

Type GU 4463/8 (codenamed 'Ursula')

This featured:

Separate shunt motor with reversing poles and end coil;

Length 1.8m (2.555m including shaft); and

Performance 427kW at 850rpm (2 hours) or 332kW at 775rpm (continuous).

The revolutions were transmitted to the propeller shaft through a cog-wheel drive. This system also ran during charging, the movable friction clutch being situated between transmission and bearing. These boats were fitted with a 'silent' motor manufactured by BBC.

Type GCR 188

The main features were:

Grooves in herring-bone gearing (for running as silently as possible);

Length 1.61m;

Diameter 0.92m;

Weight 1.997kg; and

Performance 25.8kW at 300rpm.

The motor was connected to the main shaft by means of six 'vee'-belts (gear reduction 3:1). The maximum underwater speed attained using the main motor was 12.5 knots, with a range of 3–5nm at 10 knots, and that using the 'silent' motor 4.5 knots, with a range of 194nm at 4 knots.

When, on 15 January 1958, an order for the 201 Class was placed, Ingenieur-Kontor Lübeck had already prepared a design, and this was presented two weeks later, on 30 January, The propulsion system was similar to that of the wartime Type XXIII—two fast-running diesel engines driving the shaft through a transmission unit and an electric motor serving as both generator and (underwater)

propulsion system. However, the design was not taken up as far as the propulsion system was concerned.

Now, for the first time, a diesel-electric propulsion system would be installed in a German-built submarine:

Two Daimler-Benz MB820 diesel engines of 600hp each at 1,450rpm;

Two permanently connected BBC generators; and

One SSW propulsion motor in the range 25–270rpm, with a maximum output of 1,500hp and a three-part battery.

Following this, a large number of submarines were built to IKL designs, both for the Bundesmarine and for foreign navies, many of them in German shipyards. All the boats were single-shaft submarines with diesel-electric propulsion.

To complete the picture, listed below are the German submarines and designs not included in the foregoing summary:

1. In 1957 the wartime Type XXI U-boat U 2540, which had been scuttled by her crew near the Flensburg lightvessel in 1945, was raised and rebuilt as the experimental *Wilhelm Bauer*. In place of the original propulsion system, she was equipped with a diesel-electric one-shaft drive.

2. In 1972 an agreement was signed involving IKL, Howaldt Deutsche Werke (HDW) and Vickers with the objective of building submarines to German designs under licence in British shipyards. As a result, from 1975 three submarines with a standard displacement of 540 tonnes were built for Israel to the German design, the propulsion system being two MTU diesel generators of 40kW each, one SSW electric motor of 1,800hp/290rpm and three batteries each with 120 cells (3,122Ah/1.5h, 4,650Ah/5h and 7,300Ah/1h, battery weight 98 tonnes) and a fuel reserve of 20.8 tonnes.

3. In 1982 TNSW Emden was awarded a contract by Norway for six 210 (*Ula*) class submarines with two 960hp MTU 16V 396SB diesel engines each, two Norsk Electric BBC generators and one 4,500kW Siemens electric motor.

4. 'Design 2000', developed by HDW/IKL at the end of the 1970s, was presented as an alternative to the nuclear attack submarines of the major powers. With a standard displacement of 2,000 tonnes, it was to be equipped with four MTU diesels, four 450kW generators and one 7,350kW SSW electric motor. A boat of this design was offered to the United States in 1979, but the US Navy declined it. HDW/IKL offered six boats of a slightly larger type to Australia in 1986, but in 1987 the RAN decided in favour of the Swedish Type 471.

The Development of Propulsion Motors

The changeover to diesel-electric propulsion with fast-running diesel motors is now complete. The DC generators permanently connected to the motors have in part already been replaced by synchronised generators with connected rectifiers.

With the resumption of German submarine construction in the late 1950s, the development of propulsion motors thus began with a proven concept—twin motors with two armatures which shared a common shaft but were, electrically, entirely separate; and twin batteries.

All propulsion systems for submarines built in Germany were by this time furnished by Siemens. Their performance steadily improved:

201–207 classes:	1,100kW
540 class (design):	1,326kW
209 class:	3,670kW
210 and 1500 classes:	4,500kW

Within stages II, III, IV and V the rpm were varied by changing the weakening of the field by using rotating or static converters; in Stage I the rpm were controlled by changing the tension of the armature by using a rotating or static converter while keeping the current at the same level.

The demand for a system independent of air supply from the outside, and of still higher performance, resulted in the development of a motor with closed-air circulation and built-in sea-water cooling. Siemens' observations about this 'four-circuit direct-current motor' were as follows:

> Generally, twin motors are built symmetrically, i.e. with both partial motors identical. Each motor has two separate armature circuits which can be operated independently, like two separate motors. The armature has two identical windings, each of which is connected to its own commutator. The spools of these windings are situated in the same armature grooves each; in this way, a four-tier winding is achieved compared to the usual two-tier windings. The windings have to be isolated against each other in order to achieve full voltage. Each of these windings is assigned its own and identical compensation- and reversing pole-windings, which—like the anchor windings—are sitting on the same poles and together produce the reversing field. On the main poles, however, there is only one excitor winding, and this excites both armature windings equally.

This motor was installed in the Argentinian TR1700 submarines. It had an output of 6,600kW at 200rpm. For the Design 2000 offered to the United States by IKL/HDW, a performance increase to 7,360kW was planned. However, this motor was never built.

Siemens thinks that a performance increase of roughly 10 per cent is possible for this type of motor if an increase of the length and weight of the motor can be accepted. In the long run, the DC commutator motor will probably be replaced by a synchronised motor in which the direct current is not transformed into alternating current by commutators but outside the machine by converters. This means that lower weight, smaller dimensions and more efficiency can be achieved while offering the same performance. In the meantime, Siemens has developed the 'Permasyn', a permanently excited converter-operated trials motor.

Diesel-Electric Propulsion

Diesel motors for U-boats of the Second World War were provided by three companies:

> MAN Augsburg, with the MV40/46 as an eight-cylinder unit for the Type IA boats, a six-cylinder engine for 35 Type VIIs and a nine-cylinder engine for all of Type IXs;
>
> Motorenwerke Mannheim (MWM), with the six-cylinder, four-stroke RS127S, the standard unit for Type II U-boats;
>
> Germaniawerft, Kiel—who switched from two-stroke to four-stroke engines after the First World War—with the F 42 and then the F46, which latter became the standard unit for all Type VIIs (except for the 35 equipped with MAN engines, as above).

With these engines the Type I boats achieved surfaced speeds of between 12 and 13 knots and the Types IA, VII and IX speeds of between 17 and 18 knots. The Kriegsmarine was content with this sort of performance—which, however, was hardly an improvement over that achieved by the U-boats of the Great War.

How could increased performance, and thereby higher underwater speeds, have been achieved? The performance of a diesel motor may be calculated according to the equation

$$N = V\,(z(n(P_e(C))))$$

where V is the cylinder volume, z the number of cylinders, n the rpm and P_e the average cylinder pressure. C is a constant. In order to achieve better performance, an attempt could have been made to change any of the four variable factors.

Cylinder volume (V)

The largest MAN engines of World War I had a cylinder diameter of 530mm, a stroke also of 530mm and thus a cylinder volume of 116.9dm³. During the Second World War, MAN and Germaniawerft engines had the same cylinder dimensions—diameter 400mm, stroke 460mm and thus a volume of 57.8 dm³ (less than half).

Number of cylinders (z)

The largest U-boat engine of the First World War had ten cylinders, the largest of the Second World War, the

MAN-Motor M9V40/46, only nine. As the Kriegsmarine required surfaced speeds of only 15–16 knots from 1943, the newly developed Type XXI U-boats were equipped only with six-cylinder engines.

Average cylinder pressure (P_e)

The average pressure in the cylinder could be increased by supercharging, which did not exist in the First World War. When MAN began to developing supercharged engines, it decided to use turbo-compressors driven by the exhaust gases, whereas Germaniawerft introduced an appended box compressor. The first U-boat with supercharging was U 29 (Type VII), launched on 29 August 1936 at Deschimag, Bremen. The two MAN engines were fitted with superchargers, increasing the average pressure from 5.8 to 7.75kp/cm². From U 37 (Type IX), launched on 14 May 1938, all U-boats were fitted with supercharged engines.

On the insistence of the Kriegsmarine, MAN switched from exhaust-gas compressors to the box compressors at the beginning of 1941, although the company continued with tests of the Buchi compressor on its own account and at the beginning of 1943 offered the M6V40/46 KBB, which, by using that compressor, achieved an average pressure of 10kp/cm² and had a performance weight of only 9kg/hp. The engine was intended for installation in the Type XXI boats

Number of revolutions (rpm) (n)

The engines of all First World War U-boats were run at an average speed. For example, the small MAN (Augsburg) units had a performance of 250hp for 500rpm, the medium-sized engines for a maximum of 450rpm and the largest ones for only 390rpm.

For the Type II U-boats, the MWM RS127S, with a performance of 350–1,000rpm, was selected, working on the shaft via a transmission system. This fast-running engine was chosen because the boats's small hull, with an underwater displacement of only 303–364 tonnes, allowed only two, very compact powerplant units to be fitted. This was also true for the Type XXIII, which had an even lower underwater displacement of 258 tonnes. These boats were equipped with only one engine for surfaced drive and to charge the batteries—the MWM RS134S, with an output of 575hp at 850rpm and with external reduction gearing.

All the other U-boats of the Second World War employed a medium-fast motor with a speed of up to 500rpm—as in the First World War. The only faster unit was, as we have noted, the MAN M 6V40/46KBB, completed in 1943 and destined for the new Type XXI boats. This had a designed output of 2,000hp at 520rpm.

There were no further attempts to increase the rpm in order to achieve higher performance—with one exception. According to Christoph Aschmoneit,[4] in 1940 there existed a plan to test two long-range U-boats with engines of the type fitted to Schnellboote (E-boats). The chosen boats were the Type IXD$_1$ U 180 and U 195, launched on 10 December 1941 and 8 April 1942, respectively, at the Deschimag yard in Bremen. They were each equipped with six 20-cylinder Daimler-Benz MB 501 'vee' engines, offering a performance of 2,000hp at 1,620rpm. Three engines each worked one shaft via a Föttinger liquid clutch, although for use in a U-boat the performance of each was limited to 1,500hp at 1,500rpm. The 9,000hp available made it possible for the boats to reach a maximum surfaced speed of 20.8 knots. In 1943 both U 180 and U 195 made a successful sortie to the Indian Ocean, but on their return the six E-boat engines were removed, to be replaced by two Germaniawerft F46s. After this, no further attempts to increase rpm to achieve higher performance in U-boat engines were made.

U-boats with diesel-electric propulsion system did not appear until the end of the war. Even in 1947, Heinrich Oelken's judgement on this type of propulsion was as follows:

> The freedom they [diesel-electric powerplants] provide by their installation can in general not be utilised on a submarine to its full advantage. The separation allows for noiseless diesel machinery, but this is of no use as long as propeller noise . . . exceeds that generated by the engines. It is only when propeller noise can be eliminated, even at high rpm, that diesel-electric propulsion becomes interesting for submarines.[5]

There is no logic here: Oelfken sees a connection between propulsion systems for surfaced drive—i.e., diesel-electric propulsion—and the propeller noise generated by systems for underwater drive, and he therefore dismisses diesel-electric propulsion.

Other navies understood the advantages of the fast-running diesel engine much more quickly. Captain Small, an American, wrote in 1943 to the effect that when the construction of the modern American submarine was discussed, the Navy saw the necessity to more than double the performance of the engines for the same-sized hull.[6] He commented that this is why a much lighter and more compact, fast-running motor needed to be developed. Both diesel-electric propulsion and geared transmission had been used successfully, and the normal number of pistons—six to ten—had increased to 40.

From 1935 onwards all US Navy submarines were fitted with indirect propulsion, part diesel-electric and part turbine or mixed type. The first diesel-electric submarines to enter service were the USS *Shark* (SS-174) and *Porpoise* (SS-172), launched on, respectively, 21 May and 20 June 1935. However, it is remarkable that American submarines with a diesel-electric component in addition to their direct-diesel propulsion were in service ten years before that—the *Barracuda* class, *Argonaut*, the two

Narwhals and *Dolphin*. Indeed, the first of these boats, *Barracuda* (SS-163), had been launched as far back as 17 July 1924. In Germany, however, all that apparently counted was the opinion of one civil servant who had seemingly never heard of the fact that the performance of a diesel engine can be increased proportionally to its rpm—amongst other things.

There was one exception. The only German U-boat in which the diesel engines were not directly connected to the propeller shafts was the Imperial Navy's U 2, although this was not in order to increase the performance of the unit by increasing the rpm: the diesels were each connected to two generators, one of them the main generator and the second working in sychronisation with the first. Connected to the shafts, therefore, were two motors which could operate over a range of 0–200 per cent of the battery's voltage. The result was a voltage with relatively little loss to the main engines—which was not, however, really necessary. No other submarine of the First or Second World War had this kind of circuit arrangement.

The Snorkel

The history of submarine propulsion systems would be incomplete without mentioning the snorkel, the principal catalyst in the evolution of the true submarine from the submersible. The functions of the snorkel were to provide the boat with air and to drain off the exhaust fumes of the diesel engines while proceeding at periscope depth. During this phase, the crew could both charge the batteries and go ahead at normal drive.

Two tubes were used: one was required to provide air, and had a valve which prevented the ingress of water when washed over; and the other was for discharging exhaust fumes. During a run at periscope depth, the submarine had to be steered in such a way that the exhaust fumes exited beneath the surface of the water, in order to preclude the possibility of the boat being located by the enemy as a result of emitted heat.

As an idea, the snorkel is as old as the submarine itself. When the English mathematician William Bourne presented his submarine project in 1578, he gave it a mast for ventilation. This mast was of course for ventilation only because machines which required air to operate did not exist at that time. A mast for the ventilation of a steam engine is first found in a project for a semi-submersible torpedo boat designed by the Frenchman M. Lagane in 1880.

The first snorkel-equipped craft actually to have been built was Lake's *Argonaut* of 1897. In this, the air for the petrol motor was first brought into the boat through a hose, though later through two hollow masts (one to admit air and the other to expel the exhaust fumes). These masts allowed progress to be made along the sea bed at depths of up to 15m. It is well known, however, that the US Navy had little interest in *Argonaut* and no interest at all in the 'air masts', which were not to be found on American boats until the end of the Second World War.

In 1927 the Dutch Lieutenant-Commander Wichers was granted a patent for an 'air mast' which was supposed to guarantee good ventilation inside a submarine when submerged at periscope depth, and the Dutch Navy's O 19–O 27 were so equipped. The device, however, lacked a seal (i.e., a valve or float) at its upper end and was designed not for use during diving but to guarantee an uninterrupted air supply to the diesel engines above the surface and in heavy seas.

Following the occupation of the Netherlands in 1940, O 25–O 27 were taken over by the Kriegsmarine, which, however, was not interested in the devices as the Germans had already solved the problem of supplying air to diesel engines in heavy seas in a different way. When the head valve was introduced it was soon noticed that modifications to the diesel engines themselves, and the fans, become necessary (for example, special cams for 'snorkel drive' were required in order to reduce the valve overlap between the entry and exit vents in two-stroke mode).

When the Kriegsmarine started to convert its U-boats to snorkel operation in 1943, however, there were a number of medical reservations:

Pressure fluctuations
The snorkel in general use today, and in use in the German Navy from the beginning, utilises the interior of the submarine as an 'air buffer'. The fresh air enters the inside of the boat through the entry mast, the diesel motors drawing in the air they need (as in surfaced drive). A low atmospheric pressure of 50–100 millibars results, which, however, does not cause discomfort to the crew because it is constant.

Things are different, however, if the valve at the top of the snorkel is washed over and closes, as is the case during rough seas or when an error is made steering at depth. The diesel motors still suck the air from the inside of the boat, but the pressure falls rapidly, the drop in pressure depending upon the volume of air inside the boat and on the rpm of the engine at the time.

There are reports concerning trials with a Type IXD. This boat had two nine-cylinder MAN M9V40/46s with supercharging and were four-stroke units each with an output of 2,200hp at 470rpm. During the trials the central hatch was closed, all the bulkheads were left open and fixed, and there was no snorkel mast. During normal operation—that is, running two engines at 310rpm = 2 × 750hp—a low pressure of about 50 millibars developed. During a simulated snorkel operation, while undercutting the head of the snorkel—simulated here by closing the central hatch—the following results were noted while running on one engine:

rpm	Reading below atmospheric pressure (millibars)	
	t = 0	t = 2min
200	6	62
300	20	113
400	47	160

The relatively favourable conditions of operating with only one engine could not be relied upon, there was no maximum rpm, there was a large volume of air available in a large U-boat, and undercutting was completed after two minutes in normal circumstances. (During the war, the author experienced a drop in pressure of almost 500 millibars.) The results of this sort of experience are headaches, 'popping' eyes and, perhaps, lapses into unconsciousness. The only remedy is to switch off the diesel engines and blow some pressurised air into the boat.

Combustion gases
The transit to snorkel drive starts from underwater drive. If the diesel engines are started while the exhaust flaps are still shut, or if the engine stalls because the counterpressure is too high, exhaust fumes, principally carbon dioxide, can enter the interior of the boat. However, even at very low pressure a diesel will blow CO_2 from leaking packings and flanges. Therefore, the engines have constantly to be tested for leakages. Stopping the diesel engines several times led to cases of carbon dioxide poisoning during the war and, on one occasion in the spring of 1945 on board U 1228, the death of a crew member.

Lack of sunshine
In this respect some medical authorities suspect that damage to the body may be caused, although they overlook the fact that, even during submerged operations without using a snorkel, engine-room personnel are almost completely deprived of sunlight without any apparent ill-effects. Just before the end of the war a German U-boat returned from a snorkelling operation involving a unbroken period underwater of 83 days (!), a record only bettered many years later by a US Navy nuclear-powered submarine. Here again, no damage to the health of the crew was discovered.

Summary
In heavy seas, through mistakes in deep-sea manoeuvres, or while starting the diesel engines or switching them off too late, through a drop in pressure or because of combustion gases, there can be dangers. With a well-trained crew and the almost fully automatic snorkel systems of today, however, these dangers are negligible.

In 1944–45 it was considered that snorkel operations were less demanding mentally—and thus also physically—for the crews than operations without the snorkel. This was unsurprising, since a snorkel operation offered a much greater degree of protection against surprise attacks by the enemy.

Nowadays the development of snorkel systems is more or less complete, and automated. Problems associated with undercutting, falling pressure within the submarine, and a concentration of exhaust fumes are automatically dealt with as the information is passed to regulators which close flaps and valves, drive back the levers on the diesel motor and shut down the charge. Steering at depth is also automated. With a modern snorkel system a submarine can continue to make headway, even in rough seas, without ever having to surface to charge its batteries.

After 1945 the German developments concerned with the snorkel were quickly adopted worldwide. The snorkel will be with us for as long as there are propulsion systems working with combustion motors (apart from nuclear propulsion) and for as long as alternative propulsion systems independent of an exterior air supply restrict a submarine's range.

Sensors

In submarines, it is necessary to distinguish between:
> Underwater passive reception of information (listening);
> Underwater active detection of information (sonar etc.);
> Above-water passive reception of information (radio direction-finding); and
> Above-water active detection of information (radar).

Underwater Passive Reception (Listening)
Every moving ship produces sounds in the water with its propeller(s) and the machinery that operates it. These sounds are reflected into the water by the propeller(s) or the hull and can be radiated over 360 degrees and for very long distances. The principal source of noise is the screw, which produces a regular rhythm and also very detectable soundwaves in the high-frequency ranges by causing cavitation effects as a function of its revolutions. These noises can readily be 'heard' by suitable receivers. Since low frequencies on their way through the water are deadened less than high frequencies, they can be detected at longer ranges. On the other hand, high frequencies offer the opportunity of obtaining more accurate bearings.

The propagation of acoustic waves in the water and around a moving ship has been the subject of extremely detailed investigation. Sound propagation is about 4.5 times greater in water than in air, but many factors come into play. Kinsler has suggested the following formula:[7]

$$C = 1410 + 4.21t - 0.037t^2 + 11s + 0.018d$$

where C is the speed of sound (in m/sec), t is the temperature (in °C), s is the salinity (in percentage by weight) and d is the depth of water (in metres), the range of the passive noise reception depending upon all these elements, the stratification of the water and the sensitivity of the listening equipment. The function of the sound locators—assuming other vessels are not present nearby—is to detect vessels at as great a range as possible and their bearing as accurately as possible.

Up to 1939
During the First World War, German U-boats were equipped with Geräuschemptangern ('carbon microphones'), positioned in various locations along the hull in order to pick up the noise generated by ships' propellers. The direction from which the noise came was determined by switching the individual receivers on or off. In 1918 the Kaiserliche Marine issued a patent for a direction-finder.[8] A 'compensator' already existed, albeit in primitive form, and was later taken up by the Horch group of companies (GHA and/or GHG), but it did not meet the tough specifications—suitably sensitive receivers covering the highest possible range of frequencies that did not change their characteristics over a period of time and were suitable for use at great depths.

The 'carbon microphones' used in the First World War did not, of course, have these features. Electro-dynamic receivers were tried at first, but they were unsatisfactory because of their resonance properties. In the end, the solution was the piezoelectric receiver, which functioned according to the effects discovered in 1880 by Pierre Curie in which quartz crystals develop a positive or negative charge under mechanical stress.

In co-operation with the Kaiserliche Marine, Atlaswerke A. G. of Bremen and Electroacustik in Kiel conducted research into these receivers (and into the development of listening devices in general), eventually proceeding from quartz crystals to seignette (Rochelle) salt—potassium sodium tartrate, $KNa(C_4H_4O_6)4H_2O$. Sensitivity in the range of essential audio-frequencies is about 0.1 mV/bar, and the reception surface of such a crystal receiver has a diameter of only some 5cm. With a speed of sound in the water of 1,500m/sec, the wavelengths for the frequency range in question of some 1,000–15,000 Hz are 1.5–0.1m. Because of these huge variations—5cm at one extreme and 1.5m at the other—a single crystal receiver cannot indicate direction: hanging loosely in the water, it receives sounds coming from different directions with almost the same sensitivity. (This is true also for magnetostrictive receivers, used in addition to seignette receivers.)

In an aligned receiver system, instead of a single receiver, groups, in which the individual sensors are spaced out in the water in the same arrangement as the size of wavelength to be received, are required. There are two methods in which receiver structures with certain alignment characteristics are suitable for the location of sounds:

1. The 'rotating base' method, in which the entire receiver structure, mounted on the horizontal, is rotated around a vertical axis and the maximum result is observed on the listening phone; and
2. The 'compensation method'—which works with fixed receivers—in which the alignment vector is rotated by inserting delaying or phase-levelling links between the individual receivers and the listening phone according to the configuration of the receiver alignment.

Both these systems were used on German U-boats in the Second World War.

Kristall-Dreh-Basis-Geräuschpeilanlage (KDB) (crystal rotating base sound-locating system)
This consisted of a group of six crystal receivers in a straight line built into a casing at a distance of 8cm from each other to produce a horizontal receiver base with a width of about 50cm. Later, instead of the group of six, the so-called Streifengruppe ('strip group') was used, consisting of a rectangular receiver membrane 36m in length and 4cm in width. The interior of the membrane was covered with block crystals in order to achieve a more accurate bearing of the higher frequencies at close ranges.

After swinging the device out, the base was rotated either by hand or by remote control; and by moving it back and forth, a noise source could be located with an accuracy to within a few degrees by searching for the maximum volume. By switching on electric filters it was possible to suppress the lower frequencies and get more accurate readings by allowing the higher frequencies through.

KDB devices were at first designated for use by surface ships, but were then also employed by submarines, especially in the detection of other submarines lying on the sea bed. Because of noise from the current generated by movement through the water. KDB equipment could at first only be used at speeds of up to 6 knots, but improvements came later when it was built into a streamlined casing.

Gruppen-Horch-Geräte-Anlage (GHG) ('group listening devices equipment')
The problem of obtaining good reception at high speed could only be solved by installing groups of receivers

permanently into the hull plating or into special housings at the bow or along the keel. In essence, a compensation system was used. When sound approaches at an angle, it makes the different phases of the vibrations in-phase and feeds them to the listening phone. With, for example, a group of six receivers in a straight line, and with the sound approaching from the right-hand side, the sound waves reach the individual receivers one after the other with a determinable time difference. Electrical delay networks can be switched between the individual receivers and the listening phone, these consisting of self-inductors in series and condensers connected in parallel. By switching on more or fewer segments of this delay network, it is possible to 'delay' the incoming vibrations and to feed those emanating from all the receivers to the listening phone in phase. The individual parts of this electric delay network are connected by 'decks' which can be changed at the same time with a common switchboard according to the geometrical arrangement of the receivers. When the source of a noise has been located, the position with the maximum amount of noise can be determined by changing the contacts on the slides of the electric compensator. The direction of the noise can then be read on a scale connected to the compensator.

The first GHG systems, with electrodynamic receivers, were fitted on ocean liners in 1925. Originally, straight-lined groups of 2 × 6 or 2 × 12 receivers were used, which were built into the hull on both sides towards the bows of the ship, near the keel—that is, as far as possible beneath the waterline—and with the receiver membranes fitted into the hull plating as smoothly as possible. Whereas they proved to be very accurate for diagonal readings, these straight-line receiver groups had the disadvantage of offering very inaccurate results for readings from bearings forward or astern. This is why, in the interests of better accuracy, a different spread was adopted wherein the projection of the receivers on the horizontal level approximated a circle. This was achieved by building the receivers into the hull plating at the bow of the ship in a rising and descending line. However, as the principle of the electrical compensator demanded either straight-line or circular receiver formations, in the final analysis a formation appropriate to the shape of the ship's hull had to be used.

The first submarines equipped with GHG systems had 2 × 12 receivers in 1935, but by 1939 they had two systems built into the hull each with 24 receivers. Crew training took place at the U-Boot-Abwehrschule (Submarine Defence School) using noise recordings and, subsequently, on board U-boats themselves.

Given favourable 'acoustic weather', a U-boat in 'silent' mode could pick up noise at the following ranges:

A destroyer cruising at 20 knots and at a range of 6–12nm with an accuracy of 1 degree;

A merchantman moving at a speed of 10 knots and at a range of 4–8nm to the same accuracy; and

Convoys from a far greater distance.

As an aside, an interesting isolated instance during the Second World War occurred when the heavy cruiser *Prinz Eugen* detected the British battlecruiser *Hood* at a range of 20nm.

From 1939

Because of the great tactical importance of equipping U-boats with listening devices, continuing trials were conducted throughout the Second World War in order to improve the quality of these systems. As of course the noise level of the listening ship under way and the reflection of sound from the sea bed were very important factors affecting efficiency, systematic measurements of all types of ships sailing at different speeds and in different sea states were undertaken by U-boats in the Bornholm area, in order to discover the optimum positions for the location of receivers, the optimum hull form, etc., in order to achieve the best compromise when distinguishing between 'useful noise' and 'interference'. The 'balcony' introduced later on U-boats originated with a demand by Oberkommando der Marine to make it also possible for surfaced, as well as submerged, U-boats to 'listen'. In this, the receivers were built in a horizontal 'horseshoe' projection, the two rows having a spacing of some 30cm. This shape permitted continuous direction-finding with approximately the same accuracy in all arcs apart from the sector aft between 150 and 210 degrees.

The increase in cruising and maximum speeds brought about by the Type XXI and XXIII U-boats, as well as by the Walter (Type XVII and XXVI) boats, saw the 'balcony' arrangement installed behind the hull plating and faired over as smoothly as possible, the receivers working through a 3mm thick cover of V2A steel sheeting. The demands for listening devices by the Type XXVI at maximum speed were ultimately so great that a 'balcony' with 4 × 48 (i.e., 196) receivers in eight horizontal lines had to be devised.

Considerations as to how the acquisition range could be increased even further led to proposals to explore lower frequencies—those between 100 and 200Hz—by using a larger base. However, none of these plans had become reality by the end of the war.

As there was full awareness of the dangers of using active devices to measure range, investigations were conducted into whether this sort of data—as well as bearing data—could be obtained by using passive sound locators. A project dubbed 'Felchen' was proceeded with, based on the theory that, with the help of a base of a known length, at each end of which there was a receiver, the two base angles to the target could be measured and the distance calculated from that.

Apart from the 'Felchen', the development of which was not quite ready by the end of the war, the following projects were also, according to Waas, under way at this time:

'NHG' and 'TAG': Warning systems for incoming torpedoes;

'WB-Gerät': A passive ranging device to estimate the distance of falling depth charges;

'Dorsch': A sound alarm buoy, to increase listening range; and

'SP-Anlage': A targeting device to enable a deeply submerged submarine to engage an incoming attacker. The was supposed to give the submerged U-boat the capability for engaging, for example, a destroyer by firing rockets. Using the 'sum-difference method', the horizontal and vertical angle of incidence of the propeller noise of the destroyer was calculated, using the receivers of two standard S-Anlagen. The diving depth was kept at 70m, and the distance was calculated from the angles of incidence and this known depth. During tests this device proved quite successful.

Underwater active Detection

Up to 1939

In the nineteenth century, experiments took place to determine the depth of the ocean by producing a sound signal just under the water surface, observing the echo coming back from the ocean floor and measuring the time that elapsed between the sending of the signal and the return of the echo. Tests at the beginning of the twentieth century were still unsuccessful, however, because of a lack of appropriate sound converters.

The event that stimulated research into horizontal echo-sounding was the *Titanic* disaster of 15 April 1912: within a month, on 10 May, the Englishman Lewis Richardson applied for a patent by which he proposed to send out dense clusters of ultrasound signals and to observe the echoes, even though appropriate transmitters and receivers were not yet available.[9] Behm in Germany and the Canadian Reginald Fessenden in the United States worked on soundboards. A breakthrough was achieved when, in 1917, the Frenchman Paul Langévin presented a converter which worked on the piezoelectric principle. Some ten years later, the work of the Frenchman Pierce, among others, resulted in the ultrasonic interferometer and magnetostrictive converter.

As explained in the previous section, passive listening devices existed in the First World War, but, inasmuch as base measurement analogous to optical distance could not be calculated, these devices yielded no information concerning range, i.e. distance to target. This is why, in 1929–30, the Reichsmarine initiated experiments and trials in horizontal sound location, starting with piezoelectric con-

verters—tests with which were first conducted in 1932–33 on the submarines built for Finland—and, later, magnetostrictive converters.

It is well known that low frequencies provide a wider range than high frequencies, but also demand larger oscillator measurements. A reasonable compromise is seen in the range 15–20kHz. Thus for all German instruments a frequency of 15kHz was chosen, with an impulse performance of 4–5 kW and a duration of impulse of 0.02sec. In good conditions, Kühnhold indicates, large surface ships could be detected at 5,000–10,000m by a submerged U-boat running 'silently', while submarines at 3,000–5,000m could b detected by a cruising destroyer.[10]

At the beginning of the Second World War the so-called 'Mob-S-Anlage', built by the Gesellschaft für akustische und mechanische Geräte (Gema; Society for Acoustic and Mechanical Devices), became operational.

From 1939

The dangers to a submarine employing active echo-sounding equipment such as this are obvious: not least, she is emitting signals which betray her presence to an enemy—possibly well before the submarine herself has discovered a target. For this reason there was, in the Kriegsmarine, a general order first to search the horizon with the GHG-Anlage and then to take a bearing on the enemy. This bearing was next passed on to the Mob-S-Gerät. It was only when the enemy sound was heard by the observer at his listening station that calculating a more accurate range and bearing could commence—and this had the advantage of requiring few impulses for any given direction.

From the Mob-S-Gerät, which functioned on a two-strip basis, was developed the four-strip 'S-Gerät', which reduced the opening angle to 15–20 degrees and solved the problem of ambiguous signals. The image in the cathode ray tube, which had a diameter of 9cm, was projected via a tilting mechanism on to a semi-transparent mirror where the operator could observe it. Powered by a small motor, the mirror moved from left to right at a constant speed and then quickly returned to its starting position. Through the mirror could be seen an indirectly illuminated range scale, in coincidence with the deflections originating from the Braun tube. Each time the vibrating mirror jumped back to 'zero', an impulse of 20 milliseconds at 15kHz was sent out. Depending on the degree of amplification, the nearest echoes became visible on the range scale immediately afterwards in the shape of a wild confusion of ellipses, the amplitude of which quickly faded, and the echoes from the object targeted could then be recognised clearly and their range read. The amplifiers were equipped with a timer-based automatic amplifying control which caused the sensitivity of the system to adapt to the distance from which the echo was received during each period of bearing. If the echo signals on the Braun tube were vertical, the range was read on the bearing scale of the extension instrument; if at an angle, the echo was 'straightened' by turning the bearing wheel until it was vertical.

Extending the S-Gerät with a listening instrument resulted in the 'SZ-Gerät', and the device was now able to 'hear' the echoes and to recognise the relative speeds of the listening boat and the object under observation thanks to the Doppler effect, the frequency of the echo being compared to the fixed (known) frequency of the impulse generator: an increase in frequency indicated an approaching target, while a decrease indicated that the target was moving away.

A further development in the 'S-Gerät' series was the 'Nibelung', which was tested for the first time on the Type VIIC boat U 1008 (commissioned on 1 February 1944) and was scheduled for use in the Type XXI and XXIII U-boats, which were designed to be able to launch their torpedoes from a position well below periscope depth. Whereas the S- and SZ-Geräte employed a movable mirror to indicate range, the 'Nibelung' calculated range purely electronically, with the help of 'tilting' devices to lower the point of light on the screen of the cathode-ray tube. The tube, sitting vertically in the device, was watched by the operator through a fixed, semi-transparent mirror through which the indirectly illuminated range scale was also visible. On the left side of the scale was point zero, from which the point of light moved to the right at an exponentially reduced speed.

The Type XXI had its four-strip base built in, hinged, behind the casing. Bearings were taken through this casing, which consisted of a lattice covered by thin sheet metal, permissible because of the manner in which it was built and because it tilted at an angle of some 100° to direction ahead.

At the end of the war, the 'Sarotti', 'Most' and 'Hildebrand' systems were under development as 'panoramic' additions to the S-Geräte, and an echo-printer was also being developed (for which the 'Nibelung' already had a connection point) using dampened electrolyte paper for recording purposes

Research and development for these systems was the responsibility of the Nachrichtenmittelversuchsanstalt (NVA; renamed Nachrichtenmittelversuchskommando—NVK—on 8 September 1939), which was a department of the OKM/Amtsgruppe Technisches Nachrichtenwesen (OKM/NWa). When it was suggested that the instruments developed by the NVA could not be tested and assessed sufficiently critically, the Nachrichtenmittelerprobungskommando (NEK) was founded in September 1936 and also placed under the supervision of OKM/NWa. The scientific department of the NVA/NVK was headed by Dr Rudolf Kuhnhold from October 1934 until the surrender.

The instruments themselves were built by the Electroakustik GmbH, Kiel, and Atlaswerke, Bremen. They were installed at the shipyards, where there were special departments for signals and location equipment responsible for their procurement, according to guidelines issued by the OKM.

The academic staff of the Kriegsmarine was set up in 1943, under the direction of Professor Küpfmüller, and became the driving force behind the science of underwater sound location. There was good co-operation among all the Kriegsmarine departments, and with the two manufacturing concerns in Kiel and Bremen—not least as a result of Kühnhold's strong personality. German underwater sound location instruments were already very advanced at the beginning of the war, and remained so to its end. Their superiority over the enemy's equipment was maintained.

Nevertheless, although U-boats had excellent sensors for both active and passive underwater detection, the fact remained that only rarely were they able to approach their targets underwater. With maximum speeds of only some 8 knots, and a running time of less than two hours at this speed, they were simply unable to reach a convoy while submerged, let alone fast warships. They were, as Friedman puts it, not much more than 'manned mines'.[11]

Above-Water Passive Reception (Radio Direction-Finding)

Up to 1939
At the end of the First World War—and, indeed, at the beginning of the Second—the optical sight was the most reliable method of detecting an enemy at long range. It could have been different: U-boats were equipped with direction-finders, which, however, were used only to receive wireless messages, on very long frequencies (9,000–20,000m, corresponding to 33.3–15kHz), or as navigation aids. Taking bearings on enemy radio traffic in order to discover the whereabouts of this same enemy had not yet been thought of.

From 1939
At the beginning of the war, German U-boats were equipped with the Type 280S rotating direction-finder and the Telefunken T3 PLLA8 receiver for medium, long and very long frequencies in the 13–33.3 and 70–1,200kHz ranges, as well as the short-wave 'Main' T8 K39 receiver covering the 1.5–25MHz range.

In the autumn of 1943 Kriegsmarine listening posts discovered that signals for Allied convoys had been changed to frequencies of around 2.4MHz; moreover, a lot of unnecessary personal messages were being sent over the German airwaves. As indicated above, the highest frequency for submarine instruments at that time was 2MHz, and therefore Telefunken introduced the T3 PLLA38 receiver operating at up to 2.4 Hz. In addition, a device called 'Presskohle' (literally, 'Compressed Coal', or 'Briquette') was developed for the 'Main' T8 K39 short-wave receiver (1.5–15MHz), designed to be connected to the frame of the direction-finder.

In late October 1943 the enemy began to realise that his frequencies were being located and therefore switched to short signals, undetectable by sound-location devices but only by visible direction-finders—with which U-boats were not equipped. The 'Presskohle' adaptation thus proved redundant and was not installed.

The Germans attempted to counteract the transition to short signals by introducing 'Lichtkohle' ('Light Coal'), which functioned by lobe-switching the network deflector antenna in order to get a rough estimate as to direction, but this failed to deliver satisfactory results. The solution was then believed to lie in 'Sumpfkohle' ('Swamp Coal'), wherein a crossed-coil antenna was attached between the top of the snorkel and its casing, thereby overcoming the problem of 'dampening' short frequencies. The reading was made from a display unit.

In addition to this short-range direction-finder, a 'Braunkohle' ('Brown Coal') apparatus was devised, to cover the long-range frequencies. In this, four high-frequency iron cores were positioned in pairs on the pressure hull, each crossed-coil antenna being connected to the entry point of a permanently rotating quadruple goniometer. Research into both 'Sumpfkohle' and 'Braunkohle' was incomplete at the end of the war.

At the beginning of the Second World War, radio direction-finding was employed by the Germans merely because it offered the best possible reception of friendly wireless messages and could function as a navigation aid, and for this reason only part of the whole spectrum of frequencies utilised by the enemy was covered. The gaps in the frequency bands were closed only slowly because the potential of RDF was underestimated and experimentation proceeded only fitfully. Even by the end of the war, satisfactory operational systems were still unavailable.

Above-Water Active Detection Systems (Radar)

In Düsseldorf on 30 April 1904, Christian Hülsmeyer—whom some might consider to be the inventor of radar (although the term had not been coined at the time)—received his first patent 'metallische Gegenstände mittels elektrischer Wellen . . . zu melden' (for a procedure 'for reporting . . . metal objects by means of electric waves').[12] On 17 May 1905 a presentation was made in Cologne, and the following day the *Kölner Zeitung* reported the event, stating, among other things, that 'The big advantage that this invention offers is, above all, that ships equipped with a transmitter and receiver for this system can sight . . . every other ship.'[13]

On 31 May 1904 Hülsmeyer's 'Telemobiliskop-Gesellschaft' turned to the Holland–America Line and proposed trials, and these took place from 8 to 10 June during a shipping congress in Rotterdam using the tugboat *Columbus*.[14] Important representatives from all the big shipping lines were present. On 11 November that year Hülsmeyer was granted an additional patent for his idea to measure 'die Entfernung von metallischen Gegenständen' ('the range of metal objects').[15]

However, Hülsmeyer's hopes remained unfulfilled: his invention was before its time. The participants of the successful demonstration in Rotterdam were enthralled by Marconi's work, and failed to understand that Hülsmeyer did not wish to *transmit* wireless messages but to *locate* them. Dahl writes thus in recognition of Hülsmeyer's achievements:[16]

> What followed now was the tragedy of an inventor of genius. Everywhere he encountered rejection and suspicion. Nobody realised that Hülsmeyer's invention had nothing to do with the work of Marconi. All Marconi wanted to do was to send messages, and he transmitted them in all directions without any screening. Hülsmeyer, on the contrary, shielded his messages so carefully that he transmitted in a single, defined direction.
> It appears, from his patent specifications DRP 165546 dated 30.4.1904 and 169154 dated 11.11.1904, that he used both a parabolic reflector and a horn transmitter. He deliberately used very short wavelengths, whereas Marconi was concerned with longer and longer wavelengths. Judging from the remains of one of his antennae found later, it can be deduced that he worked with decimeter wavelengths of 40–50cm.

In the autumn of 1904 Hülsmeyer approached the Kaiserliche Marine, setting down his thoughts in writing. The reaction from the Reichsmarineamt was a letter with a marginal note handwritten by Tirpitz: 'Meine Männer haben bessere Ideen!' ('My men have better ideas!')

Hülsmeyer and the Telemobiloskop-Gesellschaft also applied for foreign patents, presenting their proposals to various well-known companies—late in 1904, for example, Gesellschaft für drahtlose Telegraphie mbH (Telefunken) in Berlin, founded a year earlier, was in receipt of his enquiries—but here, too, nothing but a lack of interest and understanding was forthcoming. On 21 August 1905 Telefunken wrote: 'We are returning herewith the . . . patent specifications . . . as we do not have any use for the inventions described.'

In the end, Hülsmeyer resigned his position and pursued other interests, although he received belated recognition of his 'radar idea' after the war.

It could be argued that Hülsmeyer was unsuccessful because the necessary technical prerequisites were not in place at the time of his inventions—the electron valve, for example, was only invented in 1906 (by the Austrian physicist Robert von Lieben), the science of pulse code modulation remained unknown for a long time, and so on.

On the other hand, the Marconi company defended its monopoly with all means necessary—'Participation in communications traffic only with Marconi instruments!'— and nobody genuinely recognised the difference between transmitting communications and wireless-location.

It is, however, completely incomprehensible why the official authorities, like the RMA, and private companies, like Telefunken, did not grasp the significance of Hülsmeyer's work. A development which could have influenced world history lay fallow for decades. Leo Brandt, a radar expert acknowledged both during and after the war, wrote: 'If you look at these patent specifications today, it seems completely inexplicable why this route wasn't followed for three decades.'[17]

Practice cannot necessarily keep up with the advance of theories into hitherto unknown areas of knowledge, but in 1933 Nachrichtenmittelversuchsanstalt (NVA), which had, at the suggestion of Dr Rudolf Kühnhold, been working on sound impulse technology for four years, formulated a method of using electronic waves for locating objects. In January 1936 Kühnhold delivered a lecture at the Allgemeine Marineamt (General Naval Office), in the course of which he said:

> As location requires, above all, the measurement of distance, the objective is to locate the enemy by irradiating him and registering the waves reflected by him. A condition for such a reflection is, however, that the wavelength used is as short as possible relative to the reflecting surface. In this case, it means that the wavelength has to be shortened in relation to a variety of surfaces, for example the superstructural parts of the target, in order to avoid a dependency on the situation of the target in relation to the transmitter. On the other hand, in order to locate something one also needs to take a bearing; taking a bearing, however, is only possible with the help of a very concentrated beam. These considerations, which are of crucial importance for pinpointing a specific location, make it necessary from the start to use the shortest possible electromagnetic waves—preferably a wavelength of less than one meter.[18]

However, in 1933 science had not progressed this far. It is true that the Julius Pintsch A. G. in Berlin had built a transmitter and receiver functioning with a wavelength of 13.5m, but tests in Kiel harbour in the autumn of 1933 were negative: the performance of the tubes was too weak to obtain any reflections. The only possible method of producing the necessarily short waves was considered to be the magnetron, which was theoretically known in Germany at the time but did not actually exist. The NVA tried to persuade Telefunken to co-operate in some joint research but failed. At NVA's suggestion, a new company, the 'Gesellschaft für elektroakustische und mechanische Apparate' (Gema), was founded, but in retrospect it was a mistake for NVA to allow Telefunken to discourage them in lower-level research, because now Gema had to start from scratch in too many areas. Leo Brandt says:

> With this step, the expertise and the thirty-year tradition of the wireless industry were renounced and they had to start from scratch in every aspect, from the physical to the mechanical, from the development of tubes to their serial production. Every expert will tell you that such an approach involves major difficulties and cannot achieve the same success as co-operation on a wider basis.[19]

It is, however, doubtful whether contact at the highest level, for example between the Marineleitung and Telefunken, would have resulted in any co-operation, because at the time Telefunken thought that electric waves in the centimetre- or lower decimetre-range behaved like light waves and were reflected not back but away.

Gema started its work with magnetrons purchased from Holland working to a wavelength of 50cm. On 26 September 1935 there was a presentation in the grounds of the NVA in Pelzerhaken, attended by, amongst others, the Oberbefehlshaber der Kriegsmarine (ObdL; Commander of the Navy) Erich Raeder, the Flottenchef (Fleet Commander) and the Chef des Marinewaffenamtes (Head of the Navy Office). The demonstration was successful, the officials were impressed, and more finance was made available for research into radar location. During tests at the end of October 1935, a range of 7,000m was achieved using the light cruiser *Königsberg*. Around the turn of the year 1935/36, a joint development programme by Gema and the NVA was established, the main objectives of which were the development of an instrument in the centimetre wavelength (4–10cm), further development of the 50cm instrument as a seaborne system, and the development of an instrument using a wavelength of about 2m for use against aerial targets. At about this time, the British were beginning to build their ground-based 12m-wavelength radar warning chain.

Developments in Germany now proceeded apace. In 1937 the 2m system led to a 2.4m apparatus, 'Freya', which, given sufficient elevation, would later detect targets at ranges of up to 150km and to a precision of 2 to 3°. It could not be used to calculate height. The 50cm apparatus led on to the 60cm targeting instrument (later called 'Seetakt'), which was revealed to the ObdM in May 1937 when a range of 10,000m was demonstrated using the light cruiser *Köln*.

The first experimental systems were installed in the torpedo boat G 10, the NVA trials ship *Strahl* and the light cruiser *Königsberg* in 1937. In 1938 they were added to the pocket-battleship *Admiral Graf Spee* and in summer 1939 to the Type IX U-boats U 39 and U 41. The submarine version of 'Seetakt' (FuMO 29) had fixed dipoles on the forward face of the conning tower (see illustration, page 75). The apparatus could be rotated 10 degrees by using a compensator, but for a panoramic search the U-boats themselves had to turn circles.

The third line of development was the centimetre-wavelength apparatus, upon which the NVA began work in 1936, as recommended by Kühnhold in his lecture at the beginning. The early results were disappointing, the trials ship *Welle* being located only at 2,000m. Tests and further work were halted because of instability of the transmitter and receiver and unexpected clutter. It appears that it was this failure that led to the fateful decision, made in January 1939, to concentrate on the seemingly more promising longer wavelengths. Centimetre-wavelength investigations then remained dormant for almost six years and were only resumed when, in 1943 an example of the British H2S device was recovered from a crashed bomber near Rotterdam.

In summary, from the German point of view, the problem as to which type of wavelength was to be preferred was not examined, nor even discussed, thoroughly enough in the years 1936–1939. There could not, of course, be any operational research in this area, and the expenditure of time and money that would have been necessary for the production of an efficient centimetre-wavelength instrument was not, it was judged, worthwhile having regard to the potential of such an instrument. To put it another way, from 1936 to 1943 the 'search for an optimum wavelength' was not undertaken in Germany. During this period, in contrast, the British successfully explored the course from the 12m wavelength to the 9cm wavelength.

From 1939
Despite the fitting of decimetre-range 'Seetakt' aboard U 39 and U 41 in the summer of 1939, the fact that there was insufficient space in U-boat radio rooms for installing two active detection systems—'S-Gerät' for underwater sound location and 'Seetakt' for radio location—dissuaded Dönitz from authorising the wholesale adoption of radar. The equipment installed aboard U 39 and U 41 was removed, and the U-boat fleet began hostilities having rejected the great advantages that radar would have offered.

What happened in the area of German naval radar technology during the war is quickly told. At the end of 1941 trials took place with 80cm 'Seetakt' (FuMO 30), and there were experiments with fixed-frame and rotating antennae, albeit with scant success. Three Type IX U-boats—U 156, U 157 and U 158—were equipped with this FuMO 30, but they were lost in the Caribbean between 13 June 1942 and 8 March 1943.

In mid-1943, addressing this very unsatisfactory state of affairs, the 'Hohentwiel' system was ordered to be fitted. This was a device operating on a wavelength of 56cm, developed by the Luftwaffe and built by the Lorenz company. The advantages over the Gema apparatus were its shorter wavelength, its considerably more powerful transmitter (30kW compared to 10kW) and its more compact dimensions, permitting installation in U-boats' radio rooms. The first FuMO 30 was tested aboard U 742, a Type VIIC, in August 1943 (this boat was lost off Narvik on 18 July 1944).

By September a total of 64 U-boats had been equipped with 'Hohentwiel', which had an expected range of 8–10km against targets at sea and 15–20 km against aircraft. However, as the instrument had a lower limit ('shadow') of 1,800m, it could not deliver any data useful for launching torpedoes.

At the end of the war, two further systems were being tested. 'Berlin U II' was a retractable, tactical radar that could be used at periscope depth. It utilised a 9cm wavelength and featured a panoramic display. 'Lessing II', another retractable radar, was for air search. Operating at a wavelength of 2.4m, it had a 100kW transmitter and a range of 30km, but lacked a direction-finding facility. Both these devices were produced specifically for the Types XXI and XXVI U-boats and were supposed to have been ready for introduction in mid-1945.

Summary
Progress in German radar development can be summarised thus:

The inventor Christian Hülsmeyer fails to get backing from Tirpitz in 1904 ('My men have better ideas!').

In 1933 it is Dr Kühnhold, not the Nachrichtenmittelversuchsanstalt, who comes up with the idea of adapting the concept of underwater detection involving sound waves to one of above-water detection using electronic waves. German private industry (i.e., Telefunken) is not interested.

When, in 1936, Kühnhold proposes the way forward to centimetre-wavelength technology—and at that time the British are still working in the 12m range—he is not listened to. The successes achieved in the decimetre range seem adequate.

In 1939 Dönitz dispenses with radar technology in favour of the active sound-location instruments—which turn out to be virtually useless during the war because of their practical shortcomings.

From 1936 to 1943 practically no research is undertaken into centimetre-range wavelengths in Germany. Only when the secrets of the British airborne H2S radar are fortuitously presented to the Germans at the beginning of 1943 is a study group ('Rotterdam') set up, and what can be achieved in only a few months—and what has been missed for seven years—is rapidly demonstrated.

Armament

We now come to the third term of the equation for the fighting power of a submarine—the armament.

The MS U-boats of the First World War were equipped with one or two quick-firing 8.8cm or 10.5cm guns, and at the beginning of the Second World War the Type VII and IX U-boats had the same. The U-cruisers and the redesigned transport submarine *Deutschland* had 15cm guns. As the opportunities for using these weapons after 1939 rapidly diminished and finally disappeared altogether, we will look at the development only of the torpedo in this section.

In 1866 Robert Whitehead, the works superintendent at Stabilimento Technico Fiumano in Fiume—at that time a port in Austria-Hungry—demonstrated his first torpedo, which he had manufactured to the design of the Austrian frigate captain Johann B. Luppis.

In 1871 the Marine established a department for conducting trials with Spieren- (spar) and Schlepptorpedos (towed torpedoes). That same year Werner von Siemens submitted a paper to the Kriegsministerium (War Ministry) concerning the 'Zerstörung feindlicher Kriegsschiffe durch Torpedos' ('The Destruction of Enemy Warships by Torpedoes').

In 1874 the Berliner Maschinenfabrik Schwartzkopff (BMAG) offered its own torpedo design, which proved to be an almost identical copy of the Whitehead weapon. The same year, the Marine set up a Torpedo-Versuchs- und Prüfungskommission (Torpedo Test and Examining Commission), the work of which was in 1878 taken over by the Torpedo Versuchs-Kommando (TvK, or Torpedo Test Command) in Kiel. On 1 April 1891 the Torpedowerkstatt (TW, or Torpedo Workshop) was established, which would take on the sole responsibility for the manufacture of torpedoes from that time until 1914 and for their development until 1918.

During this period of development, torpedoes were first propelled by compressed air, then by warmed compressed air and finally by a mixture of steam and gas. Progress in Germany kept pace with international standards, except for the transition to a 21in (533.4mm) diameter, which, for the time being, was not selected for the Kaiserliche Marine.

Like the torpedoes of all other navies, these torpedoes were steam/gas weapons, with the one great disadvantage that they left a prominent wake of bubbles—a revealing pale stripe on the surface of the water as they sped towards their target. Because of this, at the beginning of the war Wilhelm von Siemens resumed trials with electrically propelled craft using remote control, continuing the work begun by his father Werner von Siemens in the 1870s. Under Wilhelm's supervision, a small group of technicians began to work on designs and calculations for electrically driven torpedoes.

By the end of the First World War, 0.6m and 0.7m torpedoes with steam/gas propulsion of adequate quality were available—showing, for example, a range of 4,000m and a speed of 37 knots. The development of electric torpedoes was a long drawn out process, but trials were by this time under way and their introduction to service was planned for February 1919. Percussion fuses worked satisfactorily, although magnetic fuses, at the experimental stage, were expected to be perfected in the near future. The problem of surgeless torpedo ejection had been solved and was expected to be introduced at the beginning of 1919. Targeting data still had to be gathered 'by hand'.

By 1939, the range, maximum speed and explosive power of the gas/steam torpedo had been improved, and the electric torpedo was available. During the Second World War this became the standard torpedo for use by submarines against merchant ships, although a possible increase in speed at the expense of range—the subject of much investigation—was, for the time being, rejected. Percussion fuses, successfully employed during the First World War, had been shown to have shortcomings, principally because of their failure to function properly at acute angles of impact; however, proximity fuses, the subject of research since 1915, were still not ready for introduction to service. Depth regulators still did not work properly—mainly a consequence of the decision to install them at the rear of the torpedo. Finally, targeting data could now be calculated mechanically.

Torpedo Propulsion from 1939

Bypass system (circulating operation)

In 1927 the TVA awarded a contract to the Versuchsanstalt für Kraftfahrzeuge (Experimental Station for Motor Vehicles) of the TH Berlin (Technical College in Berlin) for a torpedo motor with bypass system, and by 1932 just such a power source was available, developing 230hp. However, the head of the Versuchsanstalt, Dr Kaufmann, emigrated the following year and work stopped. Four years later, in 1937, the OKM placed a fresh order, with Junkers in Dessau, for a motor with an output of 420hp, giving the new torpedo a speed of 48 knots at a range of 22,000m, and when war broke out this unit was still under development. Trial-firings with the weapon, designated G7m, were reportedly conducted in mid-1943 at the Industrie-Versuchsanstalt of the OKM in Neubrandenburg (INN), but work was halted in February 1945.

In 1933 Hellmuth Walter proposed a fast underwater vehicle which would derive the necessary oxygen for burning fuel while underwater from hydrogen peroxide, and in 1938 he presented a project for a series of torpedoes utilising this propulsion system. One of these was a U-boat torpedo with a diameter of 533.4mm which would achieve 45 knots at a range of 6,830m. A rocket propulsion system was initially intended for these torpedoes, similar to those installed in the aerial rockets constructed by Walter in 1936–37, but the torpedo's speed proved to be low compared to the speed at which the exhaust gases were ejected. For this reason Walter then attempted to fuel the four-cylinder engine of the G7a with a mixture of split H_2O_2 and petroleum, but in 1939 he switched to turbine propulsion. During the war a total of 21 different H_2O_2 torpedoes were built; trials dragged on and none of them ever entered service.

Electric propulsion with primary cells

Until 1942 the Kriegsmarine considered the performance of the G7e (range 5,000m at a speed of 30 knots) to be adequate. It was achieved using a secondary (lead) battery warmed to 30°C and weighing 665kg. The weight of the battery constituted 41.3 per cent of the total weight of the torpedo ready to be launched and resulted in a negative buoyancy of 20.7 per cent. When, in 1943, it was possible to raise the negative buoyancy by using telescopic fins, the weight of the battery was increased to 845kg and a range of 7,500m could be achieved.

Apart from the enlargement of the secondary batteries, tests with primary batteries were conducted from 1941, the objective being, once again, to achieve a significant increase in range. Two systems were developed, one using a carbon and magnesium electrode with dilute nitric acid as an electrolyte (CMg), and the second having a zinc and a lead dioxide electrode and dilute sulphuric acid ($ZnPbO_2$). With the CMg system, ranges of more than 20,000m at 30 knots were expected, but some disappointing trials in September 1944 led to the abandonment of the project. With the $ZnPbO_2$ system it was hoped to reach ranges of 12,000m at 30 knots, but it appears that no trials were ever conducted.

Steering

There are four different methods of bringing a torpedo to its target:

1. Calculation of the collision course and the corresponding drift angle, a method based on estimated data and having to rely on this data not changing after the torpedo has been launched;
2. Remote control or, better, 'post-launch' steering, which can modify the track according to such changes in data as may occur;
3. Programmed steering (auto-pilot); and
4. Steering in accordance with predetermined calculations.

Until the end of the First World War, all German torpedoes were fired according to manual calculations concerning the required course. The transition to mechanical calculators was made before 1939.

Remote control

Werner von Siemens was the first German to propose that it was possible to steer a vessel containing an explosive charge from the coast via cable, submitting his ideas to the Marineministerium on 4 August 1870— 'Zerstörung feindlicher Kriegsschiffe durch lenkbare Torpedos' ('Destruction of Enemy Warships by means of Steerable Torpedoes').

In 1872–73 tests were carried out using a steam launch made available by the Navy, more thorough trials being conducted on 1 June 1874 on Lake Rummelsberg. However, it was not until 1935 that the TVA turned once again to the subject of remote-controlled torpedoes. In a project designated 'G7f' (later 'NY'), behaviour patterns were studied and tested using wavelengths of between 1,000 and 20,000m. Trials took place in 1942, but in February 1944 work on the project was suspended.

In the meantime—and resurrecting trials suspended as far back as 1916—Siemens proposed a torpedo guided by wire. This project was designated 'NYK'. The guidance was intended to enable the torpedo to change direction in the horizontal plane and to surface briefly for target-location. Experiments were also carried out using infra-red and ultra-violet light.

At the beginning of 1944 a decision was made that the wire-guided torpedo (equipped, incidentally, only with a single-core wire) should be employed chiefly for coastal defence. This project was designated 'Spinne' (Spider). Trials using land-based control consoles, and involving also miniature submarines, were carried out, but, again, these weapons were not introduced into service.

In summer 1943 the TVA proposed 'Lerche' (Lark), a project for a guided torpedo employing a magnetostrictive microphone with sharp directional characteristics and capable of being rotated by 60° to port and starboard. The signal picked up by the microphone was sent to the operator on the submarine via a 6,000m cable. The operator now had to take the torpedo either to the target by means of steering commands ('Passive Lerche') or, if the torpedo was equipped with an acoustic homer, close to the target ('Aktive Lerche'). This torpedo, too, was never used operationally.

Programmed steering

The theory behind programmed steering is to use any remaining range or time from a 'miss' in order to make a second attempt to hit the target by means of a pre-programmed, curved course. This means that the track of the torpedo has to be adapted to match the course and speed of the enemy. A change of speed by the torpedo is also possible once the latter had reached its target area.

The first such weapon was the FAT (Feder-Apparat-Torpedo; literally, 'Spring Apparatus Torpedo'), in which different semi-circular courses could be pre-set by means of control plates. The FAT was first employed in service in December 1942, utilising the pneumatically driven G7a. The FAT II was introduced in May 1943, using the electrically driven G7e and different control plates, and this was particularly useful against destroyers. Finally, in February 1944 the LUT (Lagenunabhängiger Torpedo; literally, 'Torpedo Independent of Position') was introduced. With this weapon, the course could be adapted to the relative angle of the enemy vessel(s) under attack. However, as all these pre-programmed torpedoes were introduced at a stage in the war when U-boats were finding it more and more difficult even to sight a convoy, let alone close with one, their successes—apart from the first FAT launches in early 1943—were insignificant.

Automatic steering

The idea that a torpedo might seek out a target of its own accord is not new: there are laboratory examples of a torpedo with automatic steering dating back to the beginning of 1939, at the end of which year the first test launches were carried out. However, little progress was made in respect of U-boats simply because too much basic scientific data was lacking.

At the end of 1942 the T IV *Falke* (Falcon) became available for use against merchant ships. Derived from the G7e, it had a range of 7,500m at 20 knots. In early 1943 the T V *Zaunkönig* (Wren) was introduced for use against merchant ships. Its warhead contained two magnetostrictive oscillators serving as hydrophones, their directional characteristics so orientated that sounds were identified by one from about 30 degrees starboard and by the other from 30 degrees port. Noise received predominantly from one direction caused the torpedo's rudder to be turned in that direction, and the torpedo therefore changed course towards the target. Also derived from the G7e, it had a range of 5,700m at 24.5 knots; the range of the target-seekers was some 300m. The T V was first employed in September 1943 against convoy ON.202.

These torpedoes had a minimum impact range so that they would not endanger the launching U-boat. As this range was only 400m, however, the boat was obliged to dive deeply immediately after firing them. One result of this was that success rates were vastly overestimated, end-of-run and other failed detonations frequently being counted as 'kills'. According to Rohwer, the torpedoes were launched on 761 occasions between September 1943 and May 1945 and 112 hits were achieved, giving a success rate of only 14.7 per cent.

Other projects under development but not ready by the time the war came to a close were:

'Ackermann'—a passive torpedo steered on the basis of varying pressure conditions in the wake;

'Marchen'– a passive torpedo steered by means of the distortions in a target's magnetic field;

'Pfau', 'Möwe', 'Taube'—passive-acoustic steering;

'Geier'—active-acoustic steering;

'Ibis'—steered by means of the reflection of ultrasound on the wake;

'Fasan'—transition to LUT steering when going through the wake of a ship, utilising ultrasound impulses;

'Kondor'—a long-range torpedo steered by a combination of 'Geier' and 'Fasan' technology.

Torpedoes in the Bundesmarine

The first torpedoes to be used by the Federal Navy were the G7a and G7e, stocks of which were returned from Allied war booty. The British standard Mk 8 torpedo was also used, a 21in (53.3cm) weapon with a length of 6.57m. Indigenous development began again with the DM1 *Seeschlange* (Sea Serpent), a 53.3cm torpedo with electric propulsion, wire-guided and equipped with a homing warhead. A further project was the anti-submarine torpedo *Nixe* (Mermaid) for use against underwater targets. Two methods of propulsion were envisaged, a MaK 'vee' petrol engine and a Mercedes-Benz rotary (Wankel) engine. However, development of *Nixe* was terminated in the mid-1970s in favour of the 53.3cm DM2 *Seal* by AEG-Telefunken, which hardly fulfilled the requirements demanded of *Nixe* but was considered adequate to meet the tactical demands of the day. Apart from the DM1 and DM2, the Federal Navy was also equipped with the American anti-submarine Mk 37, which had a diameter of 19in (48.3cm) and a length of 3.43m.

By about the middle of the 1970s it was becoming more and more obvious that the distinction between a surface target and an underwater target was impracticable for both tactical and logistical reasons, and so development was put in hand for a multi-role torpedo. The result was the SUT (Surface and Underwater Target) torpedo, designed by AEG-Telefunken and using many components taken from the *Seal*. A new feature, however, was its three-dimensional steering system.

Missile Submarines

This section should not conclude without at least a brief mention of the employment of U-boats for launching missiles, the first instance of which involved U 511 off Peenemünde. In February 1942 U 156 had bombarded oil tanks at night off the island of Aruba, Venezuela, but the episode was not considered successful because the boat had to surface in order to use its gun.

Research into the firing of projectiles from a submerged U-boat was accordingly conducted, and, for this purpose, in May 1942 a launching frame was constructed at a depth of seven metres off Greifwalder Ole, a small island in the Baltic Sea close to Peenemünde. From this, 30cm WkSpr 42 projectiles—which had proved their value during the Russia campaign—were fired, with encouraging results.

A launching platform was next installed on the deck of U 511, which at that time was in dock at Stettin. The projectile envisaged had a propellant charge of 15kg and an explosive charge of 30kg. However, as Dönitz needed every available U-boat for sorties against Allied convoys in the Atlantic, tests were discontinued.

At the end of 1944, in connection with the successful development of the A4N2 (V-2) rocket, a proposal was discussed to have a U-boat tow one of the 12-tonne, 14m missiles to the US coast complete with all its technical back-up, fuel and liquid oxygen on barges and to launch it from there at land targets. At this stage of the war, however, there were more important issues for the Kriegsmarine to attend to.

Air-Independent Propulsion

Although, in the following paragraphs, the closed-cycle diesel engine, the Stirling motor, the MESMA turbine and the fuel cell will be briefly covered, these systems are not, strictly speaking, air-independent propulsion (AIP) systems. They are, rather, auxiliary systems designed to increase the underwater endurance and underwater range of submarines equipped with conventional powerplants (that is, with lead batteries and electric motors), and they can achieve this only for as long as a submarine's fuel and oxygen last.

In the first three systems mentioned above, mechanical (and thus electrical) energy is produced by burning a hydrocarbon. The three technologies suffer from two problems that are connected to the burning of hydrocarbon: they produce high temperatures and they generate carbon dioxide. The heat has to be eliminated—a relatively easy undertaking in sea water, although it does mean that a submarine is easily detectable. The carbon dioxide produced has to be treated, either by storing it on board (compressed or by dissolving it in a leaching solution) or by ejecting it into the sea. In case of the latter, special attention has to be given to the 'signature' of the boat, again to avoid detection

These problems do not occur when PEM fuel cells are used. The waste heat, with its fairly low temperature levels (maximum 80°C), is used to draw out the hydrogen from the metallic hydride and to evaporate the necessary

oxygen. Further advantages of fuel cells are their high electrical efficiency and low oxygen consumption, which makes them superior to the three other technologies.

Close-Cycle Diesel Engines

Since the dawn of the submarine age, boats that can be powered by internal combustion engines yet do not, for underwater travel, require an external air supply, have been the goal of the many designers. Well before the launch of the first submarine with Walter propulsion in Germany (V 80, in 1940) and the advent of the first submarine with reactor propulsion (the USS *Nautilus*, in 1954), there was, as far back as the beginning of the twentieth century, the prospect of closed-cycle propulsion, which promised to fulfil the dream.

In a closed-cycle system, the use of fuels and pure oxygen is out of the question because, as already noted, the engine is designed to be run on the surface using the surrounding air and underwater using closed-cycle technology; furthermore, ballast tanks have to be incorporated so that submerged manoeuvres may be executed. The main problem concerns the exhaust gases generated by the engine, which will consist principally of carbon monoxide (CO), carbon dioxide (CO_2), hydrogen (H_2), steam (H_2O), nitrogen (N_2) and traces of other hydrocarbons. The majority of the surplus gas, however, consists of CO_2, which can, however, be replaced by other gases—as will be explained later. The oxygen required for the powerplant needs to be as concentrated as possible, in order to keep its volume small. Other possibilities include liquid or gaseous oxygen (O_2), hydrogen peroxide (H_2O_2), nitrogen monoxide (N_2O), nitric acid (NHO_2) and tetranitromethane ($C(N_2O)_4$), but up to the present day only oxygen has been used successfully.

In 1901 the Frenchman Georg F. Jaubert put forward an application for a patent that was also submitted in Germany that same year.[20] The application stated that the 'characteristics of this technique . . . are that the fuel-oxygen charge is mixed with redundant gases sucked from a purifier that has been fed with the gases emanating from the cylinder.' Jaubert quickly recognised that he had become involved in a pioneering invention with full relevance to submarine propulsion. In 1905 he applied for another patent: 'Propulsion for submarines, characterised by the use of internal combustion engines with closed-cycle operation for propulsion where, in the known manner, the more or less purified exhaust gases are reused to produce the combustion mixture after enrichment with oxygen or a gas containing oxygen.'[21]

On 22 May 1902 construction work began on the French submarine Y (Q 37) in Toulon. Launched on 24 July 1905, he boat had a length of 43.5m, a beam of 3m and a draught of 2.8m, and a surfaced displacement of 213 tonnes. According to Pesce and Conway's, it had a 250hp diesel motor for propulsion that was supposedly also run while the boat was underwater in closed cycle, offering a speed of 6 knots.[22, 23] Despite Jaubert's patent, progress in French closed-cycle technology was slow and generally unsuccessful; indeed, it is unclear whether the submarine Y ever travelled underwater using her diesel engine. Whatever the case, the boat failed to complete her trials and the technology was not taken up. Her intended reconstruction with a supplementary electric motor for submerged drive was abandoned at the end of 1907, and in May 1909 the submarine herself was stricken.

In 1904 the French *Guêpe* class of submarines seemed to hold promise for the future. Ten boats were envisaged, 20.5m long, 2.1m in the beam and displacing 45 tonnes in surfaced condition. Diesel propulsion would enable the craft to reach a speed of 9 knots underwater utilising closed-cycle operation, at an output of 240hp. Only two of the class *Guêpe 1* (Q 49) and *Guêpe 2* (Q 50) were laid down (in Cherbourg), and construction was brought to a halt in March 1908.[24]

The next reference to closed-cycle operation is found in a letter from Professor M. Seruys that is not dated but was composed in about 1914. He writes:

C'est en 1913 que la firme Sautter Harlé réalise sous la direction de l'Ingenieur Wisler le premier moteur Diesel pour sousmarins à circuit fermé appliquant le système Jaubert à l'injection d'oxygène . . . [In 1914 the Sautter Harlé company, under the direction of engineer Wilser, produced the first closed-cycle diesel engine for submarines according to the Jaubert system of oxygen-injection . . .][25]

In lists of ships of the French Navy, however, no such submarine is found.

Developments in Germany ran approximately concurrently. In Cologne, Paul Winand defined a patent on 17 November 1903 concerning the 'Procedure for the operation of internal combustion engines for submarines and torpedoes, characterised by taking the oxygen necessary for combustion from . . . nitrogen dioxide.'[26] Winand was granted a patent in 1905, according to the specification for which 'Two-stroke engines are especially advantageous when internal combustion engines are installed in submarines.'[27]

Gasmotoren-Fabrik Deutz agreed a contract with Winand in 1905 concerning the development of his future patents,[28] and two years later signed an agreement with the Inspektion des Torpedowesens regarding the construction of 'a reduction apparatus for NO_2 or $C(NO_2)_4$ and a diesel engine that is supposed to produce "at least 300hp in a ten-hour continuous operation at 400rpm while completely sealed from the outside atmosphere".'[29] However, although this apparatus was produced, no further success was achieved in relation to the contract.

On 1 March 1918 Oberst van Erckelenz, the 'special authorised representative' of Gasmotoren-Fabrik Deutz, had a conversation with Korvettenkapitän Arno Spindler of the Reichsmarineamt (Imperial Naval Office), upon which he reported to Cologne the following day. Spindler said of this conversation that

. . . the last discussion between GFD and the U-Boot-Inspektion in Kiel . . . took place in July 1914 after the latest trials with the apparatus produced an unfavourable result . . . The U-Boot-Inspektion had expressed their wish that it should first be clarified whether the tests should be started again from scratch or whether they should be considered to be completely finished. In the meantime, war has broken out and a decision on this question has not thus far been made.[30]

In the further course of the conversation, Spindler stressed the underlying interest of the Reichsmarineamt in a standardised engine for U-boats and left it to GFD to continue with the tests if the chances of success seemed good—but, 'of course, the plan could only be approached from both sides after the war.'[31] The tests were never resumed.

Other concerns were also working on closed-cycle diesel engines for submarines at this time. In 1905 MAN Augsburg placed a diesel motor at the disposal of the Linde company in Munich, upon which Professor von Linde conducted research using a 50/50 mixture of oxygen and nitrogen. He reported the success of his tests to the Torpedoinspektion, who wrote back to him on 19 July 1905: 'These data . . . are very interesting and hold promise for the use of diesel engines instead of accumulators on submarines under water.'[32]

It cannot be confirmed whether or not Germaniawerft in Kiel also investigated closed-cycle technology, although it may be assumed that they did. In 1913, for example, the Marinebaurat (Government Naval Surveyor) Berling, responsible for submarine construction at Germaniawerft since 1904, compared the techniques for underwater propulsion systems for submarines as they were then known: lead batteries and electric motors; compressed air (of 200atm pressure); sodium boilers and steam engines; and diesel motors operating in a closed-cycle system.[33]

Berling based his calculations on a submarine that maintained a constant volume and displacement ($84m^3$ and 59 tonnes), an came up with the following ranges for the various underwater propulsion systems:

Lead batteries	28 nautical miles
Compressed air	26.8 nautical miles
Sodium boiler	22.6—29 nautical miles
Closed-cycle system	214 nautical miles

Closed-cycle systems thus offered eight to ten times the range of the other three.

Berling also calculated the relative underwater endurance figures, assuming a speed of 8 knots, and suggested a similar superiority:

Lead batteries	3.5 hours
Compressed air	3.35 hours
Sodium boiler	2.84—3.6 hours
Closed-cycle system	26.8 hours

It might reasonably be assumed that, because of the results presented by Berling in 1913 and the trials that took place during the First World War, good progress in this technology would have been made, but in fact it was not until 1927 that the Torpedoversuchsanstalt in Eckernförde placed the order relating directly to the research undertaken, and this was with the Versuchsanstalt für Kraftfahrzeuge of the Technische Hochschule in Berlin for the development of a long-range torpedo with closed-cycle propulsion. The motor that resulted—which used benzene as fuel—demonstrated an output of 230hp in 1932. However, with the emigration of the Versuchsanstalt's director, Dr Kaufmann, in 1933, work ground to a halt. In 1937 the OKM agreed a new contract with the Junkers company in Dessau for the development of a closed-cycle torpedo, but work on this project, too, stopped before the outbreak of war.

On 1 December 1940 Dr H. Drager, of Lübeck, placed a developmental order for a closed-cycle diesel engine with the Forschungsinstitut für Kraftfahrzeugwesen und Fahrzeugmotoren of the Technische Hochschule in Stuttgart (FKFS), as a private initiative but certainly also with

a view to the business interests of his company. FKFS worked on the project for three years, and on 5 January 1944 it presented its final report.[34] As can be seen from the report, the OKM wavered for some considerable time—placing a developmental order, rescinding it, offering support once again to FKFS, then withdrawal, and so on. In May 1943, however, the OKM signalled a more positive interest just as the Wende (turning-point) of the U-boat war was demonstrating that conventional submarines had reached the limit of their potential. At the same time, the work of FKFS was being brought to a successful conclusion. On 18 December 1943 OKM/K II—in the person of Admiral Fuchs—wrote to the shipbuilding commission proposing a trials U-boat fitted with a closed-cycle system:

The examination of further testing of the closed-cycle system on board has shown that your V 80 proposal cannot be realised because the compartmentation is far too restricted. I suggest, therefore, for this purpose the use of one of the Type XVII U-boats that is at present out of commission at Germaniawerft. The study has shown that this hull—which is available complete—will be well suited for onboard testing of the closed-cycle technique. The U-boat is not to be equipped for the front line but only as a floating test vehicle capable of running and diving, with all the technical and nautical equipment necessary but no weapons.[35]

At first, everything moved speedily. On 21 December 1943 came verbal advance orders from the OKM to Germaniawerft for the trials U-boat, to Daimler-Benz for the MB 501 engines and to FKFS for the closed-cycle system. On 12 February the following year, a firm order was placed with Germaniawerft for U 798 (builder's number

G 787), and on 23 February 1944 work began in earnest. On 6 June 1944 Daimler-Benz demonstrated the engine installation in closed-cycle mode to representatives of the OKM, and on 15 June U 798 was undergoing pressure tests. Unfortunately, from that date the project slowly faded, the OKM setting other priorities for Germaniawerft. When, on 6 December 1944, it was realised that almost 100,000 more working hours were required for the completion of U 798, work stopped altogether. On 15 February 1945 the U-boat was removed from her berth and in May she was destroyed by bombing.

It will be recalled that in 1913 Berling had, following his calculations, estimated the following underwater ranges for U-boats travelling at a speed of 8 knots:

Powered by lead batteries and electric motor: 28nm
Powered by closed-cycle diesel engine: 214nm

The most ubiquitous U-boat of the Second World War was the Type VIIC, which, at its maximum underwater speed of 7.6 knots, had a range of some 22 nautical miles.

After the war there were in Norway tentative plans to convert the submarine *Knerter* (the former U 4706) into a closed-cycle boat. Apparently there was no success, since work was called off in 1953. In Sweden, however, successful tests were conducted with an eight-cylinder, 1,500hp diesel engine using liquid oxygen. Plans to convert six U 1 class submarines (U 4–U 9) launched in 1943–44 to closed-cycle operation were called off after the boats were inspected, and they were reinstated in the fleet as conventional *Abboren* class boats—a change of heart apparently brought about by the promising prospects held out by the Stirling engine.

From 1948 tests were carried out in the United States using MB501 equipment captured in Germany[36] and, later, with the General Motors 1678A (1,600hp at 750rpm). Fuel consumption registered 0.24kg/hp/hr and oxygen consumption 0.94kg/hp/hr—very similar results, in fact, to those achieved in Stuttgart in 1943. After the introduction of nuclear propulsion, however, the tests were discontinued, and a closed-cycle engine would never actually be installed in a submarine, although, in the Soviet Union, the three-shaft 'Quebec' class submarines in commission from 1954 to 1957 reputedly had a closed-cycle diesel engine as a propulsion unit for the central shaft.[38]

MAN Augsburg and Bruker Meerestechnik Karlsruhe

In 1982 the Bereich Neue Technologie (Department of New Technology) at MAN began work on a system designated 'Motark' (from 'Motor mit geschlossenem Argon-Kreislauf', or 'diesel motor with closed argon cycle'). Whereas the argon as the carrier gas remained in the cycle unused, the products of combustion, CO_2 and H_2O, had to be extracted. The extraction of H_2O is not a difficult problem but that of carbon dioxide is, and in this system it was removed by means of a cleansing plant wherein the CO_2 was absorbed by 50 per cent solution of potassium hydroxide (KOH) and the resulting liquid transferred to a leaching tank. As the water produced by the combustion was also collected in special tanks, the whole process took place without the necessity for any exchange of materials with the exterior environment and was thus completely independent of the diving depth.

A collaborative programme was then set up between MAN and the Bruker company, which had been specialising in underwater technology for many years. After a developmental and construction phase of several years, the system, together with the MAN D2566ME engine (136hp at 1,500rpm) was installed in the experimental submarine *Seahorse*, which was launched in June 1989. Following moored and shallow-water trials in the Rhine harbour at Karlsruhe, the craft was transported by rail to Kiel, which

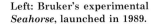

Left: Bruker's experimental *Seahorse*, launched in 1989.

served as a base for ocean trials from that September—all of which proved satisfactory.

Cosworth Engineering / Thyssen Nordseewerke
Since the early 1980s, Nordseewerke Emden (TNSW) have also been devoting considerable resources to the problem of air-independent propulsion for underwater vehicles, and one outcome of this has been a collaboration with Cosworth Engineering (CDSS), a Northampton company that has also investigated the cleansing of exhaust gases using potassium hydroxide but has since concentrated on the purification of these gases using sea water as an absorptive medium. Here the problem has concerned the introduction of sea water into the submarine and the disposal, offboard, after the absorption of the CO_2.

As the prototype system developed by CDSS involved a powerplant with an output of only 25 kW, a contract was agreed between TNSW and CDSS to develop a 120kW system in Emden. This contract provided for the construction of a compartment similar to that in a real submarine in order to be able to test an integrated system as realistically as possible. Oxygen was supplied by the ring conduit at the shipyard, and the carrier gas required, argon, was

Above: Views of TNSW's experimental closed-cycle facility with (right) the former U 1 with the AIP system in place.

bottled. The system was built in such a way as to withstand a maximum diving depth of 450m. The motor selected was a Mercedes-Benz OM42/A series developing 210hp at 1,800rpm and connected to a three-phase generator.

The test vehicle was U 1, which was decommissioned at Emden by the Bundesmarine on 29 November 1991 and transferred to TNSW on loan. U 1 was a 205 Class boat with a pressure-hull diameter of 4.5m. In December the boat was disassembled and, when ready, the new section containing the closed-cycle system was installed. She was ready for sea trials on 13 November 1992. The first diving trials with the new powerplant in operation took place on 3 March the following year. The diesel installation was an MTU 183 TE52 giving 340hp at 1,500rpm. On 14 October 1993, following the conclusion of the trials—which were successful—the closed-cycle system was shut down, and two weeks later the boat was in the breakers' hands.

In general, it has to be said that the development of the closed-cycle diesel system has not been a success story for the German Navy, and has not reflected the advances in

Above: U 1 following the installation of her new powerplant. After a year of trials, the boat was scrapped.

science and technology available, as the following time-table demonstrates:

20 July 1901	First French patent
6 Aug. 1905	First German patent
1907–1918	Collaboration between Gasmotoren-Fabrik Deutz and Inspektion des Torpedowesens
1913	Proof by Berling that, as regards range, closed-cycle system is more than eight times better than all other underwater propulsion systems.
1940–1944	Collaboration between Forschungs-institut für Kraftfahrzeugwesen und Fahrzeugmotoren (Technische Hochschule Stuttgart) and OKM.
1991	Thyssen-Nordseewerke Emden constructs and successfully tests functioning closed-cycle section in U 1.

By the 1990s the Bundesmarine had long since decided against closed-cycle diesel propulsion in favour of the fuel cell as the AIP system for the new 212 Class.

In short, before and during the First World War the closed-cycle system was probably insufficiently advanced for series production, despite considerable efforts to make it so. By the beginning of the Second World War, however, the system could have been developed to the production stage and would have given U-boats a much-needed technological edge.

Today, developments in military powerplant technology have probably consigned this form of propulsion to history: submarines travelling underwater on diesel engines would have little chance of survival in the face of modern sensors. For this reason, underwater vehicles with closed-cycle systems will probably only see development in the civilian world, for example as pleasure craft and for offshore commercial undertakings

The Stirling Motor

Next to the steam engine, this powerplant is the oldest form of thermal engine.

Ideally, the thermodynamic process of the hot-gas motor embraces four changes of state:

1. Compression at low temperature (isotherm with emission of heat);
2. Introduction of heat at a constant volume (isochore);
3. Expansion at high temperature (isotherm with addition of heat);
4. Emission of heat at a constant volume (isochore).

The 'working' gas—today generally helium—is pushed to and fro between a cold and a warm chamber in a closed system at a maximum working pressure of 140 bars. Between these chambers there is a heat accumulator (regenerator). This withdraws heat from the gas flowing into the cold chamber and gives it off again to the gas flowing back.

The advantages of the hot gas motor are:

1. External application of heat, allowing the continuous combustion of liquid, gaseous or solid fuels with a high amount of excess air;
2. Fewer toxic emissions;
3. Little noise; and
4. High efficiency.

The two types of hot-gas motor that have been developed can be distinguished by the way in which the changes of volume in the hot and cold chamber are produced. In a double-acting motor, the two chambers are fitted in different cylinders; in a displacement motor, they are fitted in one. The double-acting hot-gas motor can only be built as a multi-cylinder engine, but the displacement engine, which is connected to a rhombic gearing, can also be produced as a single-cylinder engine.

Principle of the double-acting motor

In each of the four cylinders there is a hot chamber above the piston and a cold chamber below. The hot chamber is connected to the cold chamber of the next cylinder by a heater, a regenerator and a cooler. As the first cylinder works with the second, the second with the third and the last with the first cylinder again, there is a connection between the number of cylinders and the phase displacement of the piston. With four cylinders, the phase angle is 90 degrees, with six cylinders it is 60. The piston rod has to be straightened by a double-holed capstan head so that the cold chamber can be sealed with the rod.

Principle of the displacement motor with rhombic gearing

The hot chamber, surrounded by the heating element, is located above the displacement unit; the cold chamber is between the displacement unit and the piston. Before reaching the flame, the air from the burner flows through a channel heated by the exhaust fumes. The rhombic gearing in the crankshaft housing ensures that the proper co-ordination of the discontinuous movements of piston and displacement unit is made.

Every cylinder goes through four phases:

1. Piston in the lowest displacement unit in the highest position; all the gas is in the cold chamber.
2. Displacement unit stays in the highest position; the piston has compressed the gas at a low temperature.
3. Piston remains in the highest position; displacement unit has pushed the gas into the hot chamber via the cooler, the regenerator and the heater.
4. The hot gas has expanded; the displacement unit and piston have both arrived together at the lowest position.

After this, the displacement unit pushes the gas into the cold chamber via the heater, the regenerator and the cooler (during which time the piston remains in the same position), so that the starting position is reached again.

Historical background

At the beginning of the nineteenth century the steam engine was the only power source offering a high performance. Many inventors attempted to replace the working medium—water—with air. Developments over this period included open systems using fresh air for each cycle and closed systems wherein the same volume of air was constantly recirculated. The invention of the Scottish vicar Dr Robert Stirling belongs to the second group. He applied for a patent in 1816, and today a model of his first motor, built in 1827, is with the Department of Natural Philosophy at the University of Glasgow.

Stirling progressed from the principle of the displacement motor to that of the double-acting motor. His machines, and those of his successors, were built in large numbers in the second half of the nineteenth century, some proponents believing that they could offer serious competition to the steam engine. However, without exception these powerplants demonstrated an unacceptably low efficiency, rarely surpassing 30 per cent. According to an 1895 price list from a German company, the largest Stirling motor that could be purchased had an output of a mere 2hp, but at a weight of 4,100kg, and it is therefore hardly surprising that, following the invention of the internal-combustion engine, hot-gas motors disappear virtually into oblivion.

In 1938, however, the principle was revisited by Philips Glühlampenfabrik in Eindhoven, whose theoretical and experimental research showed that, using the latest findings regarding heat transmission, aerodynamic resistance etc., the Stirling motor could be almost as efficient as the internal-combustion engine.

It is to Philips' credit that the company resuscitated Stirling's idea and developed his invention to the stage at which it was commercially viable.

The Stirling motor and the diesel engine

In comparison with a standard diesel engine:

1. The Stirling motor's efficiency is of the same order;
2. In a Stirling motor, the consumption of lubricating oil is practically zero;
3. The Stirling motor is not subject to pressure shocks by the working mechanism or to sudden accelerations of mass, which makes it extremely quiet;
4. In contrast to the diesel engine, other fuels can be taken into consideration for the Stirling motor, including even solar and nuclear energy;
5. When using the Stirling motor underwater, a light metal accumulator can be employed that is heated during surface cruising; and
6. Because of the high pressure in the combustion chamber, the exhaust fumes can be directed away from a submarine without the use of a compressor, even at great diving depths.

Practical application

In 1968 a company known as United Stirling A. B. (USAB) was established, with its headquarters in Malmö, Sweden, and a development programme was initiated under licence from Philips. In the field of conventional submarines, the company, in collaboration with Kockums, developed a powerplant comprising two Stirling motors with generators, the necessary auxiliary equipment and the liquid oxygen system. The Swedish A 19 class submarines, commissioned from 1996 to 1998, have a built-in 'hybrid' compartment for Stirling motors which offer a performance of some 200hp.

The MESMA Turbine

This turbine was developed by a syndicate comprising five French companies—Air Liquide, Bertin Technologies, DCN, Thermodyn, Technicatome—and the Spanish company E. N. Bazán.

The principle is very simple. The MESMA system is characterised by a conventional steam turbine that is fed by means of circulating fuel and oxygen, the latter being stored in a low-pressure tank. This cycle is followed by an energy cycle involving a steam generator, a turbine and a condenser. The by-products of the combustion process, with a pressure of some 60 bars, can be exhausted directly offboard without the need for a compressor.

It is unclear to the author quite why six syndicated companies were required in order to develop this simple principle: Hellmuth Walter had described it fifty years previously. There are only two (practically insignificant) differences: first, Walter decided to provide the oxygen necessary for combustion in the form of hydrogen peroxide (H_2O_2) whereas for a MESMA turbine it is in the form of a liquid at low pressure; and while Walter was designing a propulsion system offering a very high underwater speed, the MESMA turbine is designed as a propulsion system with a low underwater speed for 'stealth'.

According to information from DCN International, three such AIP propulsion systems have been sold—by France to Pakistan for the *Agosta* class boats built originally in the 1970s. The first, *Khalid*, was converted in the late 1990s at DCN in Cherbourg and the second, in a conversion lasting from 1998 until 2001, was commenced at Cherbourg and completed at Karachi. The third unit was due to have been completed at Karachi in 2002.

Fuel Cells

In electrolysis, water can be split into hydrogen and oxygen by introducing electric energy, and, as with many physical/chemical procedures, this process is reversible. It should therefore be possible, theoretically, to produce electric energy directly by bringing together hydrogen and oxygen. It is not quite as simple as that, however: bringing together gaseous hydrogen and gaseous oxygen produces not electric energy but highly explosive oxyhydrogen gas.

Historical background

The first fuel cell involving hydrogen and oxygen was built by the Englishman W. R. Grove in 1839, and at the beginning of the twentieth century the Baur'sche Schule (School of Baur) in Zürich was investigating the theory and scientific analysis in detail. However, it was only in about 1958 that scientists in Britain and the United States succeeded in producing functioning cells for the combustion of gaseous hydrogen, and these were used in the Gemini space programme amongst other projects.

In Cambridge, Francis T. Bacon built a hydrogen/oxygen cell with a working temperature of 220°C at a pressure of 20atm (kg/cm²), achieving a current density of

Below: HDW's fuel-cell research facility at Kiel.

500mA/cm² and a terminal voltage of 0.7. Union Carbide built a hydrogen/oxygen cell with electrodes manufactured from porous carbon with catalysts added. In Germany, meanwhile, Professor Dr Justi from the Technische Hochschule (Technical College) in Brunswick was also working on fuel cells

Developments at Siemens-Varta

In 1968 the Siemens-Varta team received an order, T71-802K-504, from the Bundesministerium für Verteidigung (Federal Ministry of Defence) for the development, construction and testing of a fuel-cell unit with a nominal capacity of 30kW in order to examine its suitability for use aboard submarines. Under the specifications, the unit had to function automatically and reliably, be easy to maintain and allow for extensive testing with various fuels.

Although the test results demonstrated the suitability of the system for use on submarines, the Siemens-Varta partnership was disbanded. The research undertaken resulted in a relatively heavy cell (about 60kg/kW), and there was little prospect of a practical application in the immediate future.

After 1975 Siemens concentrated on so-called 'alkaline fuel-cell technology', and in 1988 the submarine U 1 was,

Below: A cutaway showing the internal layout of a 212 Class U-boat.

prior to her use as a test-bed for closed-cycle experiments, equipped with an added hybrid fuel cell and proved its value. It also showed that, logistically, the hydrogen/oxygen supply to the cell did not create any difficulties.

At the beginning of the 1980s, however, at the request of the Bundesamt für Wehrtechnik und Beschaffung (BWB, or Federal Office for Military Technology and Procurement), Siemens switched to 'polymeric electrolyte membrane technology', because not only could this be run with pure oxygen—as with alkaline fuel cells—but it also has the potential to be run using simply air. Siemens' investigations resulted in PEM modules with a performance range of between 30 and 50kW in the 212 Class submarines intended for service in the German and Italian Navies. A further development was the 120kW module for proposed 214 Class export submarines and the second unit of the Bundesmarine's 212 Class.

The PEM fuel cell operates at a relatively low temperature (80°C). The waste heat is used to drive the hydrogen out of the metallic hydride storage unit and to vaporise the oxygen needed, which is stored in a cryogenic state (approximately normal pressure, liquid, −186°C). As the working materials hydrogen and oxygen convert almost completely into water which can be kept on board and used, there is another advantage with this technology—the mass, and thus the buoyancy, of the submarine does not alter while the fuel cells are in operation.

Walter Propulsion

Whilst it is true that the underwater performance of German U-boats of the Second World War matched that achieved in foreign navies, it was nonetheless unimpressive. The maximum speed was under 10 knots and the range less than 100nm at 4–5 knots. Figures from the First World War and from the development of U-boats up till 1936 demonstrate this, as shown in the table below. This is the situation that Hellmuth Walter encountered when he began work on his 'Unterwasser Schnellboot' (Underwater Speedboat) in the early 1930s.[39]

Helmut Walter was born on 26 August 1900 in Wedel on the Lower Elbe, the son of Ludwig and Louise. He attended primary school in Wedel. From 1910 he was a pupil at the secondary school in Hamburg-Blankenese, but he left at an early age in order to become a Marineingenieur (marine engineer). From 12 April 1917 he was a mechanical engineering apprentice at the Reiherstiegwerft in Hamburg, where he stayed for two years, and in the spring of 1921 he began to study mechanical engineering at the Technische Lehranstalten (Technical College) in Hamburg, graduating on 20 February 1923. He then joined the Vulcan-Werke Hamburg as a turbine constructor.

On 18 October 1925 he applied for his first patent, and this would be followed by almost 200 others in the course of his life. This first patent has the title 'Verfahren zur Durchführung eines Kreisprozesses, insbesondere für Gasturbinen, mit isothermischer Verichtung des Gase' (Procedure to Perform a Cyclic Process, especially for Gas Turbines, with Isothermal Compression of the Gases). After a short period of study at the Technische Hochschule (Technical College) in Berlin, in 1926 he joined the Heereswaffenamt (Army Weapons Office) in Berlin, where he was involved in the development of anti-aircraft systems.

Walter, however, maintained his fascination with the idea of propelling ships by means of gas turbines, and whenever an opportunity presented itself he pestered his colleagues from the Marineamt (Naval Office) with his theories, so much so, in fact, that they finally capitulated: in 1930 the Marineamt placed an order with Germaniawerft in Kiel for the building of a gas turbine to Walter's design—under the direction of the inventor of course. Thus he joined Germaniawerft.

From early 1933 Walter worked on his theories, concentrating on the use of hydrogen peroxide (H_2O_2) as an oxygen and energy carrier, although at that time the highest concentration available was 30 per cent. In March 1933 he wrote to Albert Pietzsch, founder of the Electrochemische Werke München (EWM), requesting information and delivery options. His powers of persuasion led to EWM working with him to raise the concentration percentage to 85.

At this point Walter approached the Navy officially, writing to the Marineleitung on 5 October 1933:

Re.: New submarine propulsion
Enclosed I am respectfully sending you draft calculations concerning the propulsive motor for a fast submarine of about 300 tonnes displacement. The same documents have been sent to the Elektrochemische Werke München AG, for the attention of President Pietzsch. In accordance with our discussions of 19 September 1933, we will begin with solving the problem of the technical apparatus, and the company mentioned above has undertaken to design the necessary apparatus to achieve the performance indicated (enclosed) and will carry out any preliminary testing in respect of that. In the meantime I myself will be endeavouring to work on individual problems such as the adjustment and changeover of the machine from using air to using oxygen.[40]

Design for an underwater speedboat (U-S-Boot)
The following design originates from the requirement to increase the surfaced and submerged speeds of submarines sufficient to enable them to be fully employed as fleet escorts. The submarine, therefore, has to be able not only to move forward with the fleet at normal combat speeds but, beyond that, to reach speeds that will allow it to manoeuvre into a favourable attacking position against a fast-moving enemy.

UNDERWATER PERFORMANCE OF U-BOATS UP TO 1936			
	Max underwater speed (kt)	Underwater range (nm @ kt)	Commissioning of first boat
Up to 1918			
MS boats	9.7	51 @ 5	U 43 (30 Apr. 1915)
UB III boats	8.0	55 @ 4	UB 60 (6 June 1917)
UC II boats	7.0	55 @ 4	UC 16 (26 June 1917)
UF design	7.0	64 @ 4	–
UG design	8.0	90 @ 3	
After 1933			
Type I A	7.3	78 @ 4	U 25 (6 Apr. 1936)
Type II A	6.9	35 @ 4	U 1 (29 June 1935)
Type VII	8.0	73–94 @ 4	U 27 (12 Aug. 1936)

On 27 December 1933 the Marineleitung placed an order for a study and on 10 April 1934 for a test unit:

Re.: Ship propulsion
On the basis of the documents presented during your last meeting with Oberbaurat (Senior Surveyor) Brandes and Baurat Braking on 15.1.1934 concerning the ship propulsion system proposed by you, I intend to go forward with the development of this system. I therefore respectfully request that you ask Germaniawerft, Kiel, to prepare the offer for the initial test unit, consisting of combustion chamber with burner, gas-circulating pipe with ventilator, and oxygen generator. At the same time, I would like to ask you to complete your proposal regarding the carbon dioxide absorption unit as soon as possible and present it at the same time.[41]

Heartened by this success, on 1 July 1935 Walter set up his own company. The fact that the 'Ingenieurbüro Walter, Kiel' could afford to employ but one co-worker for the time being did not at this stage impair its founder's enthusiasm.

The main features of Hellmuth Walter's project can be summarised thus:

1. Underwater propulsion by means of one or more turbines;
2. An oxygen supply derived from hydrogen peroxide stowed on board; and
3. An overall shape more suited to that of a genuine submarine, not a submersible that occasionally dives.

By the end of the Second World War he had produced the following:

V 80—Built at Germaniawerft, Kiel; put to sea 20 April 1940; trials on the Schiel and off Hela. Maximum underwater speed 28.1 knots, underwater range 50nm at 28 knots.
Type Wa 201—Two boats built at Blohm & Voss, Hamburg, the first (U 792) being commissioned on 16 November 1943. Maximum underwater speed 24–25 knots, underwater range 127nm at 20 knots.
Type Wk 202—Two boats built at Germaniawerft, Kiel, the first (U 794) being commissioned on 14 November 1943. Maximum underwater speed 24–25 knots, underwater range 117nm at 20 knots.
Type XVII B—Three boats completed at Blohm & Voss, Hamburg, the first (U 1405) commissioning on 21 December 1944. Maximum submerged speed 25 knots, submerged range 123nm at 25 knots.
Type XXVI W—Order for 100 U-boats placed with Blohm & Voss in 1944, and at the end of the war four were at an early stage of construction. Designed maximum underwater speed 24 knots, designed underwater range 158nm at 22 knots.

The first boat, V 80, was built by Walter as a private venture with Germaniawerft's merchant-ship division at Kiel. The other boats were developed and built by Walter in collaboration with the Kriegsmarine, although in truth the latter, and Dönitz in particular, were probably never totally persuaded of the value of Walter's ideas. For example, on 29 June 1943 Dönitz wrote to him:

Re.: Use of the Walter shapes for new U-boats
With reference to the documents provided by you regarding the design of fast submarines, and based on the development work carried out by you together with the Oberkommando der Kriegsmarine in this area, the possibility of developing a new type of submarine has emerged on the basis of a draft examined by the Oberkommando. Equipped with standard U-boat machinery, this design shows such remarkable qualities that I have ordered its speedy introduction. Irrespective of the fees that you are entitled to in such a case on the basis of the existing agreements, I would like to express my special thanks to you that, based on your ideas and preliminary work, it has been possible to initiate the development of an important new type of U-boat.
    I also hope that the initial trials of your boats, expected this autumn, are successful, because I still attach a lot of importance to the development of Walter submarines with a high underwater speed and Walter engines . . .

Hence the emergence of the Elektroboot (electrically propelled U-boat), the development of which would, apparently, be more expeditious:

Type XXI—Eleven shipyards building sections, four shipyards for assembly, the first boat (U 2501) entering service on 28 June 1944. Maximum underwater speed 17.2 knots, maximum range 30nm at 15 knots.
Type XXIII—Various shipyards, with sectional construction and assembly taking place within the same yard. First example (U 2321) commissioned 12 June 1944. Maximum submerged speed 12.5 knots, range 35nm at 10 knots.

These boats, of course, represented considerable progress with respect to the pre-war U-boats, but they did not really bear comparison with the Walter submarines, especially the Type XXVIW. At this stage of the war, however, it was probably too late for progressive ideas to take root. As Aschmoneit writes, 'The war of the engineers takes place before the war.'

None of Walter's boats ever left home waters, and none of his twenty-one different types of torpedo— also designed on the basis of turbine propulsion and hydrogen peroxide—was ever used.

Nuclear Propulsion

On 20 March 1939—a few weeks before the discovery of uranium-based nuclear fission—Ross Gunn proposed to the US Naval Research Laboratory a submarine propelled by nuclear energy. He received limited funding for research purposes but was forced to halt his work in 1942 when the 'Manhattan' project—the construction of an atomic bomb—was given the highest priority. Shortly after the war, however, Gunn resumed his research. The *New York Times* of 14 December 1945 quotes Gunn as saying that 'the main task of atomic energy is turning the wheels of the world and propelling ships.'[42]

On 5 April 1946 the American Philip Abelson designed the first atomic submarine, replacing the Walter propulsion unit of the German Type XXVIW with a sodium-graphite reactor, and that spring it was decided that a test reactor should be built at Oak Ridge, Tennessee. The US Navy participated in the project, the senior officer being Admiral Hyman G. Rickover, a man, as Rohwer writes, 'of high intelligence and iron will'.[43]

Rickover insisted that two test reactors be built immediately, in Arco, Idaho, one of them inside a trials model of a submarine's pressure hull. The units were to be pressurised-water reactors (PWR). The timetable for carrying through the project to build the world's first nuclear-powered submarine was hectic:

21 Aug. 1951	First instructions issued to Electric Boat Division and General Dynamics Corporation
14 June 1952	Keel-laying by President Truman at Groton
30 Mar. 1953	Test reactor at Arco goes critical
May 1953	Rickover makes simulated Atlantic crossing at full power with test reactor
21 Jan. 1954	*Nautilus* launched
30 Sept. 1954	*Nautilus* commissioned

All this happened in peacetime, a few years after the war, at a point in time when it was still a completely open question whether or not reactor development would follow the direction of the pressurised-water type. There was a parallel development by the General Electric Company (GEC) involving a reactor that used liquid sodium as a

Below: The USS *Nautilus*, the world's first nuclear-powered submarine.

coolant. This powerplant was later installed in the submarine USS *Seawolf*.

Nowadays the navies of China, France, Great Britain, Russia and the United States all have nuclear-powered submarines in service—ballistic-missile, cruise-missile and fleet submarines. Their sizes range from the French *Rubis* class with an underwater displacement of 2,670 tonnes to the Russian *Typhoon* class at 26,000 tonnes, with power outputs of, respectively, 9,500hp and 81,600hp.

It is difficult to judge how the development of nuclear submarines will continue. According to Weyer, today some 85 per cent of all nuclear-powered Russian submarines are not combat-ready.[44] It is not known whether other navies are planning to adopt reactor-driven main propulsion systems for submarines, but it is rather unlikely.

The cruising profile of a submarine carrying out a combat sortie will always be composed of different 'legs'—moderate speed, for example, en route to the area of operation and back, low speed while loitering and high speed for either attack or flight.

If a navy for whatever reason decides against the adoption of reactor propulsion, the only alternative, in order to cope with the different underwater cruising profiles, is some form of hybrid system. However, boats of this nature do not yet exist. All non-nuclear submarines have diesel-electric propulsion—diesel drive whilst on the surface or while snorkelling to charge their batteries and an electric motor powered by the batteries for submerged drive. The necessary additional underwater hybrid 'add-ons' are only at the developmental stage—diesel drive with closed-cycle function (Italy and Germany), Stirling motor (Sweden) or fuel cell (Germany). The performance offered by these hybrid components varies from 100kW (the experimental fuel-cell unit on the German submarine U 1) to several hundred kilowatts for the experimental diesels and Stirling motors.

If one considers that oxygen or oxygen/hydrogen supplies in these hybrid boats can last only for a limited period, and that after the consumption of these fuels the submarine once more becomes a conventional diesel-electric boat, the ideal hybrid component—the fuel resources for which last to all intents and purposes indefinitely—is a small reactor.

In this connection the experience of US space programmes is relevant. Energy converters that could be taken into consideration are turbines, thermocoupled elements and thermionic converters. Turbines and thermocoupled elements have been tested in space, although the latter have had to be eliminated for use as submarine propulsion systems because of their low efficiency and low power density. A reactor with a turbine of several 100kW of generator performance could be installed in a submarine section 6m in length and 7m in diameter—dimensions which allow for all the other auxiliary equipment shielding.

The most interesting solution, however, could be the thermionic reactor, wherein the converters are integrated into the core. Groll writes:

> With these in-core thermionic reactors, the fuel rods are surrounded by cylindrical converters that are electrically connected in series. The collectors are covered by an insulating layer which is followed by a metallic encasing tube (three layers). This makes it possible to cool the reactor in a single cycle. The cooling agent flows around the elements in an axial direction and carries the waste heat to a radiator. A number of such thermionic fuel rods make up the core, which is, again, surrounded by a reflector.
> The advantages of in-core thermionic systems are:
> (a) thermodynamically favourable direct coupling of converter and heat source at a high temperature level;
> (b) low maximum temperature of the fuel; and
> (c) its feasibility as a thermal reactor with low use of fissionable fuel.
> Disadvantages are:
> (a) possible disruptions as a consequence of chemical reactions involving fuel and emitter and diffusion of fuel and fission products by the emitter, increasing because of the release of fission gas and core growth; and
> (b) the difficulty of optimal connection of the converters—when the converters of a thermionic rod are connected in series, the breakdown of one element (for example, because of a leak) means the failure of the entire rod.[45]

In the Federal Republic of Germany, the Bundesministerium für Bildung und Wissenschaft (Federal Ministry for Education and Science) financed a research programme for a terrestrial prototype of an in-core reactor (ITR) at the beginning of the 1970s. The programme involved BBC at Mannheim, Siemens at Erlangen and Interatom at Bensberg.

During the development of the prototype, the low weight was first on the list of requirements, shielding and efficiency being of lesser importance. In a submarine, this is of course different. Nevertheless, the development of a reactor with thermionic converters offering a power output of several hundred kilowatts and its installation in a 6m by 7m (diameter) submarine compartment should be possible.

In summary, it can be said that nuclear propulsion, either as the main drive or as an auxiliary powerplant, is the most appropriate form of submarine propulsion from a technical viewpoint. In cases where such powerplants are politically unacceptable, propulsion units based on a large lead accumulator battery in conjunction with a hybrid fuel-cell battery should be the best solution for the immediate future.

The U-Boat 'Aces'

First World War

The highest military decoration of the First World War was the Pour le Mérite, and a total of 29 U-boat commanders received this award.

Below: Lothar von Arnauld de la Perière (left) and Walter Forstmann.

MOST SUCCESSFUL COMMANDERS IN THE MERCANTILE WAR, 1914–1918

Commander	Date of birth	Boat(s)	No of sorties	No of ships sunk	Aggregate tonnage (grt)
Lothar von Arnauld de la Perière	18 Mar. 1886	U 35, U 139	15	194	453,000
Walter Forstmann	9 Mar. 1883	U 12, U 39	47	146	384,000
Max Valentiner	15 Dec. 1883	U 3, U 38, U 157	24	141	299,000
Otto Steinbrinck	19 Feb. 1888	U 6, UB 10, UB 18, UC 65, UB 57	36	202	231,000
Hans Rose	15 Apr. 1885	U 53	17	79	213,000

COMMANDERS RESPONSIBLE FOR THE SINKING OF LARGE PASSENGER LINERS, 1914–1918					
Commander	Date of birth	Boat	Date of success	Name of ship	Tonnage (grt)
Walther Schwieger	7 Apr. 1885	U 20	7 May 1915	Lusitania[1]	31,600
Gustav Siess	11 Dec. 1883	U 73	21 Nov. 1916	Britannic[2]	48,200
Hans Oskar Wutsdorff	29 Nov. 1890	UB 124	20 July 1918	Justicia[3]	32,200

Over 50 other passenger ships, troop transports and auxiliary cruisers of more than 10,000grt were sunk.

Opposite, top: Max Valentiner (left) and Otto Steinbrinck.
Opposite, bottom: The *Britannic*, sunk on 21 November 1916 by Gustav Siess, commander of U 73.
Above: The RMS *Lusitania*, the sinking of which, on 7 May 1915 by Walter Schwieger (U 20), did much to bring the United States into the war against Germany two years later.
Below: The *Justicia*, sunk on 20 July 1918 by UB 124 under the command of Hans Oskar Wutsdorff.

MOST SUCCESSFUL COMMANDERS IN ATTACKS ON LARGE WARSHIPS, 1914–1918

Commander	Date of birth	Boat	Date of success	Name (type) of warship	Nationality	Displacement (tonnes)
Otto Weddigen	15 Sept. 1882	U 9	22 Sept. 1914	*Aboukir* (armoured cruiser)	British	12,000
			22 Sept. 1914	*Cressy* (armoured cruiser)	British	12,000
			22 Sept. 1914	*Hogue* (armoured cruiser)	British	12,000
			15 Oct. 1914	*Hawke* (armoured cruiser)	British	7,400
Otto Hersing	30 Nov. 1885	U 21	5 Sept. 1914	*Pathfinder* (light cruiser)	British	2,900
			25 May 1915	*Triumph* (battleship)	British	11,800
			27 May 1915	*Majestic* (battleship)	British	14,900
			11 Feb 1916	*Admiral Charner* (armoured cruiser)	French	8,700

Above: The First World War U-boat U 9, which accounted for three British armoured cruisers in the space of just over an hour on 22 September 1914.
Right: Otto Weddigen, the successful commander of U 9.
Opposite page: Two of Weddigen's victims: the armoured cruisers *Aboukir* (top) and *Cressy*.

MOST SUCCESSFUL COMMANDERS IN ATTACKS ON WARSHIPS, 1914–1918

Commander	Date of birth	Boat	Date of success	Name (type) of warship	Nationality	Disp'ment (tonnes)
Egewolf Freiherr von Berckheim	2 July 1881	U 26	11 Oct. 1914	*Palladev* (armoured cruiser)	Russian	7,800
Bernd Wegener	22 May 1884	U 27	31 Oct. 1914	*Hermes* (light cruiser)	British	5,700
Rudolf Schneider	13 Feb. 1882	U 24	1 Jan. 1915	*Formidable* (battleship)	British	14,500
Heino Adolf von Heimburg	24 Oct. 1889	UB 14	7 July 1915	*Amalfi* (armoured cruiser)	Italian	10,400
Georg Haag	23 Apr. 1889	UC 7	11 Feb. 1916	*Arethusa* (light cruiser)	British	4.,300
Franz Becker	3 June 1888	UC 14	16 Apr. 1916	*Regina Margherita* (battleship)	Italian	13,215
Gustav Siess	11 Dec. 1883	U 73	27 Apr. 1916	*Russell* (battleship)	British	14,000
Curt Beitzen	21 May 1885	U 75	5 June 1916	*Hampshire* (armoured cruiser)	British	10,900
Hans Walther	25 Dec. 1883	U 52	19 Aug. 1916	*Nottingham* (light cruiser)	British	5,500
Otto Schultze	11 May 1884	U 63	20 Aug. 1916	*Falmouth* (light cruiser)	British	5,300
Hans Walther	25 Dec. 1883	U 52	26 Nov. 1916	*Suffren* (battleship)	French	12,500
Wolfgang Steinbauer	6 May 1888	UB 47	27 Dec. 1916	*Gaulois* (battleship)	French	11,100
Gustav Siess	11 Dec. 1883	U 73	4 Jan. 1917	*Peresvyet* (battleship)	Russian	12,700
Kurt Hartwig	21 Jan. 1887	U 32	9 Jan. 1917	*Cornwallis* (battleship)	British	13,700
Robert Wilhelm Morath	7 Sept. 1884	U 64	19 Mar. 1917	*Danton* (battleship)	French	19,800
Georg Gerth	3 Mar. 1888	UC 61	27 June 1917	*Kléber* (armored cruiser)	French	7,600
Otto Steinbrinck	19 Dec. 1888	UC 65	26 July 1917	*Ariadne* (armoured cruiser)	British	11,000
Otto August Theodor Rohrbeck	8.12 1882	U 79	2 Oct. 1917	*Drake* (armoured cruiser)	British	14,200
Hans Hermann Wendland	5 June 1887	UC 38	14 Dec. 1917	*Châteaurenault* (armoured cruiser)	French	7,900
Richard Feldt	24 Sept. 1882	U 156	19 July 1918	*San Diego* (armoured cruiser)	US	15,100
Ernst Hashagen	24 Aug. 1885	U 62	7 Aug. 1918	*Dupetit Thouars* (armoured cruiser)	French	9,400
Heinrich Kukat	2 Mar. 1891	UB 50	9 Nov. 1918	*Britannia* (battleship)	British	15,900

U 35: THE MOST SUCCESSFUL U-BOAT OF WORLD WAR I

Commander	Date of birth	No of sorties	Ships sunk	Aggregate tonnage (grt)
Waldemar Kophamel	16 Aug. 1880	8	35	89,000
Lothar von Arnauld de la Perière	18 Mar. 1886	14	189	447,000
Ernst von Voigt	16 June 1888	2	–	–
Heino von Heimburg	24 Oct. 1889	1	–	–
		25	224	536,000

U 39, U 38: THE NEXT MOST SUCCESSFUL U-BOATS

Commander	Date of birth	Boat	Ships sunk	Aggregate tonnage (grt)
Walter Forstmann	9 Mar. 1883	U 39	151	399,000
Max Valentiner	15 Dec. 1883	U 38	136	293,000

Opposite, top: The British pre-dreadnought battleship *Majestic*.
Opposite, bottom: The British pre-dreadnought *Triumph*.
Left: Otto Hersing (U 21), who was responsible for sinking both of these elderly vessels.

Amongst the smaller U-boats of the First World War, the following, from U-Flottille Flandern (Flanders Flotilla) were the most successful:

UB 40 Commanders Karl Neumann, Karl Dobberstehn and Hans J. Emsmann between them made 28 sorties and sank a total of 106 vessels with an aggregate tonnage of 160,000.

UC 21 Commanders Reinhold Salzwedel and Werner von Zerboni accounted for 93 enemy ships totalling 130,000grt, 10,000grt of which were as a result of mines.

The most successful sorties were conducted in the Mediterranean. There, under the command of Lothar von Arnauld de la Perière, U 35 sank 54 ships totalling 90,000grt between 26 July and 20 August 1916.

Right: Kapitänleutnant von Arnauld de la Perière (right) with a Maat and a Wachoffizier on the bridge of U 35.

Second World War

High military decorations during the Second World War began with the Ritterkreuz zum Eisernen Kreuz (Knight's Cross of the Iron Cross), and a total of 121 U-boat commanders received this award. More outstanding achievements were marked with the Eichenlaub (Oak Leaves) to the Knight's Cross, in receipt of which were 28 command-ers. During the course of the war three grades were established: the award of Schwerter (Swords) was made five times and the very highest decoration, Brillianten (Diamonds), went to Wolfgang Lüth and Albrecht Brandi.

The Iron Cross was also awarded to fourteen Chief Engineers and seven other-ranks in the U-Boat Service.

MOST SUCCESSFUL COMMANDERS IN THE MERCANTILE WAR, 1939–1945

Commander	Date of birth	Boat(s)	No of sorties	No of ships sunk	Aggregate tonnage (grt)
Otto Kretschmer	1 May 1912	U 23 (Type IIB), U 99 (Type VIIB)	16	44	266,000
Wolfgang Lüth	15 Oct. 1913	U 9 (Type IIB), U 13 (Type IIB), U 138 (Type IID), U 43 (Type IXA), U 181 (Type IXD$_2$)	15	43	225,000
Erich Topp	2 July 1914	U 57 (Type IIC), U 552 (Type VIIC), U 3010 (Type XXI), U 2513 (Type XXI)	14	34	193,000
Karl Friedrich Merten	15 Aug. 1906	U 68 (Type IXC)	5	29	180,000
Viktor Schütze	16 Feb. 1906	U 25 (Type IA), U 103 (Type IXB)	7	34	171,000
Herbert Emil Schultze	24 July 1909	U 25 (Type IIA), U 2 (Type IIA), U 48 (Type VIIB),	8	26	171,000

Opposite (left to right): Otto Kretschmer, Wolfgang Lüth and Erich Topp.
Above (left to right): Karl-Friedrich Merten, Victor Schütze and Herbert Emil Schultze.

COMMANDERS RESPONSIBLE FOR THE SINKING OF LARGE PASSENGER LINERS, 1939–1945

Commander	Date of birth	Boat	Date of success	Name of ship	Tonnage (grt)
Engelbert Endrass	2 Mar. 1885	U 20 (Type VIIB)	6 June 1940	*Carinthia*	20,300
Hans Jemisch	19 Mar. 1913	U 32 (Type VII)	28 Oct. 1940	*Empress of Britain*[4]	42,300
Werner Hartenstein	27 Feb. 1908	U 156 (Type IXC)	12 Sept. 1942	*Laconia*[5]	19,700
Carl Emmermann	6 Mar. 1915	U 172 (Type IXC)	10 Oct. 1942	*Orcades*	23,500
Hans Ibbeken	20 Sept. 1899	U 178 (Type IXD$_2$)	10 Oct. 1942	*Duchess of Atholl*	20,100
Ernst-Ulrich Brüller	23 Sept. 1917	U 407 (Type VIIC)	11 Nov. 1942	*Viceroy of India*	19,600
Gustav Poel	2 Aug. 1917	U 413 (Type VIIC)	14 Nov. 1942	*Warwick Castle*	20,100
Horst Hamm	17 Mar. 1916	U 562 (Type VIIC)	21 Dec. 1942	*Strathallan*	23,700

Over 130 other passenger ships, troop transports, auxiliary cruisers, tankers and whaling vessels of more than 10,000grt were sunk.

MOST SUCCESSFUL COMMANDERS IN ATTACKS ON WARSHIPS, 1939–1945

Commander	Date of birth	Boat	Date of success	Name (type) of warship	Nation-ality	Disp'ment (tonnes)
Otto Schuhart	1 Apr. 1909	U 29 (Type VII)	17 Sept. 1939	*Courageous* (aircraft carrier)	British	22,500
Günther Prien	16 Jan. 1908	U 47 (Type VIIB)	14 Oct. 1939	*Royal Oak* (battleship)	British	31,250
Friedrich Guggenberger	6 Mar. 1915	U 81 (Type VIIC)	13 Nov. 1941	*Ark Royal* (aircraft carrier)	British	27,000
Hans Dietrich Freiherr von Thiesenhausen	22 Feb. 1913	U 331 (Type VIIC)	25 Nov. 1941	*Barham* (battleship)	British	31,300
Helmut Rosenbaum	11 May 1913	U 73 (Type VIIB)	11 Aug. 1942	*Eagle* (aircraft carrier)	British	22,600

Left, upper: The *Empress of Britain*.
Left, lower: *Laconia*, sunk by U 156.
This page: U-boat commanders and
their victims: (top to bottom) Schuhart
(HMS *Courageous*), Prien (HMS *Royal
Oak*) and Guggenberger (HMS *Ark
Royal*).

Above: The British battleship HMS *Barham*, sunk by Thiesenhausen (U 331).
Below: The aircraft carrier HMS *Eagle*, victim of U 73 (Rosenbaum, seen at right).

OTHER SUCCESSFUL COMMANDERS IN ATTACKS ON WARSHIPS, 1939–1945

Commander	Date of birth	Boat	Date of success	Name (type) of warship	Nation-ality	Disp'ment (tonnes)
Joachim Mohr	12 June 1916	U 124 (Type IXB)	24 Nov. 1941	*Dunedin* (light cruiser)	British	4,850
Ottokar Paulsen	11 Nov. 1915	U 557 (Type VIIC)	15 Dec. 1941	*Galatea* (light cruiser)	British	5,300
Gerhard Bigalk	28 Nov. 1915	U 751 (Type VIIC)	21 Dec. 1941	*Audacity* (escort carrier)	British	11,000
Johann Jebsen	21 Apr. 1916	U 565 (Type VIIC)	10 Mar. 1942	*Naiad* (light cruiser)	British	5,600
Max-Martin Teichert	31 Jan. 1915	U 456 (Type VIIC)	30 Apr. 1942	*Edinburgh*[6] (light cruiser)	British	10,600
Franz Georg Reschke	26 May 1908	U 205 (Type VIIC)	16 June 1942	*Hermione* (light cruiser)	British	5,600
Hans Joachim Neumann	29 Apr. 1909	U 372 (Type VIIC)	30 June 1942	*Medway* (submarine depot ship)	British	14,700
Werner Henke	13 May 1909	U 515 (Type IXC)	11 Nov. 1942	*Hecla* (destroyer depot ship)	British	11,000
Adolf Cornelius Piening	16 Sept. 1910	U 155 (Type IXC)	15 Nov. 1942	*Avenger* (escort carrier)	British	13,785
Albrecht Brandi	20 June 1914	U 617 (Type VIIC)	1 Feb. 1943	*Welshman* (fast minelayer)	British	2,650
Horst-Arno Fenski	3 Nov. 1918	U 410 (Type VIIC)	18 Feb. 1944	*Penelope* (light cruiser)	British	5,300
Detlev Krankenhagen	3 July 1917	U 549 (Type IXC/40)	29 May 1944	*Block Island* (escort carrier)	US	9,400
Hans-Jürgen Sthamer	26 July 1919	U 354 (Type VIIC)	22 Aug. 1944	*Nabob* (escort carrier)	British	11,400
Jürgen Kuhlmann	3 Mar. 1920	U 1172 (Type VIIC)	15 Jan. 1945	*Thane*[7] (escort carrier)	British	11,400

U 48 (TYPE VIIB): THE MOST SUCCESSFUL U-BOAT OF WORLD WAR II

Commander	Date of birth	No of sorties	Ships sunk	Aggregate tonnage (grt)
Horst Schulze	24 July 1909	8	28	183,000
Hans Rudolf Rösing	28 Sept. 1905	2	12	60,000
Heinrich Bleichrodt	21 Oct. 1909	2	14	78,000
		12	54	321,000

Bleichrodt also sank one naval vessel of 1,000 tonnes.

U 99, U 103, U 124, U 107: THE NEXT MOST SUCCESSFUL U-BOATS

Commander(s)	Date of birth	Boat	Aggregate tonnage (grt)
Otto Kretschmer	1 May 1912	U 99 (Type VIIB)	245,000
Viktor Schütze,	16 Feb. 1906		
Werner Winter	26 Mar. 1912	U 103 (Type IXB)	231,000
Gustav-Adolf Janssen	9 Apr. 1915		
Johann Mohr	12 June 1916	U 124 (Type IXB)	218,000
Günther Hessler	16 Sept. 1909		
Harald Gelhaus	24 July 1915	U 107 (Type IXB)	217,000
Volker Simmermacher	1 Feb. 1919		

The most successful sortie was that led by Hessler between 19 March and 2 July 1941, during which U 107 sank fourteen ships totalling 86,000grt.

Above: Diamonds holder Albrecht Brandi.

U-Boat Decoys

As a defence against the threat posed by submarines, the Royal Navy and the French, Italian and German Navies all employed 'traps'. These were inconspicuous, often small steam or sailing ships equipped with concealed guns, and in some instances also with torpedoes and depth charges. Some of these decoy ships even towed a small submarine (British 'C' class) by means of a telephone cable.

The idea behind decoy ships was that enemy submarines would be attracted by seemingly defenceless targets and surface in order to attack them with gunfire. The vessel's gun crew lay low as the submarine approached and the so-called 'Panikcrew' abandoned ship in order to lull the attacker into a false sense of security. Once this had happened the deceit was revealed and the ship opened fire.

In the First World War the British employed this tactic extensively: over 200 of these armed vessels—'Q-ships'—were put into service, and the ploy was successful on fourteen occasions: U 23, U 27, U 36, U 40, U 41, U 68, U 83,

U 85, UB 4, UB 19, UB 37, UC 18, UC 29, UC 72 fell victim in this way. The Austro-Hungarian Navy did not lose any U-boats by this means, however.

A number of engagements, for example that between the Q-ship *Prince Charles* against U 36 on 24 July 1915[1] and that involving *Baralong* and U 27 on 16 August 1915,[2] were not fought in a chivalrous manner as survivors were, reportedly, fired at while in the water. During the course of the First World War German U-boats sank nineteen Q-ships,[3] and the Austro-Hungarian U 28 sank one.[4]

With the appearance of British submarines in the Baltic Sea, the Kaiserliche Marine also employed decoy ships in 1915 and 1916, one of them, *Hermann* (2,030grt) sinking two submarines, the Russian *Gepard* and the British E 18.[5]

During the Second World War these ploys were used again by both the Allies and the Germans, but their significance was limited.

U-Tankers

It was the original intention of the Marineführung (German Naval Command) to use surface vessels for supplying U-boats at sea, but during the early 1930s these plans were put on hold in favour of constructing combat submarines for the purpose. This was the genesis for the Type XIV supply boat of 1940. The design was based on the Type IXD$_1$, but the hull was shorter, beamier and deeper in draught, and had a flatter upper deck to facilitate the transfer of supplies. Many components from the Type VII were incorporated, and the Type IX's conning tower structure was retained.[1]

The stowage capacity, for delivery to U-boats on patrol, included 430 cubic metres of diesel oil, lubricants, fresh water, foodstuffs and spare parts. In addition, each Type XIV could carry out basic repairs, offer medical facilities, exchange crews and even deliver freshly baked bread. Their armament comprised only 3.7cm and 2cm anti-aircraft guns. Diving time was relatively long, at about 50–60 seconds.

All ten of these U-boats were built by Deutsche Werke, Kiel:

Boat	Commissioned	No of supply sorties
U 459	November 1941	6
U 460	December 1941	6
U 461	January 1942	6
U 462	March 1942	7
U 463	April 1942	5
U 464	April 1942	1
U 487	December 1942	2
U 488	February 1943	3
U 489	March 1942	1
U 490	March 1943	1

All ten of the boats were lost during the war: four were discovered by chance and six were lost either because their wireless transmissions were intercepted and decoded or because they were detected by radar.[2] U 462 and U 489 were sunk by surface vessels, the other eight boats by air attack. A further three boats of the type—U 491, U 492 and U 493—were cancelled when 75 per cent complete.[3]

Large Type XB minelayers were also employed as supply boats, all eight being built by Germaniawerft, Kiel:

Boat	Commissioned	No of sorties
U 116	July 1941	3
U 117	October 1941	4
U 118	December 1941	4
U 119	April 1942	3 (2 as supply boat)
U 219	December 1942	1 (plus 1 supply sortie to Japan, May 1943)
U 220	March 1943	1
U 233	September 1943	1 as minelayer
U 234	March 1944	1 supply sortie (boat surrendered in Central Atlantic, May 1945)

In addition to a few operational sorties as a combat submarine, U A (ex *Batiray*) also carried out one supply sortie. To begin with, the transfer of supplies was conducted by means of hoses under tow, but then she and the receiving boat ran abeam of each other at 3–5 knots.

One supply boat could extend the deployment of twelve Type VIIs by four weeks,[4] and it has been estimated that altogether some 500 supply rendezvous were conducted during the war.

U-Boat Bunkers

As well as the submarine, the First World War witnessed the introduction of another revolutionary type of weapon—the aeroplane. Now the seas could be observed from aloft, especially the waters traversed by submarines entering or leaving port; moreover, the boats themselves became obvious targets for attack while moored, prompting measures designed to offer protection for these valuable resources.[1]

The first protective structures, technically and organisationally primitive, were built at Brügge, where two roofed-over berths—Kragunterstände, literally 'overhanging shelters'—70m and 20m in length were constructed alongside the quay. Iron 'T' girders 0.5m in width were laid over the quay walls and connected to each other, with a covering consisting of sheet metal, sacks of cement and planks. However, this only provided screening from prying eyes and a small measure of splinter protection.

Two shelters with roofs measuring 70m by 10m were then constructed. The covering consisted of planks, earth and concrete supported by wooden beams. Each of these shelters could accommodate five UC type boats and provided protection against light bombs.

Finally at Brügge, one bunker with eight compartments, each measuring 62m in length, 8.8m in width and 6m in internal height, was built using wooden beams and with a roof strong enough to offer protection against bombs (although it was never tested). Its characteristics were similar to the later bunkers of the Second World War.

At Zeebrügge, two Kragunterstände were built, together with two shelters some 70m by 10m in dimensions, similar to those Brügge but with a concrete roof supported by pillars. At Ostend, two Kragunterstände, a shelter similar to those at Brügge and Zeebrügge, a floating dock shelter and a roofed dry dock were constructed.

Bombs used during the early months of the First World War weighed as little as 5kg, though they were reaching some 700kg towards the end of the conflict. Even so, none of these structures, nor the U-boats they were designed to protect, were ever damaged.

Plans for more viable U-boat bunkers were well advanced before the beginning of the war in 1939. The first objective was, again, to protect berths and equipment, and to enable workers to carry out minor repairs unmolested. Further developments, however, led to the demand in 1940 for the building of complete independent shipyard bases

Below: U-boat bunker at Brügge, First World War.

U-BOAT BUNKER FACILITIES IN GERMANY, 1939–1945

Location	Name	Size (length × breadth) (m)	Roof thickness (m)	No of compartments (dry + wet = total)	Capacity (no of boats)	When built
Hamburg	*Elbe II*	137 × 62	3	0 + 2 = 2	6	Dec. 1940–1941
	(Fitting-out and repair bunker at the Howaldtswerft shipyard.)					
Hamburg	*Fink II*	151 × 153	3.6	0 + 5 = 5	15	Mar. 1941–1944
	(Deutsche Werft fitting-out facility for Type IXC and XXIII U-boats.)					
Heligoland	*Nordsee II*	156 × 88	3	0 + 3 = 3	9	Jan. 1940–June 1943
	(Satellite base for Kriegsmarinewerft Wilhelmshaven—Wilhelmshaven Naval Dockyard—capable of undertaking minor repair work.)					
Kiel	*Kilian*	176 × 79	4.8	0 + 2 = 2	12	Nov. 1941–Nov. 1943
	(Howaldtswerft facility for completion and new construction for Germaniawerft, Deutsche Werke and Howaldts and repairs for front-line and training boats.)					
Kiel	*Konrad*	163 × 35	3.5	1 + 0 = 1	5	Apr. 1943–Oct. 1944
	(Roofed Dock III at Deutschen Werke for completion and new construction and for building sections of Type XXI U-boats and Seehunde.)					
Bremen	*Hornisse*	362 × 68	4.5	–	–	Mar. 1944 (not completed)
	(Bunkered building facility for building sections of Type XXI U-boats.)					
Bremen	*Valentin*	450 × 100	7.3	–	–	Feb. 1943 (not completed)
	(Bunker with production line for final assembly of Type XXI U-boat sections. Work halted Mar. 1945 when 90 per cent complete following two air raids which devastated the site.)					

U-BOAT BUNKER FACILITIES IN FRANCE, 1941–1944

Location	Name	Size (length × breadth) (m)	Roof thickness (m)	No of compartments (dry + wet = total)	Capacity (no of boats)	When built
Brest	–	192 × 333	6.2	10 + 5 = 15	20	Jan. 1941–July 1942
	(For Kriegsmarinewerft, Wilhelmshaven, and from 1943 Deschimag, Bremen. First compartment used from Sept. 1941. Largest bunker built, requiring over 500,000 cubic metres of concrete.)					
Lorient	*Dom*	81 × 16	1.5	2 + 0 = 2	2	Feb.–May 1941
	(From Nov. 1942 used only for storage of equipment etc.)					
	Scorff	129 × 51	3.5	0 + 2 = 2	4	Apr.–Aug. 1941
	(Fitting-out facility)					
	Keroman I	403 × 146	3.5	5 + 0 = 5	5	Mar.–Sept. 1941
	Keroman II	403 × 146	3.5	7 + 0 = 7	7	May–Dec. 1941
	Keroman III	168 × 142	7.5	5 + 2 = 7	13	Oct. 1941–July 1943
	Keroman IVa	160 × 130	7	4 + 1 = 5	24	July 1943 (not completed)
	Keroman IVb	95 × 150	7	3 + 0 = 3	–	–
	(For Type XXI U-boats. Construction halted Apr. 1944.)					
	(Lorient was the site of the largest U-boat bunker complex. Construction and workforce via Wilhelmshaven.)					
St-Nazaire	–	291 × 124	7	8 + 6 = 14	20	Mar. 1941–Jan. 1942
	(Personnel predominantly from Kriegsmarinewerft, Wilhelmshaven. Four compartments ready after four months' work; in commission June 1941.)					
La Pallice	–	195 × 165	7.3	7 + 3 = 10	13	Apr. 1941–Mar. 1943
	(Construction and workforce via Wilhelmshaven and Bremer Werft Weser A. G.)					
Bordeaux	–	232 × 160	5.6	7 + 4 = 11	15	Sept. 1941–May 1943
	(Construction, personnel and materials via Blohm & Voss, Hamburg.)					
Marseille	*Martha*	? × 230	?	? + ? = 13	20	Jan. 1943 (not completed)
	(Concrete prepared for workshop facility only; abandoned Aug. 1944.)					

with dry docks for major repairs, and in 1942 there were even plans for complete, bunkered shipyards.

With the occupation of Norway and France, new operational bases became available to the U-boats, offering short—and safer—outbound transits into the Atlantic. As a result, plans for bunkers in Germany assumed less importance, in favour of protective structures in the occupied countries. The accompanying tables give details of all U-boat bunkers either built and put into commission or begun but not completed.

There was also serious consideration of the further expansion of bunker capacities. Apart from German sites at Bremen, Danzig, Hamburg and Kiel, additional bunkers on the Atlantic and Mediterranean coasts of France as well as in Constanta (Romania) and Salonika all came into the reckoning However, none of these plans saw fruition.

Experiences from the early years of bunker construction resulted in improvements towards the end of the war. For example, there was better co-operation between construction and shipyard experts at the planning stage: in order to be able provide first-class equipment and repair facilities for U-boats, a complete and self-sufficient integration of all the various tasks had to be achieved.

Despite numerous air attacks, the threat to the bunkers was negligible until 1943–44, but the introduction by the Royal Air Force of new, more powerful bombs in 1944–45—the 5.4-tonne 'Tallboy', the 10-ton 'Grand Slam' and the 2-tonne armour-piercing, rocket-propelled projectile—made them vulnerable. Numerous direct hits were scored, and although the 3–7m thick concrete roofs held well, in a number of instances they were penetrated. Plans to introduce further concrete reinforcement (7–10m), although in some instances put in hand, were never completed.

Most of these bunkers were ready on schedule, making it possible for the Kriegsmarine to equip and repair its U-boats through to the last months of the war.

U 136 at Lorient, showing part of the bunker complex.

U-BOAT BUNKER FACILITIES IN NORWAY, 1941–1944

Location	Name	Size (length × breadth) (m)	Roof thickness (m)	No of compartments (dry + wet = total)	Capacity (no of boats)	When built
Bergen	*Bruno*	131 × 143	6	3 + 3 = 6	9	Nov. 1941–July 1944
	(Care and maintenance site for Danziger Werft, usable from July 1944 though only 85 per cent complete.)					
Trondheim	*Dora I*	153 × 105	3.5	3 + 2 = 5	7	Apr. 1941–July 1943
	(Supervised by Germaniawerft with facility for repairing 15 U-boats or seven from July 1943.)					
	Dora II	167 × 102	3.5	2 + 2 = 4	6	Jan. 1942 (not completed)
	(Only 65 per cent completed; not suitable for use.)					

U-Boats in the Mediterranean and Black Sea

First World War

From 28 July 1914, the First World War saw Austria-Hungary and Germany on the one side drawn up against Serbia, Russia, France, Great Britain and Japan on the other. Initially, Austria-Hungary's navy controlled the Adriatic Sea, but this situation changed with Italy's declaration of war on the Dual Monarchy on 23 May 1915. Turkey (1914) and Bulgaria (1915) joined the Central Powers; later Romania (1916) and Greece (1917) joined the Entente.

The relationship between Germany and Italy needs to be explained. When Italy declared war on Austria-Hungary, Germany broke off diplomatic relations with Italy and let her know that she, Germany, supported the Austro-Hungarian monarchy. On 28 August 1916 Italy also declared war on Germany. The *de facto* circumstances thus became *de jure*.

The weakness of the Austro-Hungarian submarine forces and problems with their Turkish allies in the Dardanelles and Black Sea areas prompted the Kaiserliche Marine to prepare to transfer German U-boats to the theatre. To begin with, UB and UC type boats were dismantled and taken to Pola by rail, reassembly in the Marinearsenal Pola requiring some two weeks' work. The first three U-boats—UB 7, UB 8 and UB 3—were ready for combat from the end of March onwards. In May 1915 all three put to sea for Constantinople, though UB 3 was lost to unknown causes. Gradually, more U-boats arrived from Germany, and by 1915 they were also operating in the Adriatic Sea and the Mediterranean, resulting in clashes with Italian naval forces and merchant ships.

UB 15, for example, was reassembled at Pola and recommissioned on 4 June 1915. On 10 June she sank the Italian submarine *Medusa* off Venice. On 18 June she was handed over to the Austro-Hungarian Navy and put into service as U 11. UC 12 was placed in service at Pola on 27 June the same year but was lost on 16 March 1916 when one of her mines detonated as she was laying them in the harbour at Taranto. When these events came to pass, Italy and Germany were not technically at war. The Italians later raised UC 12 and, following repairs, put her back into service on 13 April 1917 as X 1.

The Entente partners gradually came to realise that German U-boats were at large in the Mediterranean; the Central Powers, for their part, were anxious to forestall diplomatic incidents, create confusion as to the number and bases of the U-boats operating there and organise a simple system of co-ordination. For this reason, all German U-boats in the theatre received an Austro-Hungarian number designation and flew the Austro-Hungarian flag. The Austro-Hungarian Navy did not distinguish between fleet, coastal and minelaying submarines and allocated these numbers consecutively. The U-boats were always under German command, manned by German crews in German uniforms, although, in a change of policy, from 1 October 1916 only U 35 (SM 35), U 38 (SM 38) and U 39 (SM 39) flew the Austro-Hungarian flag.

The first fleet submarine to arrive at Pola was U 21 (Hersing), on 13 May 1915. She was quickly into action, sinking two old British battleships on 25 and 27 May off the Dardanelles, thereby making a considerable contribution to the relief of Gallipoli. The torpedo-boats A 51 (250 tonnes) and A 82 (380) were also shipped to the Marine-arsenal, by rail, to serve as tenders at Pola.

During the war a total of 59 German U-boats (13 fleet submarines, 26 UB type and 20 UC type) operated in the Mediterranean and Black Seas. The 59 deployed in the Mediterranean area sank over 3,000,000grt of merchant tonnage together with numerous warships.[1] Deployments at Pola, Cattaro and Constantinople, and in the Black Sea (Varna), were organised flexibly according to requirements. The biggest successes were achieved against merchant traffic in the Mediterranean.

The formidable Russian Black Sea Fleet, comprising five battleships, two cruisers, ten torpedo boats, several minelayers and a number of submarines, threatened the Turkish coast and especially the transportation of coal from Anatolia for the industrial areas around Constantinople as well as for the requirements of the Turkish Navy. The mine played an important role in this theatre, and on occasion as many as ten U-boats were transferred from the

DEPLOYMENT OF U-BOATS IN THE MEDITERRANEAN, 1915–1918 (KuK no = Austro-Hungarian number)

No	KuK no	Remarks	No	KuK no	Remarks
Fleet boats (13)			UB 50	81	Returned to Germany
U 21	51/36	First boat in-theatre via sea route, 13 May 1915; returned to Germany 5 Feb. 1917; surrendered	UB 51	82	Returned to Germany
			UB 52	83	Sunk
			UB 53	84	Sunk
			UB 66	66	Sunk
U 32	37	Sunk	UB 68	68	Sunk
U 33	33	Returned to Germany	UB 69	69	Sunk
U 34	34	Sunk	UB 70	70	Sunk
U 35	35	Returned to Germany 7 Sept. 1918; surrendered	UB 71	71	Sunk
			UB 105	97	Returned to Germany
U 38	38	Returned to Germany 9 July 1918; surrendered	UB 128	54	Returned to Germany
			UB 129	55	Scuttled
U 39	39	Interned in Spain; surrendered			
U 47	36	Scuttled at Pola	*UC (coastal) minelayers (20)*		
U 63	63/83	Returned to Germany	UC 12	24 B	Sunk
U 64	64	Sunk	UC 13	25 B	Sunk
U 65	65	Scuttled at Pola	UC 14	18 B	Decommissioned at Pola 22 October 1916; returned to Germany by rail
U 72	72	Scuttled at Cattaro			
U 73	73	Scuttled at Pola	UC 15	19 B	Sunk
			UC 20	60	Returned to Germany
UB ((coastal) boats (26)			UC 22	62	Returned to Germany
UB 1	10 B	KuK U 10 from 12 July 1915	UC 23	63/83	Decommissioned st Sevastopol; surrendered
UB 3	9 B	Sunk			
UB 7	7 B	Sunk	UC 24	88	Sunk
UB 8	8 B	To Bulgaria 25 May 1916	UC 25	89	Scuttled
UB 14	26 B	Decommissioned at Sevastopol; surrendered	UC 27	90	Returned to Germany
			UC 34	74	Scuttled
UB 15	11 B	KuK U 11 from 18 June 1915	UC 35	75	Sunk
UB 42	42 B	Decommissioned at Sevastopol; surrendered	UC 37	77	Decommissioned at Sevastopol, surrendered
UB 43	43 B	KuK U 43 from 30 July 1917	UC 38	78	Sunk
UB 44	44 B	Sunk	UC 52	94	Returned to Germany
UB 45	45 B	Sunk	UC 53	95	Scuttled
UB 46	46 B	Sunk	UC 54	96	Scuttled
UB 47	47 B	KuK U 47 from 30 July 1917	UC 67	91	Returned to Germany
UB 48	79	Scuttled	UC 73	92	Returned to Germany
UB 49	80	Returned to Germany	UC 74	93	Interned in Spain; surrendered

Mediterranean to the Black Sea in order to disrupt the Russians' activities. A ceasefire was agreed with Russia with effect from 15/16 December 1917, but the negotiations with the Soviets were finalised only in February of 1918. Nevertheless, restlessness in the region continued

The war ended on 1 November 1918 following the conclusion of treaties with the Entente. The last German U-boats in the Black Sea—UB 14, UB 42, UC 23 and UC 37—were decommissioned at Sevastopol.

Second World War

The Mediterranean
On 10 June 1940 Italy declared war on France and Great Britain, leading to the outbreak of hostilities in the Mediterranean. Italian attacks were directed at the Alpine region and the south coast of France, just before the end of the German Western campaign on 22 June 1940. In Libya—

at that time an Italian colony—an offensive in the direction of Egypt was launched, but, after some initial successes, this was halted and beaten back by British troops.

From October 1940 onwards Italy attacked Greece (from Albania), but the assault got bogged down. The Italian Fleet, the strongest in the Mediterranean,[2] could neither achieve naval supremacy nor assure the safety of the supply line to North Africa—nor, for that matter, neutralise the strategically vital island of Malta, with its British bases and facilities—despite that fact that the Italian submarine fleet was, in terms of numbers of vessels, more than twice as big as its surface fleet. The French Navy had by this time been removed from the war under the terms of the Armistice with Germany.

In February 1941 German troops started to be deployed to North Africa (the Afrika Korps, under Rommel), and, against the firm advice of the Befehlshaber der U-Boote (BdU, or Commander U-Boats) the Seekriegsleitung (SKL, or Naval Warfare Command) recommended sending

U-BOATS DEPLOYED IN THE MEDITERRANEAN, 1941–1944			
U 73	U 303	U 450	U 595
U 64	U 331	U 453	U 596
U 75	U 343	U 455	U 602
U 77	U 371	U 458	U 605
U 79	U 372	U 466	U 616
U 81	U 374	U 471	U 617
U 83	U 375	U 557	U 642
U 95	U 380	U 559	U 652
U 133	U 409	U 562	U 755
U 205	U 410	U 565	U 952
U 223	U 414	U 568	U 960
U 224	U 421	U 573	U 967
U 230	U 431	U 577	U 969
U 259	U 433	U 586	
U 301	U 443	U 593	

German U-boats to the Mediterranean, thereby weakening the 'tonnage war' being waged in the North Atlantic.

Whereas the numerous German motor torpedo boats and minesweepers were transferred to the Mediterranean theatre via rivers and canals, all the U-boats had to use the sea route and pass through the Strait of Gibraltar. A total of 62 U-boats—four Type VIIBs and 58 Type VIICs—reached the Mediterranean for combat duty between September 1941 and September 1944. All were lost

The returns for this deployment comprised one battleship, two aircraft carriers, five cruisers, nineteen destroyers, thirteen other warships and 116 merchantmen with an aggregate tonnage of 470,000.[3] The Italians dropped out of the war after a truce was agreed with the Allied forces on 3 September 1943, making German U-boat activities that much more difficult, and, in terms of tonnage sunk, the U-boats force could not hope to match the successes in the First World War in the region.

The Black Sea

With the opening of the 'Barbarossa' campaign—the war with the Soviet Union—the Black Sea quickly became a combat zone. Although the Sea is, in effect, a gigantic Soviet inland lake,[4] comparable in size to the Baltic Sea, it hosted considerable naval forces in June 1941, the Soviet strength including one battleship, five cruisers, fourteen destroyers, 44 submarines and 84 motor torpedo boats.[5] These vessels were deployed wherever and whenever possible in order to disrupt the German advance, and enabled Soviet land forces—and, significantly, their weapons and equipment—to be evacuated when circumstances demanded. Thus it was not until the middle of 1942 that the stronghold of Sevastopol was taken by German forces. German successes were continually thwarted, not least because the Navy kept control of the harbours on the Caucasus coast.

Following the transfer of motor torpedo boats and minesweepers,[6] the Germans made preparations to deploy three U-boats (U 9, U 19 and U 24) in the region.[7] However, whereas an uninterrupted rail route to Pola was available in the First World War and the Black Sea could be accessed through the Turkish-held strait, this route was closed off because of Turkey's neutrality (in fact, in February 1945 Turkey declared war on Germany). Moreover, in selecting the means for transporting these U-boats, their length—some 43m—also had to be considered, although the UB I type were only 28m long and could be dismantled into three sections to facilitate transport by rail.

A number of options were discussed, but the decision was finally taken in favour of a Baltic Sea–Kaiser Wilhelm Canal (nowadays Kiel Canal)–River Elbe route to Dresden, then via the Autobahn to Ingolstadt, where the boats were prepared for transport by water on the Danube to Galatz, Romania. From here, after being reassembled, the boats continued their journey under their own power to the base at Constanta.[8] A second group, comprising U 18, U 20 and U 23, followed a few months later, and, under the designation 30.U-Flottille, these boats once more raised the German ensign in the Black Sea.

It was of course impossible for the Germans to gain any semblance of naval supremacy, bearing in mind the weakness of the flotilla: indeed, securing their own supply lines and endeavouring to disrupt those of the enemy were as much as they were able to accomplish. After the turning point in the war with the Soviets—Sevastopol was lost again in April–May 1944—securing the evacuation of German troops became a priority. When Romania changed sides on 25 August 1944 the boats lost their bases.

Nevertheless, amongst numerous achievements these U-boats accounted for some twenty enemy vessels totalling about 47,000grt. The end came with a heavy air raid on Constanta on 20 August 1944, during which U 9 was sunk and U 18 and U 24 severely damaged, to be scuttled on 25 August 1944 offshore from Constanta. U 20 and U 23, having no homeport, were scuttled on 10 September 1944 off the Turkish coast and U 19 followed suit the next day, whereupon 30.U-Flottille ceased to exist.

Commercial U-Boats: *Deutschland* and *Bremen*

When, in 1915, important strategic raw materials such as rubber and nickel began to become scarce, Germaniawerft drew up designs for a submarine that would have the specific role of bringing these materials from America to Germany as a blockade-runner.[1]

Construction—which the Friedrich Krupp company originally wished to carry out as a private venture—was prepared for by means of outline designs drawn up when a group of businessmen from Bremen who had the same idea, independently of Germaniawerft, learned about the latter's intentions and contacted them. Following the establishment of Deutsche Ozeanreedereigesellschaft GmbH (German Ocean Shipping Company Ltd) on 8 November

1915 by Norddeutsche Lloyd, the Deutsche Bank and Herr Alfred Lohmann in Bremen, negotiations were quickly concluded: *Deutschland* and *Bremen* were ordered by Ozeanreederei, to be followed by six submarines of similar size later. After the setting-up of Ozeanreederei, Germaniawerft withdrew from investing in the company.

Although the design of these civilian submarines was altogether much more straightforward than that of combat U-boats, their construction nevertheless presented a number of new challenges to Germaniawerft. Their displacement, for example, was substantially in excess of that for

Below: Outline sketch plans for *Deutschland*.

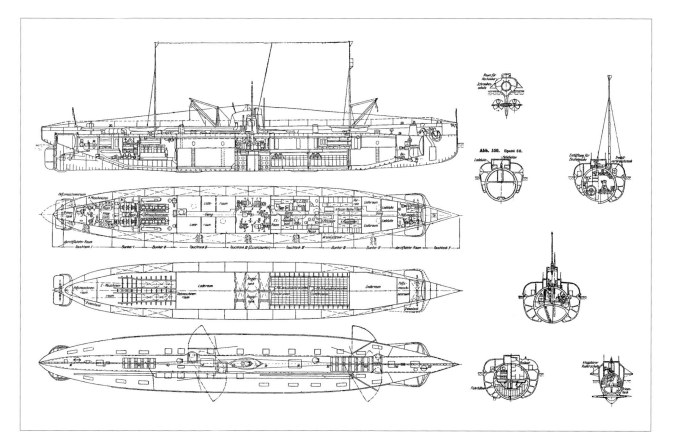

any U-boat built hitherto, although the hull length was comparable, which meant that poor depth-keeping and handling were to be expected. However, calculations in this area and the experience gained with U-boats already built suggested that these qualities would be acceptable at least for the purposes of merchant shipping. In any case, the overriding priority was to complete the boats quickly, and this was assisted in large measure by taking existing drawings and adapting them.

Standard marine diesel engines originally intended for ocean liners were selected as the powerplants: these were available for the first boats, although they had to be specially manufactured for subsequent boats. Again for the sake of simplicity, it was decided to install non-reversing engines, which meant that movement astern would only be possible using the electric motors—a feature, however, quite commonly found in submarines of foreign navies.

The main electric motors (designed as double-armature units) would be taken from open commercial-size models, with the entire propulsion system based on that used for the MS boats. The conning tower approximated the shape of a truncated, elliptical cone and had only one periscope, although the emergency periscope would be retained. The generous diameter of the pressure hull made it possible for the first time to contemplate a solid deck above the accumulator batteries and to install a movable platform beneath it to facilitate their servicing and removal.

The other major consideration was to allow sufficient space for the cargo of raw rubber, which has a relatively low weight-to-volume ratio. By reducing the size of the machinery spaces and omitting any weapons, however, it was discovered that there was insufficient 'in-built' ballast, and so a considerable amount of heavy metal ballast had to be introduced in addition to the raw rubber in order to make the boat submersible. It was therefore decided to stow further considerable quantities of raw rubber outside the pressure hull in flooded compartments—possible without really changing the composition of the interior cargo since raw rubber has a specific density of about 0.94 (i.e., just below that of water).

The pressure hulls of the two boats were built by Flensburger Schiffbau A. G., with completion undertaken by Germaniawerft. It should also be mentioned that See-Berufs-Genossenschaft, Germanische Lloyd and other concerns were involved in the project, as was common practice with the building of merchant ships; in fact, the boats were considered as nothing other than merchantmen during the entire building process: the *Deutschland*'s tonnage certificate indicates 791 gross and 414 net registered tons.

Within five months of the placing of the original order, the *Deutschland* and, soon afterwards, the *Bremen* were ready for trials, the former completing hers in the space of six weeks. *Deutschland* made two successful voyages under the command of Käpitan Paul König, bringing home on her first sortie 349 tonnes of rubber (257 tonnes of which were stowed outboard), 327 tonnes of nickel and 79 tonnes

of tin. On their outbound leg, the boats carried useful cargoes in the shape of aniline and tar dyes very much in demand in the United States, and mail was also transported, although because of the low stowage weight of this cargo considerable amounts of ballast had also to be shipped; for example, on her first trip the *Deutschland* carries 163 tonnes of dye and mail and 354 tonnes of ballast in the shape of pig-iron, 81 tonnes of which was outboard.

The *Bremen* (Kapitän Karl Schwartzkopf) was lost without a trace on her maiden voyage, the most probable explanation being that she ran on to a mine.

As Germaniawerft were unable to handle the construction of the six merchant submarines ordered later at their own shipyards, the company arranged to have them built according to their designs by Atlaswerke A. G. in Bremen, Reiherstieg-Schiffswerft in Hamburg and H. C. Stülcken

Sohn at Hamburg-Steinwarder. However, these yards could only carry out major construction and assembly work, Germaniawerft installing the machinery and completing the hulls. The diesel units were all provided by Germaniawerft. These later boats were never completed as merchantmen: like the *Deutschland*, they were converted into combat U-boats and thus become the first U-Kreuzer (U-cruisers).

U 155 (ex *Deutschland*), U 151–U 154, U 156, U 157

With the declaration of war by the United States of America in 1917, trade links with Germany were cut, posing the problem of how work for the *Deutschland* and her six sister-boats might be generated in order to further the war effort: halting construction seemed unreasonable, given the amount of building work already done. From among many options , the following were short-listed:

Left, upper: Another view of *Deutschland*, described as an 'Unterwasser Frachtschiff' (underwater freighter) in its publicity material.
Left, lower: The ill-fated *Bremen*, *Deutschland*'s sister-boat, which perished on her maiden voyage.
Above left: Herr Alfred Lohmann of Deutsche Ozeanreedereigesellschaft, the company which initiated the production of the U-Frachtschiffe.
Above centre: Kapitän Paul König of the *Deutschland*.
Above right: Kapitän Karl Schwartzkopf, commander of the *Bremen*.

1. Conversion to tankers and/or submarine depot boats;
2. Conversion to minelayers; and
3. Conversion to U-Kreuzer.

The Marine soon decided in favour of the last option, which also happened to be that recommended by Germaniawerft, the designers.

The very generous radius of action offered by these boats made them eminently suitable for use as cruisers, although their relatively low surfaced speed was a disadvantage. Adding 15cm guns, however, was seen as a way partly to offset this disadvantage.

Efforts were also made to increase their speed by installing new propellers, of such dimensions that, during a surfaced drive, they could take up the performance of both the diesel motors and the electric motors at revolutions still compatible with the former, although the use of the electric-motor 'booster' was only possible for short periods because some part of the battery capacity had to be kept in reserve for submerged cruising. Clearly, however, the consequence this form of drive was that the diesels could not achieve full revolutions—and thus full performance—without the auxiliary power provided by the electric motors, which meant in turn that with the new propeller arrangement speeds on diesel power alone were slightly lower than hitherto.

Fairly major changes were called for in order to be able to use these boats as combat vessels. Decks had to be installed in the cargo holds so that the upper compartments could be used as quarters for the enlarged complement and the lower for ammunition and torpedo stowage. Moreover, as mentioned, these U-boats were equipped with 15cm guns, taken from obsolete battleships—although that fact did not cause particular problems. The high internal capacity of the boats enabled them to take aboard 1,672 rounds—an exceptionally generous accommodation by U-boat standards. Some of the class were fitted with two 8cm guns in addition to the 15cm pieces.

In order to be able to deploy *Deutschland* as a combat boat at the earliest opportunity, she was equipped with torpedo gear consisting of six launching frames below the upper deck; the remaining six boats, incomplete in 1917, were equipped with two bow tubes each and stowage for eighteen torpedoes.

The conversion work for these boats was carried out by the Kaiserliche Werft at Wilhelmshaven, the Germaniawerft offices drawing up the conversion plans and drawings in the remarkably short time of just under five days.

These unique U-boats could be deployed in waters not normally associated with submarine activity, and for this reason enemy counteractivity was relatively ineffective and the boats were able to achieve a reasonable degree of success despite their low speed.

U-Boats Preserved

The presentation that follows lists, in chronological order according to the date of entry into service, German U-boats, or sections thereof, that are preserved in museums etc.

Brandtaucher

Brandtaucher, built in 1850, foundered on 1 February 1851 at Kiel as a result of a diving accident. The boat was discovered again after 36 years and raised on 5 July 1887. After a short period at Kiel, the boat was displayed in the Berliner Museum für Meereskunde (Museum of Ocean-ography).

    Brandtaucher was severely damaged during the Second World War but was restored between 1963 and 1965 and displayed at Potsdam, and since 1972 Wilhelm Bauer's submersible has been exhibited in the Militärhistorische Museum (Museum for Military History) in Dresden.

U 1

U 1 was decommissioned on 14 December 1906 and used solely for crew training and trials. She was stricken on 19 February 1919 and removed from the German Navy List, but was saved when Germaniawerft, Kiel, handed her over to the Deutsches Museum in Munich, where she has been on display since 1921.

U 20

U 20, which first entered service on 5 August 1913, gained lasting notoriety as the boat which, under the command of Kapitänleutnant Schwieger, torpedoed and sank the passenger liner *Lusitania* (30,396grt) on 7 May 1915, leading to heavy loss of life.

    On 5 November 1916 the boat ran aground in heavy fog off Jutland, Denmark, the crew being rescued by German naval forces. By 1925 the wreck had been broken up *in situ,*

Left: U 1, in the Deutsches Museum in Munich.
Opposite: U 505, a Type IXC U-boat on display in Chicago.

but the conning tower was saved and put on display outside the Strandingsmuseum St George in Thorminde, Denmark. A propeller can be seen in the Orlogmuseum Kopenhagen, and the gun is kept in the museum's repository.[1]

UB 46 (Type UB II)
UB 46 was commissioned on 12 June 1916 and during the Great War was broken down into sections for transportation to Pola, Austria-Hungary, by train. The boat was reassembled in the Marinearsenal and served operationally in Turkish waters. On 7 December 1916 she ran into a mine in the Black Sea and was lost with all hands.

Today, parts of the hull are displayed in the grounds of the Turkish Naval Museum (Demiz Muzesi) in Istanbul.

U 61
U 61, which entered service on 2 December 1916, was sunk in the Irish Sea on 26 March 1918 by depth charges and ramming. The Bayerische Armeemuseum at Ingolstadt has an 8.8cm gun from this boat.

U 9 (Type IIB)
U 9 was first commissioned on 21 August 1935. On 18 April 1942 she was taken out of service with the Schulflottille (Training Flotilla) at Pillau and readied for transfer to the Black Sea, re-entering service on 28 October 1942 at

Galatz on the River Danube, Romania. She was sunk by Soviet aircraft at Constanta on 20 August 1944.

The traditional emblem of U 9 was the Iron Cross, which she carried on her conning tower in memory of the first U 9 (Weddingen). The Soviets raised the boat and salvaged the emblem, and it is now in the Marine Museum of the Black Sea Fleet at Sevastopol.[2]

U 505 (Type IXC)
Only a very few German U-boats from the Second World War survive today, but U 505, a Type IXC, which was first commissioned on 28 August 1941, has been preserved in the United States. She was captured by a US Navy escort group accompanying the carrier *Guadalcanal* on 4 June 1944 north-west of Dakar after a boarding party managed to prevent her foundering. She was towed to the East Coast via Bermuda and repaired, following which she was commissioned into the US Navy as the USS *Nemo*. She was stricken in 1953, and since 25 September 1954 she has been on display in the grounds of the Museum of Science and Industry in Chicago.

U 995 (Type VIIC/41)
U 995 entered service on 16 September 1943 and at the end of hostilities, on 5 May 1945, was taken over by the British as war booty. In October 1948 she was transferred to the Norwegian Navy, with which she served from 1 December

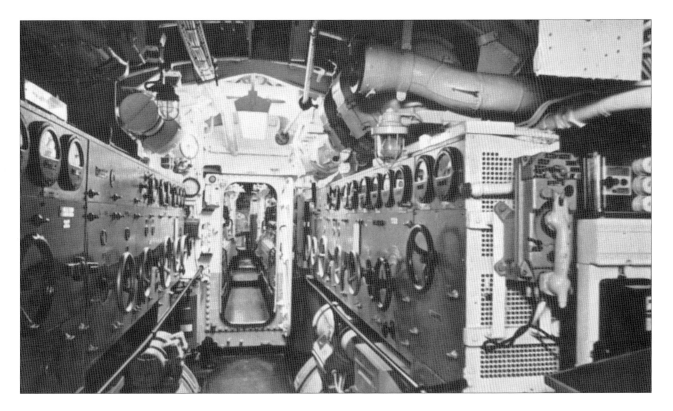

1952 until 15 December 1965 under the name *Kaura*. The Norwegians then offered to return her, the last remaining Type VIIC U-boat, for the symbolic price of one mark. Funding her restoration was a tedious and long-winded business, and there were also legal problems of ownership, but finally, on 2 October 1971, the U-boat was officially handed over in the grounds of the Marinearsenal in the presence of representatives of the Norwegian Navy.

Since 13 March 1972 U 995 has been on public display in front of the Marineehrenmal Laboe (Navy Memorial, Laboe) as both a memorial and an exhibit of twentieth-century technology.

Opposite, top: U 995, the only Type VII U-boat in the world today, preserved and open to the public at Laboe. Opposite, bottom: The torpedo room aboard U 995. Above: U 995's electric-motor compartment. Left: U 534, the preserved Type IXC/40 at Birkenhead, near Liverpool.

U 534 (Type IXC/40)

U 534 was placed into service on 23 December 1943. She was sunk by British aircraft in the Kattegat to the east of Anhalt, Denmark, on 5 May 1945, but in 1993—after 48 years—she was raised by a Danish consortium. Repaired in Norway, she arrived at Birkenhead near Liverpool in February 1977 for display.

U 2540 (Type XXI)

U 2540, which first entered service on 24 February 1945 was scuttled by her crew on 4 May that year near the Flensburg lightvessel. After twelve years—in 1957—she was raised, repaired and refitted, returning to service, unarmed, in the Bundesmarine on 1 September 1960. She served until 26 April 1968 as a training and trials boat under the name *Wilhelm Bauer*. From 20 May 1970 she was used, crewed by civilians, at the Erprobungsstelle der Bundeswehr (Federal Armed Forces Test Centre), finally decommissioning on 15 March 1982.

A great deal of support from the German citizenry, and from the people of Bremerhaven in particular, ensured that the boat was saved for posterity, and since 24 April 1984 she has been moored in Bremerhaven's Alter Hafen (Old Harbour) as the Technikmuseum Wilhelm Bauer.

Walter Turbine[3]

In 1991 the Walter factory offered the stern section of a U-boat sitting in its grounds in Kiel-Projendorf (and containing the only Walter propulsion system preserved in Germany) to the Technikmuseum Wilhelm Bauer in Bremerhaven, and, following restoration at Rostock, it was transferred there. The Technikmuseum Wilhelm Bauer donated the exhibit to the Deutsches Schiffahrtsmuseum (German Shipping Museum), in the grounds of which it is currently displayed.

Other U-Boat-Related Exhibits

Miniature submarines—*Hecht* (Type XXVII) and *Seehund* (Type XXVII B)—and small weapons such as *Neger*, *Marder*, *Biber* and *Molch* can be seen in museums in Germany and many other countries, for example the United States, Canada, Japan, the Netherlands, Norway and Denmark.

U 9 (S 188, 205 Class)

U 9 was placed into service on 11 April 1967, this 205 Class boat joining the Fleet with sister-boats U 9–U 12, U 1 (ii) and U 2 (ii) in the years 1966–69. Two of these boats remained in service as target and sonar trials vessels, U 9 decommissioning on 3 June 1993.

The Federal Navy transferred U 9 to the Technikmuseum Speyer, where she has been on display in the grounds since August 1993.

U 10 (S 189, 205 Class)

U 10 was commissioned on 28 November 1967 and taken out of service on 4 March 1993. The city of Wilhelmshaven acquired the boat in 1996, handing her over to the custody of the Deutsches Marinemuseum in Wilhelmshaven. She opened to the public on 25 April 1998.

Right: The U-boat section containing the Walter turbine is lowered into position for display at the Deutsches Schiffahrtsmuseum.

Right: U 10 on display at the Deutsches Marinemuseum, Wilhelmshaven.

Right: The control room aboard U 10.

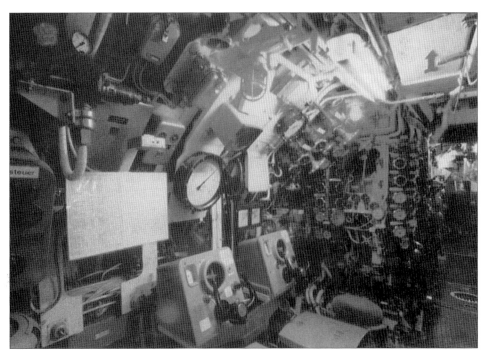

Left: *Wilhelm Bauer* at the Deutsches Schiffahrtsmuseum, Bremerhaven.

U-Boats of the Austro-Hungarian Navy

The Kaiserlich und Königlich (KuK, or Imperial and Royal) Marine (Austro-Hungarian Navy), like the Kaiserliche Marine in Germany, was persuaded of the value of submarines somewhat later than the other leading navies of the world. In 1904 the engineer Siegfried Popper presented a project for such a boat during a meeting with Navy commanders, and the following year a list of requirements was drawn up and put out to tender. The specifications included a displacement of 200 tonnes, a diving depth of 50m, a surfaced speed of 10 knots and a submerged speed of 7 knots, and an armament of two bow torpedoes.

In order to diversify and offer shipyards experience in building this type of vessel, the Marine placed orders for two boats each with three different shipyards:

U 1, U 2: 'Lake boats'—after the designer Simon Lake[1]—to be built using American drawings, documents and components at the Seearsenal Pola (contract dated November 1906);

U 3, U 4: Germaniawerft, Kiel (contract dated March 1907); and

U 5, U 6 : Holland-type submarines,[2] to be built under licence from the American company Electric Boat & Co. near Whitehead, Fiume (contract dated December 1907).

In January 1910 the Marine-Kommission reviewed progress thus far. There was a great deal in favour of the boats built by Germaniawerft, but the Hollands had superior diving capabilities and generated less smoke because their exhaust outlets were under water. Insufficent data concerning the Lake boats built at Pola meant that no firm conclusions could be drawn at this stage.

However, larger and longer-range boats were clearly desirable. Whitehead was by this time successfully exporting its products to Denmark, so Germaniawerft offered to develop U 3 and U 4 further and plans from Germany were revised and adapted in co-operation with naval engineers from the KuK's Marinetechnik-Komitee (MTK, or Naval Technical Committee). In 1913 Germaniawerft accepted an order for five submarines, with the provisional designations U 7 to U 11.

The outbreak of war in 1914 precluded the delivery of these boats, however, because transferring them upon completion to Adriatic harbours was deemed impossible. In compensation, on 28 November 1914 the Kaiserliche Marine requisitioned the boats as U 66–U 70 in an agreed takeover, refunding the deposit paid by the Austrians when the order was placed. As a result of these developments, the KuK Marine's submarine operations were restricted to the Adriatic.

Following on from U 5 and U 6, Whitehead built an improved Holland-type boat as a private venture. This was launched on 14 March 1911, and the yard then made efforts to sell it (as SS 3) both at home and overseas. Nobody showed interest at first, but when war broke out the KuK Marine agreed to purchase it. For her trials the boat was designated U 7, but on commissioning this was changed to U 12.

Further developing the blueprints for U 5 and U 6, Whitehead then produced three submarines for Denmark. (*Havmanden* class); five others were built indigenously. However, although the basic design had been altered and improved, patent and licensing problems stood in the way of the construction of additional boats for the Austrian Navy, and so, in a move not unique in times of war, the necessary data were confiscated under the Kriegsleistungsgesetz (literally, War Obligation Law) and transferred to the newly founded Ungarische Unterseebootsbau A. G. (UBAG, or Hungarian Submarine Construction Co. Ltd). Staff from the Whitehead company were made available to UBAG.

A larger class of U-boats was then considered, but in March 1915 Admiral Haus,[3] the Austro-Hungarian Marinekommandant, approved the construction of only four, to be designated U 20 to U 23: Seearsenal Pola was nominated as the builder for U 20 and U 23 and UBAG, at Fiume, for U 21 and U 22.

On 20 December 1914 the French submarine *Curie* became trapped in the net defences while attempting to penetrate the harbour at Pola. She was unable to break free and was sunk. The Austrians immediately began work to raise her, a task completed on 2 February 1915. After

AUSTRO-HUNGARIAN U-BOAT CONSTRUCTION

Builder	Boats in commission	Boats under construction	Total	Remarks
In Austria-Hungary				
Whitehead, Fiume	U 5, U 6, U 12	–	3	U 12 provisionally designated U 7 at first
Seearsenal, Pola	U 1, U 2	–	4	Plus U 20, U 23 built in collaboration with UBAG; also assembly of German-built boats
Cantiere Navale Triestino (CNT), Seearsenal, Pola	U 27, U 28, U 40, U 41	U 48, U 49, U 101–U 106	12	Work undertaken 1915–18 following evacuation of Montfalcone at Seearsenal, Pola. From 1918, following recapture, the yard was partly restored. U 104–U 106 building at Montfalcone in 1918, remaining five at Seearsenal. Hulls for U 101–U 106 built at Budapest works of Erste-Donau-Dampfschiffahrts-Gesellschaft (DDSG), Vienna, and delivered to Pola and Montfalcone by rail.
Ganz & Danubis, Budapest (Fiume yard)	U 29–U 32	U 50, U 51, U 107–U 110	10	Hulls only built at Budapest
Ungarische Unterseebootsbau A. G. (UBAG), Fiume	U 21, U 22	U 52, U 53	4	Construction in collaboration with Linz branch of Stabilimento Tecnico Trieste (STT)redesignated U 2 and U 22 at Austria Werft.
In Germany				
Germaniawerft, Kiel	U 3, U 4, U 10	–	3	U 10 ex UB 1
A. G. Weser, Bremen	U 11, U 15, U 16, U 17, U 43, U 47			U 11 ex UB 15, U 43 ex UB 43, U47 ex UB 47
In France				
Arsenal de Toulon	U 14	–	1	Ex *Curie* (Q 87)

repairs the Navy commissioned the boat as U 14 on 1 June 1915.

The Austrian Naval Attaché in Berlin, enjoying good contacts both with the Marine and with German shipbuilders, negotiated, first, to purchase blueprints and components for the German UB I design but then changed his mind and accepted an offer from A. G. Weser to build and deliver three complete submarines. As a result, the order for U 15, U 16 and U 17 was placed on 1 April 1915. The three boats were built in Bremen and delivered in sections by rail to Pola, where they were assembled.

Further sales were concluded with the purchase of UB 1 (which had entered service with the Kaiserliche Marine on 29 January 1915) and UB 15 (commissioned on 4 April 1915). Having been transported to the Seearsenal at Pola and assembled with the help of German shipyard personnel, both U-boats were initally placed into operational service with the Kaiserliche Marine in the Mediterranean in June 1915, but, following the training of Austrian crews under German supervision, the KuK Marine took them over as U 10 (on 12 July 1915) and U 11 (on 18 June), respectively.

The search for a larger submarine design continued, and this eventually resulted in a number of offers, from amongst which Grossadmiral Haus decided to acquire a licence from Germany for UB II production. In the meantime, Italy had entered the war against Austria-Hungary (23 May 1915). The German licence was acquired in August and, again, it was considered politically expedient to split the orders between the two halves of the Empire. On this occasion the agreed compromise was to build four boats (U 29–U 32) at Danubius, Fiume, and two (U 27 and U 28) at Cantiere Navale Triestino (CNT).[4] Thanks to a financial donation by the Flottenverein (Fleet Association), U 40 was ordered on 26 January 1916; the order for U 41—substituting for U 6—followed on 28 August that year. The diesel motors still available from the early loss of U 6 were installed in U 41, which, as it transpired, would be the last new-build submarine placed in service by the Austrians during the war.

On 30 July 1917 the KuK Marine took over the Type UB II boats UB 43 and UB 47 from the Germans, redesignating them U 43 and U 47, respectively.

By the end of the hostilities there were sixteen submarines—U 48–U 53 and U 101–U 110—under construction for the KuK Marine, at stages of completion varying from 15 to 90 per cent . Orders had been placed and preparatory work undertaken for sixteen further units—U 54–U 59 and U 111–U 120—displacing between 500 and 850 tonnes each.

MOST SUCCESSFUL AUSTRO-HUNGARIAN COMMANDERS IN THE MERCANTILE WAR, 1914–1918

Commander	Date of birth	Boats	No of ships sunk	Aggregate tonnage (grt)
Zdenko Hudecek	22 June 1887	U 17, U 28	12	44,828
Georg Ritter von Trapp	4 Apr. 1880	U 5, U 14	12	44,495

The largest merchantman sunk was the Italian steamer *Micazzo*, by U 14 (von Trapp) on 29 August 1917.

MOST SUCCESSFUL AUSTRO-HUNGARIAN COMMANDERS IN ATTACKS ON WARSHIPS, 1914–1918

Commander	Date of birth	Boat	Date of success	Name (type) of warship	Nationality	Disp'ment (tonnes)
Georg Ritter von Trapp	4 Apr. 1888	U 5	27 Apr. 1915	*Léon Gambetta* (armoured cruiser)	French	11,959
Heinz Adolf von Heimburg	24 Oct. 1889	U 11[7]	10 June 1915	*Medusa* (submarine)	Italian	248
Franz Wäger	7 Jan. 1888	U 10[7]	26 June 1915	5-PN (torpedo boat)	Italian	120
Rudolf Singule	8 Apr. 1883	U 4	18 July 1915	*Giuseppe Garibaldi* (armoured cruiser)	Italian	7,234
Georg Ritter von Trapp	4 Apr. 1888	U 5	5 Aug. 1915	*Nereide* (submarine)	Italian	225
Hugo von Falken hausen	11 Aug. 1888	U 6	18 Mar. 1916	*Renaudin* (destroyer)	French	756
Friedrich Fähndrich	8 Jan. 1887	U 15	23 June 1916	*Fourche* (destroyer)	French	720
Zdenko Hudecek	22 June 1887	U 17	10 July 1916	*Impetuoso* (destroyer)	Italian	672
Orest Ritter von Zopa	20 Nov. 1888	U 16	17 Oct. 1916	*Nembo* (destroyer)	Italian	325
Josef Holub	31 Dec. 1885	U 27	14 May 1918	*Phoenix* (destroyer)	British	778
Hugo Freiherr von Seyfferitzt	23 Nov. 1885	U 47	20 Sept. 1918	*Circé*/Q 47 (submarine)	French	351

Operations, Successes, Losses, Commanders[5]

Altogether the Austrian Navy had 27 U-boats at its disposal during the First World War. Nine—U 3, U 5, U 6, U 10, U 12, U 16, U 20, U 23, U 30—were lost to enemy action, although two of these were salved, U 5 being raised and then used as a training boat and U 10, stranded after striking a mine, towed free but not repaired. At the end of the war thirteen boats were surrendered to Italy and seven to France.

The boats were generally confined to the Adriatic, only U 14 and the Type UB Is having the necessary range to be able to patrol in the Mediterranean. Thirteen of the 27 boats were in service prior to 1915, the other fourteen only becoming available from 1917. Nevertheless, considerable success was achieved: altogether more than 200,000grt of merchant tonnage and numerous warships were sunk or torpedoed.

The loss of personnel during Austrian combat operations totalled 99.[6] Of the 48 U-boat commanders, most were German-Austrians, followed by Czechs and Moravians, with a few Croats and Hungarians. Georg Ritter von Trapp, Rudolf Singule and Rigele were made Ritter des Militär-Maria-Theresia-Ordens (Knights of the Military Order of Maria Theresia), the highest honour for military personnel.

The First World War ushered in a new weapon to combat the menace of the submarine—the aeroplane—and Austrian seaplanes achieved their first successes against these boats. On 9 August 1916, for example, twenty aircraft and various Army aeroplanes attacked Venice, during the course of which the British submarine B 10 (287 tonnes, and commissioned in 1906) was sunk in dock.

On 15 September 1916 a seaplane sighted a submerged enemy submarine near the entrance to Cattaro. Two seaplanes from the base at nearby Kumbor carried out an attack and the intruder was sunk, although the entire crew were rescued. It proved to be the French submarine *Foucault* (Q 70), a *Brumaire* class boat similar to U 14 (ex *Curie*). This is the first undisputed sinking of a submarine from the air.[8]

U 1, U 2

Design and development	Single-hull type, US (Lake) design. Unusual in having two retractable wheels beneath the keel and an underwater exit chamber for divers.
Builder	Seearsenal, Pola; some components supplied by USA
In service	1911
Type displacement	230 tonnes surfaced, 270 tonnes submerged
Dimensions	30.48 (30.76 after 1915 conversion) × 3.62 × 3.85m
Speed	10.3 knots surfaced, 6.0 knots submerged
Range	950nm at 6 knots surfaced, 15nm at 5 knots submerged
Propulsion	
surfaced	Two Lake benzene engines (from 1915: Leobersdorfer Maschinenfabrik diesel engines) = 720hp
submerged	Two combined motor/generators = 144kW
Armament	Two 45cm bow and one 45cm stern torpedo tubes, plus (from 1915) one 3.7cm quick-firing gun
Crew	Three officers and 14 men
Fates	
U 1	Stricken January 1918; transferred to Italy 1920, scrapped at Pola
U 2	Stricken January 1918; transferred to Italy 1920, scrapped at Pola

Left: The Austro-Hungarian U 1, built to an American design.

U 3, U 4

Design and development	Double-hull type, Germaniawerft design
Builder	Germaniawerft, Kiel (towed to Pola by sea)
In service	1909
Type displacement	240 tonnes surfaced, 300 tonnes submerged
Dimensions	43.2 (44.4 after conversion) × 3.8 × 2.95m
Speed	12.0 knots surfaced, 8.5 knots submerged
Range	1,200nm at 8 knots surfaced, 40nm at 3 knots submerged
Propulsion	
surfaced	Two 8-cylinder, two-stroke Körting petrol engines = 600hp
submerged	Two combined motor/generators = 235kW
Armament	Two 45cm bow torpedo tubes, plus (from 1915) one 3.7cm quick-firing gun and (U 4 only, from 1916) one 7cm gun
Crew	Three officers and 18 men
Fates	
U 3	Sank 13 August 1915 as a result of sinking of French destroyer *Bisson* (7 fatalities)
U 4	Transferred to France 1920; scrapped

Above: U 3 and U 4, which were German designs.
Right: The American-designed, Holland-type U 5.

U 5, U 6

Design and development	Single-hull type, American (Holland-type) design
Builder	Whitehead, Fiume
In service	1911
Type displacement	240 tonnes surfaced, 273 tonnes submerged
Dimensions	32.09 × 4.23 × 3.9m
Speed	11.0 knots surfaced, 9.0 knots submerged
Range	800nm at 8.5 knots surfaced, 48nm at 6 knots submerged
Propulsion	
surfaced	Two 6-cylinder, four-stroke benzene engines = 500hp (U 5 after conversion in October 1916: two Grazer Waggon- und Maschinenfabrik diesel engines = c. 200hp)
submerged	Two combined motor/generators = 170kW
Armament	Two 45cm bow torpedo tubes, plus one 3.7cm quick-firing gun (U 5 from July 1915: one 4.7cm quick-firing gun; U 5 from autumn 1916: one 7.5cm gun)
Crew	Four officers and 15 men
Fates	
U 5	Sunk by mine in the Canale di Fasana (6 fatalities); raised June 1917, returned to service August 1918 as training boat; to Venice 1919; scrapped 1920
U 4	Trapped in net defences in Strait of Otranto 13 May 1916, surfaced, cornered by armed trawler, scuttled

U 10

Design and development	Coastal, single-hull type. Design by Dr Techel, Germaniawerft. Specimen boat, ex UB 1, purchased.
Builder	Germaniawerft, Kiel (transported in sections by rail to Pola)
In service	12 July 1915 (in KuK Marine)
Type displacement	127 tonnes surfaced, 142 tonnes submerged
Dimensions	28.1 × 3.15 × 3.03m
Speed	6.5 knots surfaced, 5.5 knots submerged
Range	1,650nm at 5 knots surfaced, 45nm at 4 knots submerged
Propulsion	
surfaced	One 4-cylinder, four-stroke Daimler RS164 diesel engine = 60hp
submerged	One SSW combined motor/generators = 90kW
Armament	Two 45cm bow torpedo tubes, plus one 3.7cm quick-firing gun
Crew	Two officers and 13 men
Fate	Sunk 9 July 1918 by mine off Caorle, beached; repaired at Trieste but not recommissioned; to Italy postwar, scrapped 1920

Below: U 10, formerly the German UB 1, purchased from Germany by the Austro-Hungarian Navy.

U 11

Below: U 11 (ex UB 15), built for the Austro-Hungarian Navy by A. G. Weser, Bremen.

Design and development	Coastal, single-hull type. Design by Dr Techel, Germaniawerft. Specimen boat, ex UB 15, purchased.
Builder	A. G. Weser, Bremen (transported in sections by rail to Pola)
In service	18 July 1915 (in KuK Marine)
Type displacement	127 tonnes surfaced, 142 tonnes submerged
Dimensions	27.88 × 3.15 × 3.03m
Speed	7.5 knots surfaced, 6.3 knots submerged
Range	1,500nm at 5 knots surfaced, 45nm at 4 knots submerged
Propulsion	
surfaced	One 4-cylinder, four-stroke Körting diesel engine = 60hp
submerged	One SSW combined motor/generators = 90kW
Armament	Two 45cm bow torpedo tubes, plus (from December 1915) one 3.7cm quick-firing gun or (from Ocotber 1916) one 7.5cm gun
Crew	Two officers and 13 men
Fate	To Italy postwar; scrapped 1920 at Pola

U 12

Design and development	Single-hull, modified Holland type. Speculative venture by builders, designated SS 3, first operated by KuK Marine as trials boat U 7.
Builder	Whitehead, Fiume
In service	21 August 1914 (as U 12)
Type displacement	240 tonnes surfaced, 273 tonnes submerged
Dimensions	32.09 × 4.23 × 3.9m
Speed	10.75 knots surfaced, 8.5 knots submerged
Range	800nm at 8.5 knots surfaced, 48nm at 6 knots submerged
Propulsion	
surfaced	Two 6-cylinder, two-stroke benzene engines = 500hp
submerged	Two combined motor/generators = 170kW
Armament	Two 45cm bow torpedo tubes, plus (from July 1915) two 35cm external torpedo launchers and one 3.7cm quick-firing gun
Crew	Three officers and 15 men
Fate	Sunk 12 August 1915 off Venice; raised 1915 by the Italians, scrapped

U 14

Design and development	Double-hull, French (Laubeuf) design. *Pluviose* type, *Brumaire* class.
Builder	Arsenal de Mourillon, Toulon
In service	1 June 1915 (as U 14)
Type displacement	407 tonnes surfaced, 544 tonnes submerged
Dimensions	52.15 × 5.4 × 3.2m
Speed	12.2 (12.6 after conversion) knots surfaced, 8.5 (9.0 after conversion) knots submerged
Range	1,200nm at 10 knots surfaced, 85nm at 4.5 knots submerged
Propulsion	
surfaced	Two 6-cylinder, four-stroke, licence-built MAN diesel engines = 840hp
submerged	Two combined motor/generators = 485kW
Armament	Four swivelling broadside launching frames (Dzevechiy system; from 1918 replaced by tubes aft) and two fixed superstructure tubes for 45cm torpedoes
Crew	Three officers and 15 men
Fate	Foundered 20 December 1914 on net defences off Pola, salved February 1915, commissioned into KuK Marine; returned to France postwar, recommissioned (original name); finally decommissioned 29 March 1928, scrapped

Below: U 14—the former French *Curie*, trapped off Pola, captured and commissioned into the KuK Marine in 1915.

U 15–U 17

Above: U 12 (ex SS 3), built by Whitehead of Fiume.

Design and development	Coastal, single-hull, German UB I type
Builder	A. G. Weser, Bremen (transported to Pola by rail)
In service	6 October 1915
Type displacement	127 tonnes surfaced, 142 tonnes submerged
Dimensions	27.88 × 3.15 × 3.03m
Speed	16.5 knots surfaced, 5.5 knots submerged
Range	1,650nm at 5 knots surfaced, 45nm at 4 knots submerged
Propulsion	
surfaced	One 4-cylinder, four-stroke Körting diesel engine = 60hp
submerged	One SSW combined motor/generator = 90kW
Armament	Two 45cm bow torpedo tubes plus one 3.7cm quick-firing gun
Crew	Two officers and 13 men
Fate	
U 15	To Italy postwar; scrapped 1920 at Pola
U 16	Rammed and sunk 17 October 1916 by Italian steamer *Bormida* (2 fatalities)
U 17	To Italy postwar, scrapped 1920 at Pola

Right: U 15, U 16 and U 17 under construction at A. G. Weser, Bremen.

U 20–U 23

Design and development	Single-hull, *Havmanden* type (development of Holland-type U 5 and U 6)
Builder	Seearsenal, Pola (U 21, U 22: Ungarische Unterseebootbau A. G., Fiume)
In service	August–October 1917
Type displacement	173 tonnes surfaced, 210 tonnes submerged
Dimensions	38.76 × 3.97 × 2.75m
Speed	12.0 knots surfaced, 9.0 knots submerged
Range	750nm at 12 knots surfaced, 40nm at 6 knots submerged
Propulsion	
surfaced	One 6-cylinder, four-stroke MAN diesel engine (licence-built by Stabilimento Tecnico Linz, Fiume) = 450hp
submerged	One combined motor/generator = 220kW
Armament	Two 45cm bow torpedo tubes plus one 3.7cm quick-firing gun and one machine gun
Crew	Three officers and 15 men
Fate	
U 20	Sunk 4 July 1918 by Italian F 12; raised
U 21	Handed over to Italy 25 March 1919; scrapped 1920
U 22	Handed over to France 1920 for scrapping
U 23	Sunk 21 February 1918 by the Italian torpedo-boat *Airone*

Above: A photograph of
U 17. These boats were built
to the German UB I type
design.

U 27–U 32, U 40, U 41

Design and development	Coastal, single-hull (German UB II) type with saddle tanks (licence acquired from A. G. Weser by Cantiere Navale Triestino, CNT)
Builder	Cantiere Navale Triestino, Pola (U 29–U 32: Ganz & Co, Danubius Budapest and Fiume)
In service	January 1917–February 1917
Type displacement	268 (U 41: 275) tonnes surfaced, 306 (U 41: 320) tonnes submerged
Dimensions	36.9 × 3.75 × 3.7m (U 41: 37.7 × 4.37 × 3.72m)
Speed	9.0 knots surfaced, 7.5 knots submerged
Range	6,250nm at 7.5 knots surfaced, 20nm at 5 knots submerged
Propulsion	
surfaced	Two 6-cylinder, four-stroke Daimler RS206 (U 30: Körting, U 41: Grazer Waggon- und Maschinenfabrik) diesel engines = 450hp (U 41: 400hp)
submerged	Two combined motor/generators = 206kW
Armament	Two 45cm bow torpedo tubes plus one 7.5cm gun and one machine gun
Crew	Five officers and 14 men
Fate	
U 27	Handed over to Italy postwar, scrapped 1920
U 28	Transferred from Pola to Venice 23 March 1919; scrapped there 1920
U 29	To Italy postwar; scrapped 1920
U 30	Missing and declared sunk with all hands 31 March 1917
U 31	To France postwar; scrapped 1920
U 32	To Italy postwar; scrapped 1920 at Venice
U 40	To Italy postwar; scrapped 1920 at Venice
U 41	To France postwar; scrapped

Left: The launch of U 27.

U 43, U 47

Design and development	Coastal, single-hull (German UB II) type with saddle tanks
Builder	A. G. Weser, Bremen (transported to Pola by rail)
In service	30 July 1917 (in KuK Marine)
Type displacement	272 tonnes surfaced, 306 tonnes submerged
Dimensions	36.9 × 4.37 × 3.68m
Speed	8.8 knots surfaced, 6.2 knots submerged
Range	6,940nm at 5 knots surfaced, 45nm at 4 knots submerged
Propulsion	
surfaced	Two 6-cylinder, four-stroke Daimler diesel engines = 284hp
submerged	Two SSW combined motor/generators = 280kW
Armament	Two 45cm bow torpedo tubes plus one 8.8cm gun
Crew	Two officers and 21 men
Fate	
U 43	To France postwar; scrapped 1920
U 47	To France postwar; scrapped 1920

Left: U 43 receives some
routine maintenance.

Reflections

First World War

The Kaiserliche Marine began the construction of submarines rather later than other navies, the reason being that the Staatssekretär im Reichsmarineamt (Secretary of State in the Imperial Naval Office), Grossadmiral Tirpitz, had as his priority the building of an ocean-going surface fleet for his emperor, Wilhelm II—one that could rival the Royal Navy in terms of size and strength. Moreover, and unfortunately, the Kaiserliche Marine elected to opt for petrol engines as surface propulsion for its U-boats, and these were installed in the first eighteen (U 1 to U 18). From U 19 onwards, however, the changeover was made to diesel engines, a decision that had been taken some time before by the rest of the world's navies. The Marine then made another mistaken choice. It was unable to decide between four-stroke or two-stroke powerplants, and so four-stroke engines were ordered from MAN Augsburg and two-stroke from Germaniawerft. Problems arose, and the so-called pre-war U-boats U 31–U 41 were not in fact ready for service at the outbreak of the First World War. The Kaiserliche Marine therefore opened hostilities with a 'paper' strength of thirty U-boats (U 1–U 30), though by no means all of these were combat-ready. Nevertheless, lost time was quickly made up.

Between the Wars

Under the terms of the Treaty of Versailles, Germany was prohibited from having submarines in commission in her navy: all existing U-boats had to be surrendered, marking, it appeared, the demise of such construction in Germany. A way round the ban was quickly found, however, when, in Amsterdam, the Ingenieur Kantoor for Scheepsbouw (IvS) was set up to deal with matters of U-boat design, Thus, using the wartime UB I type as a starting point, the submarine *Saukao* was developed, and later built in Finland. There was no requirement for this type of boat in Germany because in 1926 the Marine had already settled on a minimum displacement of 250 tonnes. (Despite this, no orders were forthcoming for boats based on the 640-tonne UG type, the large fleet U-boat being planned under the designation 'Project 51a' by the Germans in 1918.)

IvS attempted to stoke up some interest in Spain, offering a slightly larger boat, P 111, and was rewarded with the laying down in 1929 at the Echovarrieta y Larringa Shipyard in Cadiz of a submarine. The yard went bankrupt in 1931, but work continued and E 1 was launched on 22 October 1932. Spain failed to exercise her option on the purchase of the boat after the downfall of the monarchy, and it was sold to Turkey in 1934 and commissioned into the Turkish Navy with the name *Gür*. The Kriegsmarine's Type IA was developed from this Spanienboot (Spanish boat), as it continued to be called. The differences between this type and the UG design of the former Kaiserliche Marine were insignificant.

Meanwhile, the wartime UF design served as the basis for the Finnish submarine *Vesikko*, from which, in turn, the Type IIA of 1935 was produced. The ubiquitous Type VII can be traced back to the UB III of the Imperial Navy and, finally, the Type IX was developed from the large U 115 and U 166. Thus, despite the Treaty of Versailles, the U-boats produced in Germany between 1935 to 1938— and hence the boats with which she entered the Second World War—were very similar to the final designs of the first great conflict.

The question then arises: why? The answer is unclear. While it is true that Germany was banned from developing and constructing submarines, her designers, engineers and technicians were not prohibited from thinking. Despite IvS and the programmes for Spain, Turkey and Finland, no significant progress was made after the First World War.

Fleet Submarines

A number of authors who write about the Kaiserliche Marine divide the submarines of the Imperial Navy into three groups—UB and UC types, and fleet U-boats, the last-mentioned including all the designs that do not fall into either of the first two categories and thus comprising prewar boats, the UAs, MS boats, UE I minelayers, UE II minelayers, 'Grosse U-boote' (large submarines, the predecessors of the U-Kreuzer), U-Kreuzer proper, and converted mercantile submarines. However, none of these is

HELLMUTH WALTER'S U-BOATS				
	V 80	**Wa 201**	**Wk 202**	**Type XVIIB**
Builder	Germaniawerft, Kiel	Blohm & Voss, Hamburg	Germaniawerft, Kiel	Blohm & Voss, Hamburg
Designated numbers	V 80	U 792, U 793	U 794, U 795	U 1405, U 1406, U 1407
First in service	19 Apr. 1940	16 Nov. 1943	14 Nov. 1943	21 Dec. 1944
Maximum underwater speed (kt)	28.1	24–25	24–25	25
Undewater range (nm @ kt)	50 @ 28	127 @ 20	117 @ 20	123 @ 25

a genuine Flotten-U-Boot: fleet submarines are boats which, because of their high surfaced performance, can accompany the ocean-going navy, at least at cruising speeds. The British, by contrast, built, for example, the 'K' class, seventeen units being completed, the first of which was placed into service on 22 September 1916 and the last on 18 October the following year. These submarines were equipped with 10,500hp geared turbines, enabling them to reach 24 knots on the surface, and had a crew of 48.

Germany, it is true also had at least formulated plans for a submarine cruiser, an official 1917 design designated Project 50, with a surfaced displacement of 3,800 tonnes and an underwater displacement of 4,500. The combined performance of both sets of turbines was 24,000hp, providing a maximum surfaced speed of 25 knots, and the crew was to number 9 officers and 95 men. The construction of the boats began in February 1918 at the Kaiserliche Werft, Kiel, but of course in November that year all work halted, the materials stockpiled being diverted for other uses.

Helmuth Walter

This, then, was the state of affairs that Hellmuth Walter discovered when he first approached the Marine on 5 October 1933 with his proposals for a 'schnell Unterwasserschiff' (fast underwater ship). His ideas may be briefly summarised thus:

1. Underwater propulsion by means one or more turbines;
2. Oxygen derived from onboard hydrogen peroxide; and

3. A refined, streamlined hull-form appropriate to a true submarine, not for a vessel that dives occasionally.

Walter constructed his first submarine, V 80, on his own initiative, albeit with support from Germaniawerft. Although his next three designs were developed in co-operation with the Navy, it would appear that neither the latter nor, in particular, Dönitz himself were persuaded of the excellence of Walter's projects. For example, in the last letter written by Dönitz to Walter (29 June 1943), the only reference to the latter's innovations is that concerning the underwater geometry of the boat. Dönitz opted for the Types XXI and XXIII and suggested that, although Walter's inventions might have some application in the future, they were of little importance for the present because the Wende im U-Boot-Krieg (turning-point in the U-boat war) had been reached. The outline characteristics of Walter's boats are summarised in the accompanying table.

One hundred and eighteen Type XXI U-boats were commissioned in 1944–45. They could attain 17.2 knots underwater and had a submerged range of 30nm at 15 knots; the Type XXIIIs had a maximum submerged speed of 12.5 knots and a range of 83nm at 4 knots. Neither type was deployed on the sort of missions for which they were designed, and the U-boat war in 1944–45 continued to be waged using the old, 'reliable' (and often refitted) Type VIIs and Type IXs. As a result, during this period 134 of the former and 49 of the latter were lost. The decline in the effectiveness of the U-Boat Arm can be deduced from the statistics offered in the table below.

U-BOAT LOSSES, FIRST AND SECOND WORLD WARS (EUROPEAN WATERS ONLY)			
	First World War	Second World War, 01.09.39–31.05.43	Second World War, 01.06.43–08.05.45
No of U-boats lost	178	234	396
No of merchant ships sunk	6,386	2,494	346
Tonnage sunk (grt)	11,937,994	12,604,770	1,728,312
Ratio of merchantmen sunk to U-boats lost	35.8:1	10.7:1	0.87:1
Tonnage of merchantmen sunk per U-boat lost	67,067	53,867	4,364

Dönitz's predictions concerning his new U-boats, as outlined in his letter of 29 June 1943, have therefore to be considered very optimistic. In reality, hardly anything changed as a result of the introduction of the Types XXI and XXIII, and certainly nothing changed the factors which led to Germany's defeat in the Battle in the Atlantic:

1. The Allies' ability to decode German wireless transmissions and the Kriegsmarine's stubborn refusal to believe that this was possible;
2. The very efficient convoy system practised by the Allies, the organisation of which no type of U-boat, however advanced, could influence;
3. The Allies' use of radar, and the Germans' lack of faith in close-range radar systems; and
4. The absence of any offensive aerial reconnaissance on the part of the Germans—and, indeed the absence of any semblance of co-operation between the Kriegsmarine and the Luftwaffe.

In summary, therefore, the Type XXI and XXIII U-boats, while of course representing considerable progress compared to the pre-war types, could not have altered the course of the war, even had hostilities been further protracted.

The final paragraph of Dönitz's letter to Walter reads:

> I also hope that the initial trials of your boats, expected this autumn [1943], are successful, because I still attach a lot of importance to the development of Walter submarines with a high underwater speed and Walter engines . . .

In truth, however, even though in 1944 an order for 100 Type XXVIs had been placed with Blohm & Voss, by the end of the war only four were even at the early stages of sectional construction and work on the remaining 96 had been suspended in favour of the Type XXI. Thus ten years of intensive work by Hellmuth Walter had achieved precisely nothing: none of his U-boats ever left home waters, and none of his 21 hydrogen-peroxide torpedo designs was ever used.

Notes

Introduction

1 See Dönitz, Karl, *10 Jahre und 20 Tage*; Herzog, Bodo, *60 Jahre deutsche U-Boote*; Rohwer, Jürgen, *Die U-Boot-Erfolge der Achsenmächte*; and U-Boot-Kameradschaft Kieler e.V. (ed.), *Das U-Boot Ehrenmal Möltenort an der Kieler Förde*

Early Submersibles

1 Burgoyne, Alan H., *Submarine Navigation Past and Present*, p. 28.
2 Vogel, W., *Friedrich Otto Vogels U-Boot-Versuche in den Jahren 1867–69*, p. 4.
3 *Ibid.*
4 Delpeuch, Maurice, *La navigation sous-marine à travers les siècles*, p. 374.
5 Burgoyne, *op. cit.*, p. 29.
6 Mitteilungen aus dem Gebiete des Seewesens, Pola, vol. XXX, 1902, p. 925
7 Letter from Inspektion des Torpedowesens (B.N. 15085 T.B., 14 November 1902) to the Staatssekretär des Reichsmarine-amtes, pp. 35–6.
8 Designated 'Leps'sches Tauchboot' (literally, 'Diving Boat') by Techel.
9 Mitteilungen, vol. XXVI, 1898, p. 1108
10 See Lawrenz, Hans-Joachim, *Die Entstehungsgeschichte der U-Boote*, p. 130; Techel, Hans, *Der Bau von Unterseebooten auf der Germaniawerft*, pp. 73–5; and Fock, Harald, 'Das U-Boot *Forelle* der Germaniawerft', *Marineforum*, 1987, issue 5, pp. 180ff.
11 'Die Versuche mit dem Howaldtschen Unterwasserboot . . .', (handwritten note from Inspektion des Torpedowesens dated 18 March 1901).

Manned Torpedoes and Miniature Submarines

1 A deliberate pun—*Neger* and *Mohr* are both German words for 'black man'.

Machinery, Sensors and Weapons

1 Busley, Carl, 'Die modernen Unterseeboote', *Jahrbuch der STG*, 1900, p. 123.
2 Papenburg, Notizen zur Aufstellung einer Geschichte der Entwicklung der Unterseeboottechnik in der deutschen Marine, p. 142.
3 Schnauffer, K., 'Die Motorenentwicklung im Werk Nürnberg der MAN, 1897 bis 1918,' p. 19.
4 Aschmoneit, Christoph, 'MB 501 als U-Bootmotor', U-Boot-Archiv, Cuxhaven.
5 Oelfken, Heinrich, 'Diesel-elektrischer Antrieb', Kressbronn, 10 October 1947 /1.

6 Small, 'Dieselmotoren für die US-Marine -Insgesamt 12 000 000 PSe für US-Marinefahrzeuge, Übersetzung des Verfassers', *The Motor Ship*, September 1943, p. 4.
7 Kinsler, L. E., *Fundamentals of Acoustics*, p. 435.
8 Reichspatentamt, Nr. 320/29, 27. August 1918, 'Verfahren zur Richtungsbestimmung van Schallsignalen'.
9 British Patent Office, No. 11125, 27 March 1913
10 Kühnhold, Rudolf, 'Anwendungen und Erfahrungen auf dem Schallortungsgebiet bei der ehemaligen deutschen Kriegsmarine' p. 31
11 Friedman, Norman, *Submarine Design and Development*, p. 138.
12 Kaiserliches Patentamt, Patentschrift Nr. 165546, 30 April 1904:Hülsmeyer, Christian, 'Verfahren, um entfernte metallische Gegenstände mittels elektrischer Wellen einem Beobachter zu melden'.
13 Das Telemobiloskop, eine Erfindung des Ingenieurs Chr. Hülsmeyer, *Kölner Zeitung* , 18 May 1904.
14 Letter from Telemobiloskop-Gesellschaft to the Generaldirektor of the Holland-America-Linie, Herr Wierdsma, Frau Anneliese Hecker's archive, Düsseldorf. Frau Hecker is Hülsmeyer's daughter.
15 Kaiserliches Patentamt, Nr. 169154, 11 November 1904.
16 Dahl, A., 'Radartechnik se it mehr als 60 Jahren: Zum Andenken an Christian Hulsmeyer', *Ortung und Navigation*, Düsseldorf, 11/1964, p. 30.
17 Brandt, Leo, 'Rückblick auf die deutsche Funk-messtechnik', *Interavia*, Vol. 5, No 6, 1950, p. 1.
18 Reuter, Franz, *Funkmess: Die Entwicklung und der Einsatz des Radar-Verfahrens in Deutschland bis zum Ende des Zweiten Weltkrieges*, p. 18.
19 Brandt, *loc. cit.*
20 Kaiserliches Patentamt, Patentschrift Nr. 1387 30, 20 July 1901: Jaubert, Georg F., 'Arbeitsverfahren für Explosions-Kraftmaschinen, in denen aus Brennstoff und Sauerstoff bestehende Gemische entzündet werden'.
21 Kaiserliches Patentamt, Patentschrift Nr. 188825, 6 August 1905: Jaubert, Georg F., 'Antrieb für Unterseeboote'.
22 Pesce, G.-L., *La navigation sous-marine,* p. 434.
23 *Conway's All the World's Fighting Ships 1906–1921*, p. 208.
24 *Ibid.*, p. 209.
25 Serruys, Max, 'Concernant des moteurs Diesel proprement dits', ca. 1914, MAN-Archiv, 3.36.3/8.
26 Winand, Paul, MS relating to his patent, pp. 6–8.
27 Kaiserliches Patentamt, Patentschrift Nr. 196266, 25 November 1905: Winand, Paul, 'Verfahren zum Betriebe mehrzylindriger Zweitaktexplosionskraftmaschinen'.

28 Letter from Gasmotorenfabrik Deutz dated 22 February 1905 to Paul Winand.

29 Agreements between Inspektion des Torpedowesens and Gasmotorenfabrik Deutz of 19 October 1907.

30 Comments by Korvettenkapitän Arno Spindler to Reichsmarineamt in conversation with Oberst (rtd) van Erckelens of completed Gasmotorenfabrik Deutz on 1 March 1918.

31 *Ibid.*

32 Letter from Inspektion des Torpedowesens, 19 July 1905, to Professor von Linde, Munich.

33 Berling, Gustav, 'Die Entwicklung der U-Boote und ihrer Hauptmaschinenanlagen', *Jahrbuch der STG: 14. Jahrgang*, pp. 141–50.

34 'Die Entwicklung und der Stand des Kreislaufbetriebes', Secret Report No 452 by Forschungsinstituts für Kraftfahrzeugwesen und Fahrzeugmotoren.

35 Letter OKM/K 11 dated 11 December 1943 to the Schiffbaukommission.

36 Aschmoneit, Christoph, transcript dated 11 July 1960 of discussion in Annapolis, 21 June 1960.

37 *Conway's All the World's Fighting Fhips 1947–1982*, Vol 2, p. 493.

38 Hollund, Achim; Meyer, Freek; and Regensdorf, Uwe, *Das Kreislaufdieselsystem als aussenluftunabhangiger U-Bootsantrieb: Entwicklung und Erprobung im Zeitraum, 1986–1993*, pp. 37–41.

39 A detailed discussion can be found in Möller, Eberhard, *Marine Geheimprojekte: Hellmuth Walther und seine Entwicklungen*. See also Möller, 'Die Entwicklung der Antriebe von Unterwasserfahrzeugen vom 17. Jahrhundert bis zur Gegenwart', dissertation, 1989, pp. 197–271.

40 Walter, Hellmuth, letter to Marineleitung dated 5 October 1933.

41 Chef der Marineleitung, letter to Walter dated 10 April 1934.

42 Whitestone, Nicholas, *U-Boote: Superwaffe der Zukunft?*, p. 15.

43 Rohwer, Jürgen, *66 Tage unter Wasser*, p. 15.

44 *Weyers Flottentaschenbuch: 64. Jahrgang 1999–2001*, p. 250.

45 Löb, H., *et al.*, *Kerntechnik für Satelliten und Raketen*, pp. 106–7.

The U-Boat 'Aces'

1 In 1907 the *Lusitania* (Cunard Line, Liverpool) was the largest ship in the world. At the beginning of 1915 Germany declared the waters around the British Isles to be part of the war zone, and, in New York, American citizens were warned by means of newspaper advertisements against sailing on ships entering that zone. In London, the Admiralty knew about U 20's operations: a few days before the tragedy, she had sunk several merchant ships in the same area. British warships were diverted accordingly, but the *Lusitania*'s captain apparently received no such information, instructions or warnings. A torpedo struck the ship on 7 May 1915, and half a minute later there was a second explosion. The liner went down in less than twenty minutes, and 1,198 dead—amongst them 140 US citizens—were mourned as a result. It is believed that the ship was carrying ammunition. Was this, therefore, a 'calculated' loss, engineered in order to influence public opinion in the United States? The rumours continue to this day, although there is no proof one way or the other.

2 The *Britannic* was a sister ship to the *Olympic* and *Titanic* (White Star Line, Liverpool), launched in early 1914 and completed as a hospital ship at the end of 1915. She sank about an hour after being hit by a mine, and fewer than 30 of the 1,134 people on board lost their lives. The *Britannic* was the largest ship to be sunk by a submarine.

3 The *Justitia* was launched as the *Statendam* (Holland–Amerika Lijn, Amsterdam) in 1914, following which her fitting-out was suspended. However, in 1917 she was completed, with the name *Justitia*, as a British troop transport. On 19 July 1918 UB 64 (Otto von Schrader) managed to hit the ship with a torpedo. Three more attacks were unsuccessful, and U 54, which had arrived in the meantime, also unsuccessfully launched two torpedoes. However, when UB 124 arrived on the scene *Justitia*'s fate was sealed with two torpedo strikes.

4 The *Empress of Britain* belonged to Canadian Pacific and had served as a troop-carrier since 1939. On 26 October 1940 she was hit by a German long-range bomber and caught fire; abandoned, she was taken in tow by a destroyer. On 28 October, still afloat, she was struck by two torpedoes from U 32.

5 The *Laconia* (Cunard Line, Liverpool) was first used as an auxiliary cruiser in 1939, and then as a troop transport from 1940. She was sunk in the South Atlantic by two torpedoes from U 156; some 2,800 people were on board, 1,800 of them Italian prisoners of war. A dramatic rescue mission got under way, Hartenstein sending an uncoded wireless message for help. U 506, U 507 and an Italian submarine arrived at the scene, and Dönitz also asked the French Vichy Government for help, in response to which the cruiser *Gloire* and two other ships were despatched. On 16 September 1942, however, before they arrived, U 156 was attacked and damaged by a US bomber; she received the attentions of another aircraft on 17 September but on this occasion was able to dive out of harm's way. The next day the French ships rescued more than 1,000 people, including about 400 Italians. Following this incident Dönitz gave orders that survivors should not in future be rescued—the so-called 'Laconia order'. This is why Dönitz was indicted by the British at the Nuremberg Trials (though not the reason he was convicted).

6 *Edinburgh* was at first taken in tow, but then was hit by another torpedo from Z 24 . With any chance of saving the cruiser now gone, she was finished off by HMS *Foresight* on 2 May 1942.

7 *Thane* was brought home but not repaired.

U-Boat Decoys

1 Schmalenbach, Paul, 'Deutsche-U-Boot-Fallen in zwei Weltkriegen', *Leinen los*, 1968, issue 6, p. 23.

2 Kemp, Paul, *Die deutschen und Österreichischen U-Boot-Verluste in beiden Weltkriegen*, p. 14ff.

3 Herzog, Bodo, *60 Jahre deutsche U-Boote*, 1906–1966, p. 128.

4 Aichelburg, Wladimir, *Die Unterseeboote Oesterreich-Ungarns*, vol. 2, p. 390.

5 Schmalenbach, *op. cit.*, p. 23ff.

U-Tankers

1 See Miller, David, *Deutsche U-Boote bis 1945*, p. 57.

2 White, John F., *U-Boot-Tanker 1941–1945*, p. 246.

3 Bagnaso, Erminio, *U-Boote im 2. Weltkrieg*, p. 57.

4 White, *loc. cit.*

U-Boat Bunkers

1 For a discussion of U-boat bunkers see Heitzel, Soenke, *Die deutschen U-Boot-Bunker und Bunkerwerften*; Schmeelke,

Karl-Heinz, and Michael, *Deutsche U-Boot-Bunker gestern und heute*; Ryheul, Johan, *Marinekorps Flandern 1914–1918*; and Kähling, Rolf, 'Die Unterseeboot-Bunker-Werft "Valentin"', *Hamburger Rundbrief*, 2001, issue 1.

U-Boats in the Mediterranean and the Black Sea

1 Greger, René, 'Über den Anteil der k.u.k. U-Boot-waffe am Handelskrieg im Mittelmeer', *Marinerundschau*, 1970, issue 3, p. 167.
2 According to Weyer, it comprised six battleships (with a further two under construction), seven heavy cruisers, fourteen light cruisers, 61 destroyers, 63 torpedo boats and 106 submarines (with 27 more under construction).
3 Alman, Karl, *Graue Wölfe in blauer See*, p. 305.
4 According to the *Brockhaus-Enzyklopaedie*, 17th edn, 1972–1973, the Baltic covers 420,000 square kilometres and has an average depth of 55 metres and a maximum depth of 459 metres; the equivalent figures for the Black Sea are 423,000, 1,270 and 2,240.
5 *Conway's All the World's Fighting Ships 1922–1946*.
6 Meister, Jürg, *Der Seekrieg in osteuropaischen Gewassern, 1941–45*, p. 232. In total, more than 500 warships and merchantmen of up to 250grt were transferred, amongst them sixteen speed boats and 23 minesweepers.
7 Enders, Gerd, *Deutsche U-Boote zum Schwarzen Meer*.
8 Enders, 'Von der Ostsee zum Schwarzen Meer', *Schiffahrt International*, 1989, issue 3, pp. 100–10.

Commercial U-Boats: *Deutschland* and *Bremen*

1 A good reference is Techel, Hans, *Der Bau von Unterseebooten auf der Germaniawerft*.

U-Boats Preserved

1 Lipsky, Florian and Stefan, *Faszination U-Boot*, p. 119.
2 Enders, Gerd, *Deutsche U-Boote zum Schwarzen Meer*, p. 17.
3 Möller, Eberhard, *Marine Geheimprojekte: Hellmuth Walther und seine Entwicklungen*, p. 198ff.

U-Boats of the Austro-Hungarian Navy

1 Simon Lake (1866–1945).
2 John Philip Holland, born 29 February 1840 in Ireland, died 12 August 1914 in the United States.
3 Grossadmiral Anton Haus (born 13 June 1851, died 8 February 1917), Flotteninspekteur (Fleet Inspector) from 12 July 1912, Marinekommandant (Naval Commander) from 24 February 1913.
4 The Cantiere Navale Triestino (CNT) yard at Monfalcone was founded by Österreichische Schiffahrts A. G. and Skoda Werke A. G. The company headquarters at Monfalcone were evacuated during the war and transferred to Budapest and Pola.
5 See Greger, René, 'Über den Anteil der k.u.k. U-Boot-waffe am Handelskrieg im Mittelmeer', *Marinerundschau*, 1970, issue 3, p. 167ff., and 'Wer war der erfolgreichste U-Boot-Kommandant Österreich-Ungarns im Handelskrieg?', *Marinerundschau*, 1972, January and February 1972, p. 104ff.
6 Aichelburg, Wladimir, *Die Unterseeboote Oesterreich-Ungarns*, vol. 2, p. 480ff.
7 The successes were gained while the boats were still under German command, although Austrian officers were on board undergoing training.
8 Schupita, Peter, *Die k.u.k. Seeflieger*, pp. 190, 192.

Sources

Primary Sources

Aschmoneit, Christoph, transcript dated 11 July 1960 of discussion in Annapolis, 21 June 1960, U-Boot-Archiv, Cuxhaven, Aschmoneit Estate.

———, 'MB 501 als U-Bootmotor', U-Boot-Archiv, Cuxhaven.

Comments by Korvettenkapitän Arno Spindler to Reichsmarineamt in conversation with Oberst (rtd) van Erckelens of Gasmotorenfabrik Deutz on 1 March 1918, Rheinisch-Westfälisches Wirtschafts-Archiv, Cologne, 107-VII-33.

Letter from Inspektion des Torpedowesens (B.N. 15085 T.B., 14 November 1902) to the Staatssekretär des Reichsmarineamtes, (handwritten document), Bundesarchiv/Militärarchiv, Freiburg, RM 3/3877.

Letter from Telemobiloskop-Gesellschaft to the Generaldirektor of the Holland-America-Linie, Herr Wierdsma, Frau Anneliese Hecker's archive, Düsseldorf.

Letter from Inspektion des Torpedowesens dated 19 July1905 to Professor von Linde, Munich,MAN-Archiv, Augsburg, Torpedoinspektion, Versuchsmotor, VIII, 3 a-d, Box 12 C.

Letter OKM/K 11 dated 11 December 1943 to the Schiffbaukommission, Bundesarchiv/Militärarchiv, Freiburg, RM 7/1257.

'Die Entwicklung und der Stand des Kreislaufbetriebes', Secret Report No 452 by Forschungsinstituts für Kraftfahrzeugwesen und Fahrzeugmotoren, Technischen Hochschule, Stuttgart (FKFS), 5 January 1944, author's archive, Reg. Nr. 522.

Mitteilungen aus dem Gebiete des Seewesens, Pola, vol. XXVI, 1898.

———, vol. XXX, 1902.

Oelfken, Heinrich, 'Diesel-elektrischer Antrieb', Kressbronn, 10 October 1947, Bundesarchiv/Militärarchiv ,Freiburg, N 5/8/1.

Papenburg, Notizen zur Aufstellung einer Geschichte der Entwicklung der Unterseeboottechnik in der deutschen Marine, Bundesarchiv/ Militärarchiv, Freiburg, 11 M 113/7.

Schnauffer, K., 'Die Motorenentwicklung im Werk Nürnberg der MAN, 1897 bis 1918,' Document 1956, MAN-Archiv, Augsburg.

Letter from Gasmotorenfabrik Deutz dated 22 February 1905 to Paul Winand, Rheinisch-Westfalisches Wirtschafts-Archiv, Cologne, 107-VI-33.

Serruys, Max, 'Concernant des moteurs Diesel propement dits, zweiseitiger Schriftsatz, etwa 1914', MAN-Archiv, Augsburg, 3.36.3/8.

Das Telemobiloskop, eine Erfindung des Ingenieurs Chr. Hülsmeyer, Kölner Zeitung , 18 May 1904.

'SM Unterseeboote: Neubauten und Neuentwürfe', Secret report by Reichsmarineamt, Berlin, 1917.

Agreements between Inspektion des Torpedowesens and Gasmotorenfabrik Deutz of 19 October 1907, Rheinisch-Westfälisches Wirtschafts-Archiv, Cologne, 107-VI-33.

'Die Versuche mit dem Howaldtschen Unterwasserboot . . .', handwritten note from Inspektion des Torpedowesens dated 18 March 1901, Bundesarchiv/Militärarchiv Freiburg, RM 3/3876.

Winand, Paul, MS relating to his patent, Rheinisch-Westfälisches Wirtschafts-Archiv, Cologne, 107-VI-33.

Patents

Kaiserliches Patentamt, Patentschrift Nr. 138730, 20 July 1901: Jaubert, Georg F., 'Arbeitsverfahren für Explosions-Kraftmaschinen, in denen aus Brennstoff und Sauerstoff bestehende Gemische entzündet werden'.

Kaiserliches Patentamt, Patentschrift Nr. 165546, 30 April 1904: Hülsmeyer, Christian, 'Verfahren, um entfernte metallische Gegenstände mittels elektrischer Wellen einem Beobachter zu melden'.

Kaiserliches Patentamt, Nr. 169154, 11 November 1904: Hülsmeyer, Christian, Verfahren zur Bestimmung der Entfernung von metallischen Gegenstanden (Schiffen o. dgl.)'.

Kaiserliches Patentamt, Patentschrift Nr. 188825, 6 August 1905: Jaubert, Georg F., 'Antrieb für Unterseeboote.'

Kaiserliches Patentamt, Patentschrift Nr. 196266, 25 November 1905: Winand, Paul, 'Verfahren zum Betriebe mehrzylindriger Zweitaktexplosionskraftmaschinen'.

Reichspatentamt, Nr. 320/29, 27 August 1918: 'Verfahren zur Richtungsbestimmung van Schallsignalen'.

Secondary Sources

Aichelburg, Wladimir, *Die Unterseeboote Oesterreich-Ungarns*, 2 vols, Graz, 1981.

Alman, Karl, *Ritter der sieben Meere*, Raststatt, 1975.

Bagnaso, Erminio, *U-Boote im 2. Weltkrieg*, Stuttgart, 1994.

Bekker, Cajus, *Einzelkämpfer auf See. Die deutschen Torpedoreiter, Froschmanner und Sprengbootpiloten im Zweiten Weltkrieg*, Oldenburg, 1968.

Benderf, Harald, D*ie UB-Boote der Kaiserlichen Marine, 1914–1918*, Hamburg, 2000.

———, *Die UC-Boote der Kaiserlichen Marine, 1914–1918*, Hamburg, 2001.

Berling, Gustav, 'Die Entwicklung der U-Boote und ihrer Hauptmaschinenanlagen', *Jahrbuch der STG: 14. Jahrgang*, Berlin, 1913.

Blair, Clay, *Der U-Boot-Krieg: Die Jäger, 1939–1942*, Munich, 1998.

———, *Der U-Boot-Krieg: Die Gejagten, 1943–1945*, Munich, 1999.

Botting, Douglas, *Die Unterseeboote*, Time-Life Books, 1981.

Bracke, Gerhard, *Die Einzelkampfer der Kriegsmarine*, Stuttgart, 1981.

Brandt, Leo, 'Rückblick auf die deutsche Funk-messtechnik', *Interavia*, Vol. 5, No 6, 1950.

Breyer, Siegfried, and Koop, Gerhard, *Die deutsche Kriegsmarine 1935–1945*, vol. 3, Friedberg, 1987.

Büchner, H., *Energiespeicherung in Metallhydriden*, Vienna/New York, 1982.

Burgoyne, Alan H., *Submarine Navigation Past and Present*, London, 1903.

Busch, Rainer; and Roll, Hans-Joachim, *Der U-Boot-Krieg 1939–1945*, 4 vols, Hamburg, 1996–2001.

Busley, Carl, 'Die modernen Unterseeboote', *Jahrbuch der STG*, Year 1, Berlin, 1900.

Chesneau, Roger, *et al.*,(eds), *Conway's All the World's Fighting Ships*, 5 vols, Greenwich,1979–89.

Dahl, A., 'Radartechnik se it mehr als 60 Jahren: Zum Andenken an Christian Hulsmeyer', *Ortung und Navigation*, Düsseldorf, 11/1964.

Dallies-Labourdette, Jean-Philippe, *U-Boote: Eine Bildchronik 1935–1945*, Stuttgart, 1998.

Delpeuch, Maurice, *La navigation sous-marine à travers les siècles*, Paris, 1898.

Dönitz, Karl, *10 Jahre und 20 Tage*, Frankfurt a.M., 1964.

Enders, Gerd, *Auch kleine Igel haben Stacheln*, Herford, 1984.

——, 'Von der Ostsee zum Schwarzen Meer', *Schiffahrt International*, 1989, issue 3.

——, *Deutsche U-Boote zum Schwarzen Meer*, Hamburg 1997.

Ewerth, Hannes, 'Die dritte deutsche U-Boot-Waffe', *Marine-rundschau*, 1984, issue 8.

——, *Die U-Flottille der deutschen Marine*, Hamburg 1995.

Le Fleming, H. M., *Warships of World War I: Submarines* (British and German), London, 1925.

Fock, Harald, *Flottenchronik*, Hamburg, 2000.

——, 'Das U-Boot *Forelle* der Germaniawerft', *Marineforum*, 1987, issue 5.

——, *Marine-Kleinkampfmittel*, Hamburg, 1996.

Friedman, Norman, *Submarine Design and Development*, Greenwich, 1984.

Garrett, Richard, *U-Boote,* Herrsching, 1977.

Gray, Edwyn, *Die teuflische Waffe*, Oldenburg, 1975.

Greger, Rene, 'Über den Anteil der k.u.k. U-Boot-waffe am Handelskrieg im Mittelmeer', *Marinerundschau*, March 1970.

——, 'Wer war der erfolgreichste U-Boot-Kommandant Österreich-Ungarns im Handelskrieg?', *Marinerundschau*, January and February 1972.

Gröner, Erich, *Die deutschen Kriegsschiffe 1815–1945*, vols 3, 6 and 8/2, Koblenz, 1985, 1989 and 2000.

Haws, Duncan, *Merchant Fleets*, vol. 12, Cunard Line, 1989.

Heitmann, Jan, *Unter Wasser in die Neue Welt*, Berlin, 1999.

Heitzel, Sönke, *Die deutschen U-Boot-Bunker und Bunkerwerften*, Koblenz, 1991.

Herzog, Bodo, *60 Jahre deutsche U-Boote*, 1906–1966, Munich, 1968.

Hollund, Achim; Meyer, Freek; and Regensdorf, Uwe, *Das Kreislaufdieselsystem als aussenluftunabhangiger U-Boots-antrieb: Entwicklung und Erprobung im Zeitraum, 1986–1993*, Sonderdruck der Thyssen Nordseewerke GmbH, Emden 1994.

Howe, Hartley Edward, *North America's Maritime Museums*, 1982.

ITR (Incore Thermionic Reactor), *Prospekt der Firmen BBC, Inteatom und Siemens*, 1987.

Kähling, Rolf, Die Unterseeboot-Bunker-Werft "Valentin"', *Hamburger Rundbrief*, 2001, issue 1.

Karschawin, Boris A. *Das deutsche Unterseeboot U 250*, Jena, 1994.

Kemp, Paul, *Bemannte Torpedos und Klein-U-Boote im Einsatz 1939–1945*, Stuttgart, 1999.

——, *Die deutschen und Österreichischen U-Boot-Verluste in beiden Weltkriegen*, Munich, 1998.

Kinsler, L. E., *Fundamentals of Acoustics*, New York, 1950.

Kühnhold, Rudolf, 'Anwendungen und Erfahrungen auf dem Schallortungsgebiet bei der ehemaligen deutschen Kriegsmarine' (lecture, 19 October 1953, in Bremen), *Sonderbücherei der Funkortung: Beiträge zur Schallortung*, 1953, issue 1.

Kludas, Arnold, *Die grossen Passagierschiffe der Welt*, vols 1–4, Oldenburg, 1972–1974.

Lanitzki, Günter, *Kreuzer Edinburgh*, Herford, 1991.

Lau, Manfred, *Schiffssterben vor Algier. Kampf-schwimmer, Torpedoreiter und Marine-Einsatzkommandos im Mittelmeer 1942–1945*, Stuttgart, 2001.

Lawrenz, Hans-Joachim, *Die Entstehungsgeschichte der U-Boote*, Munich, 1968.

Lipsky, Florian and Stefan, *Faszination U-Boot*, Hamburg , 2000.

Löb, H., *et al.*, *Kerntechnik für Satelliten und Raketen*, Munich, 1970.

Mallmann-Showell, Jak P., *Die U-Boot-Waffe: Kommandanten und Besatzungen*, Stuttgart, 2001.

——, *Uboote gegen England*, Stuttgart, 1975.

Mayer, Horst-Friedrich, and Winkler, Dieter, *Als die Schiffe tauchen lernten: Die Geschichte der k.u.k. U-Boot-Waffe*, Vienna, 1998.

Meister, Jürg, *Der Seekrieg in osteuropaischen Gewassern, 1941–45*, Munich, 1958.

Miller, David, *Deutsche U-Boote bis 1945*, Zürich and Stuttgart, 2000.

Möller, Eberhard, *Marine Geheimprojekte: Hellmuth Walther und seine Entwicklungen*, Stuttgart, 2000.

Möller, Eberhard, and Brack, Werner, *Einhundert Jahre Dieselmotoren für fünf deutsche Marinen*, Hamburg, 1998.

Müller, Wolfgang, *Schiffsschicksale in der Ostsee*, 1945, Hamburg, 1996.

Müller-Urban, Christiane, and Müller, Eberhard, *Schiffsmuseen*, Bielefeld, 2001.

Neill, Peter, *Great Maritime Museums of the World*, 1991.

Neitzel, Sonke, *Die deutschen Ubootbunker und Bunkerwerften*, Koblenz, 1991.

Padfield, Peter, *Der U-Boot-Krieg 1939–1945*, Berlin, 1996.

Pawlik, Georg, *S. M. Unterseeboote: das k.u.k. Unterseeboots-wesen, 1907–1918*, Graz, 1986.

Pesce, G.-L., Franz, *La navigation sous-marine*, Paris, 1906.

Reuter, Franz, *Funkmess: Die Entwicklung und der Einsatz des Radar-Verfahrens in Deutschland bis zum Ende des Zweiten Weltkrieges*, Opladen, 1971.

Rohwer, Jürgen, *66 Tage unter Wasser*, Oldenburg, 1962.

Rössler, Eberhard, *Geschichte des deutschen Ubootbaus*, vol. 2, Koblenz, 1987.

Ryheul, Johan, *Marinekorps Flandern 1914–1918*, Hamburg, 1997.

Schmalenbach, Paul, 'Deutsche-U-Boot-Fallen in zwei Welt-kriegen, *Leinen los*, 1968, issue 6.

Schmeelke, Karl-Heinz, and Michael, *Deutsche U-Boot-Bunker gestern und heute*, Wolfersheim-Berstadt, 1996.

Schupita, Peter, *Die k.u.k. Seeflieger: Chronik und Dokumentation der österreichisch-ungarischen Marineluftwaffe, 1911–1918*, Koblenz, 1983.

Sieche, Erwin, *Die Unterseeboote der k.u.k. Marine*, Wolfersheim, 1998.

Small, 'Dieselmotoren für die US-Marine -Insgesamt 12 000 000 PSe für US-Marinefahrzeuge, Übersetzung des Verfassers', *The Motor Ship*, September 1943.

Techel, Hans, *Der Bau von Unterseebooten auf der Germania-werft*, Berlin, 1922.

U-Bootkameradschaft Kiel, (ed.), *Das U-Boot-Ehrenmal Möltenort an der Kieler Förde*, 8th edn, Kiel, 1995.

Vogel, W., *Friedrich Otto Vogels U-Boot-Versuche in den Jahren 1867–69*, Essen, 1911.

Welham, Michael, *Kampfschwimmer: Geschichte, Ausrüstung, Einsätze*, Stuttgart 1996.

Wetzel, Eckard, U 2540: *Das U-Boot beim Deutschen Schiffahrts-museum in Bremerhaven*, Erlangen, 1989.

———, *U 995: Das U-Boot vor dem Marine-Ehrenmal in Laboe*, Erlangen, 1995.

Weyers Flottentaschenbuch: 64. Jahrgang 1999–2001, Bonn. 2000 (and earlier edns).

White, John F., *U-Boot-Tanker 1941–1945*, Hamburg, 2000.

Whitestone, Nicholas, (trans. Merten, Karl-Friedrich), *U-Boote: Superwaffe der Zukunft?*, Munich, 1975.

Whitley, Mike, *Deutsche Seestreitkrafte 1939 –1945: Einsatz im Küstenvorfeld*, Stuttgart 1995.